Theoretical Frameworks in Qualitative Research

To the ongoing forum
about the role of theory in qualitative research

Theoretical Frameworks in Qualitative Research

EDITORS

Vincent A. Anfara, Jr.
University of Tennessee

Norma T. Mertz
University of Tennessee

SAGE Publications
Thousand Oaks ▪ London ▪ New Delhi

For information:

Sage Publications, Inc.
2455 Teller Road
Thousand Oaks, California 91320
E-mail: order@sagepub.com

Sage Publications Ltd.
1 Oliver's Yard
55 City Road
London EC1Y 1SP
United Kingdom

Sage Publications India Pvt. Ltd.
B-42, Panchsheel Enclave
Post Box 4109
New Delhi 110 017 India

Printed in the United States of America on acid-free paper

Library of Congress Cataloging-in-Publication Data

Theoretical frameworks in qualitative research / editors, Vincent A. Anfara, Jr., Norma T. Mertz.
    p. cm.
Includes bibliographical references and index.
ISBN 1-4129-1416-7 (pbk.)
    1. Qualitative research. 2. Social sciences—Research—Methodology.
I. Anfara, Vincent A. II. Mertz, Norma T.
H62.T427 2006
001.4'3—dc22

                                  2005030919

06   07   08   09   10   9   8   7   6   5   4   3   2   1

Acquiring Editor:	Lisa Cuevas Shaw
Editorial Assistant:	Karen Gia Wong
Production Editor:	Sanford Robinson
Copy Editor:	Taryn Bigelow
Typesetter:	C&M Digitals (P) Ltd.
Indexer:	Karen A. McKenzie
Cover Designer:	Janet Foulger

Contents

List of Figures and Tables

Preface

The idea for this book developed from our experiences as teachers of qualitative methods. Graduate students seemed to lack an understanding of the role of theory in qualitative research, specifically the use of a theoretical framework. Our students' confusion was a reflection of the fact that discussions about qualitative research are not generally clear and precise about the use of theory in its development and conduct.

When we discussed theory and, in particular, theoretical frameworks, in our classes, students seemed puzzled and would ask a litany of questions: What is a theoretical framework? How do you find it? Where do you use it? What effect does it have on your research? Typical queries would include concerns like

- "How do I find something that fits what I'm doing?"
- "What happens if I can't find one?"
- "Does this mean I need to do another review of the literature?"

As students attempted to explore the literature on this topic to answer their questions, they reported finding competing conceptualizations of the relationship between theory and qualitative research in the literature as well as divergent definitions of what a theoretical framework is and how it is used. Unfortunately, our students were left with more questions than answers.

In January 2004, we shared our common experiences related to teaching qualitative methods. We both acknowledged that we had searched for a book that would clearly explicate these issues. This led us to begin a discussion about writing a book that would directly address the role of theory in qualitative research. We intensified our discussions as we carefully reviewed the literature and by February 2004, a proposal for the book was on its way to Sage. It seemed to be the likely publisher for such a book, because almost every book we had used in our qualitative research courses had been published by Sage.

We were excited to receive a quick, positive response from Lisa Cuevas Shaw, Acquisitions Editor at Sage. We met with her in April during the American Educational Research Association (AERA) meeting in San Diego. During that breakfast meeting, she expressed great interest in the book and asked a series of important questions about the book proposal. It was obvious to us that she had done her homework. We left AERA and San Diego with the promise that Lisa would discuss this project with her editorial team and that we would consider the reviews she intended to solicit. These reviews proved to be helpful in revising the original book proposal.

Once Sage offered us a book contract, a "call for manuscripts" was widely issued. More than 90 submissions were received. As we carefully read through these submissions, we found that many of these proposals did not "fit" our definition of a theoretical framework (e.g., the purported theoretical framework was methodological or paradigmatic in nature) or did not provide evidence of any self-conscious understanding of the effect of the theoretical framework on the study conducted. After months of reading, e-mailing, and talking with potential contributors, we settled on the 10 proposals that are presented in this book.

The potential contributors were then asked to develop more complete drafts of their chapters, attending to questions we had posed to them. While in Montreal for the 2005 AERA meeting, we had our first opportunity to meet face-to-face with the authors and discuss the initial drafts of the chapters. We also presented comprehensive feedback to the selected contributors on their chapters. Not surprisingly, the authors did a fantastic job in discussing their research and the theoretical framework they used. But most of them had not revealed enough of the "behind-the-scenes" processes of working with a theoretical framework, of how the framework had affected specific aspects of their study. We wanted more of the researchers' thoughts and actions exposed so that future qualitative researchers could get inside the heads of these researchers. The contributing authors then had 4 additional months to revise and resubmit their manuscripts. It is our hope that these normally tacit decisions and actions will provide both guides for the reader to follow and mental stimulation for imagining the pervasive effects of a theoretical framework on qualitative research.

We would be remiss if we did not thank Lisa Cuevas Shaw, Acquisitions Editor; Karen Wong, Editorial Assistant; Taryn Bigelow, Copy Editor; and Sanford Robinson, Project Editor, all at Sage, who guided us through this process and made a very difficult task seem relatively simple. Finally, we want to thank each of the contributing authors for allowing readers to see many of the aspects of the research process that are often hidden. It is our hope that this book will contribute in some special way to the ongoing dialogue about theory in qualitative research, and with and among those who teach it. This discussion about the role and place of theoretical frameworks in qualitative research is one that needs to take place.

Vincent A. Anfara, Jr.
Norma T. Mertz

Introduction

Vincent A. Anfara, Jr.
Norma T. Mertz

S tudents as well as experienced researchers who employ qualitative methods frequently have trouble identifying and using theoretical frameworks in their research. This trouble is typically centered on finding a theoretical framework and understanding its pervasive effects on the process of conducting qualitative research.

Currently, no comprehensive discussion of theoretical frameworks exists to assist those engaged in qualitative research. Therefore, our overarching goal is to provide a book that effectively explains, through discussion and example, what a theoretical framework is, how it is used in qualitative research, and the effects it has on the research process. In short, this is a guidebook into the mysteries of theoretical frameworks in qualitative research.

To begin our journey, we look at what theory is and review the literature that currently exists on the use of theory in qualitative research. Ongoing confusion about the use of theory and theoretical frameworks in qualitative research makes it all the more important to openly address this issue, look closely at what researchers do, and subject their use of theory to review by others. We, then, provide readers with the definition of theoretical frameworks that is used throughout this book and exemplified in Chapters 1 through 10. The contributors of these chapters focus on published research studies and address where and in what ways the theoretical framework affected their studies. We conclude this introduction with a discussion of the organization of the book and guidelines for readers to maximize its use.

What Is Theory?

Although Flinders and Mills (1993) argued that "precise definitions [of theory] are hard to come by" (p. xii), theory has been defined in a variety of ways by philosophers of science and scholars in the academic disciplines. Examples include Kerlinger (1986), who defined theory as "a set of interrelated constructs, definitions, and propositions that presents a systematic view of phenomena by specifying relations among variables, with the purpose of explaining and predicting phenomenon" (p. 9). In similar fashion, Argyris and Schon (1974) defined theory as "a set of interconnected propositions that have the same referent—the subject of the theory" (pp. 4–5), and LeCompte and Preissle (1993) stated that "theorizing is simply the cognitive process of discovering or manipulating abstract categories and the relationships among these categories" (p. 239). In a somewhat different vein, Strauss (1995) noted that theory provides a model or map of why the world is the way it is. He further explained that whereas theory is a simplification of the world, it nonetheless is aimed at clarifying and explaining some aspect of how the world works.

Discussing this myriad of definitions, Silver (1983) purported that formal definitions of theory rob it of its true beauty, its emotional significance, and its importance to everyday life. She defined theory as a unique way of perceiving reality, an expression of someone's profound insight into some aspect of nature, and a fresh and different perception of an aspect of the world.

Although we favor Silver's (1983) conceptualization of theory, it is evident from what she says that understanding theory and its relationship to the research process requires effort. To understand a theory is to travel into someone else's mind and become able to perceive reality as that person does. To understand a theory is to experience a shift in one's mental structure and discover a different way of thinking. To understand a theory is to feel some wonder that one never saw before what now seems to have been obvious all along. To understand theory, one needs to stretch one's mind to reach the theorist's meaning.

The Building Blocks of Theory

In many discussions of theory (e.g., Babbie, 1986; Silver, 1983; J. Turner, 1974), important points are made about its components parts—the relationship of concepts, constructs, and propositions to theory. As one moves from concepts to the level of theory, there is also a movement from concrete experiences to a level of abstract description.

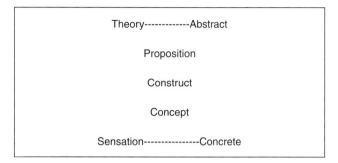

Figure I.1   The building blocks of theory.

Working from the most concrete level of sensations and experiences, concepts are words that we assign to events. Concepts enable us to distinguish one event or sensation from another. Concepts also allow us to relate events in the past to ones in the present or future. Often these concepts will cluster and form a higher-order unit of thought known as a construct. Silver (1983) provides the example of IQ as a construct. This construct incorporates the concepts of age (the amount of time one has lived) and intelligence (the amount of knowledge one has).

Moving to the next level of abstraction we encounter propositions. Propositions are expressions of relationships among several constructs. Because propositions are new inventions, they must be carefully defined and explained to others. Because one proposition is usually insufficient to explain a new insight about an aspect of reality, researchers use a set of propositions that are logically related. It is this relationship of propositions that constitutes a theory. When we develop theory, we have completed a highly abstract thought process with ideas being removed in successive stages from the world of immediate experience and sensation. Even though abstract, theories are profoundly helpful for understanding the experienced world. To help understand the relationship between and among the building blocks of theory and to assist in comprehending the movement from concrete experience to abstract explanation, we offer Figure I.1.

Some Examples

Within the social sciences, one can find a multitude of efforts to describe, explain, or predict phenomena. The nature of theory (what it is and its component parts) might be clarified by reference to two particular theories that are familiar to most readers. Let us then briefly turn to the work of Abraham Maslow and Leon Festinger.

Self-Actualization

(to develop into what one is capable of becoming, autonomy, self-direction)

Esteem

(self-esteem and recognition by peers)

Social Affiliation

(love, belonging, acceptance by others)

Security and Safety

(physical safety, financial security)

Basic Physiological Needs

(food, water, shelter, sex, air)

Figure I.2   Hierarchy of needs as used in Maslow's theory of motivation.

One of the most powerful ways of understanding human motivation was developed by Abraham Maslow (1954). According to Maslow, human beings have a variety of needs (concepts), some more fundamental than others. Maslow grouped these needs into five basic categories (constructs), arranged hierarchically from "lower" to "higher" (propositions). Lower needs dominate behavior when they are not satisfied. Higher needs become salient only after the lower needs have been satisfied. From these concepts, constructs, and propositions, Maslow concluded that behavior is an expression of one's drive to reduce deficiencies by gratifying the most salient type of needs (theory). This hierarchy is shown in Figure I.2.

As a second example, let us look at Festinger's theory of cognitive dissonance. Published by Leon Festinger in 1957, *A Theory of Cognitive Dissonance* has been one of the most influential and widely debated theories in social psychology. Festinger's theory begins with the beliefs one has about "the environment, about oneself, or about one's behavior" (1957, p. 3). These beliefs (concepts) are called cognitions, and the theory deals specifically with pairs of cognitions (constructs). Pairs of cognitions may relate to each other in relevant or irrelevant ways (propositions). Irrelevant pairs of cognitions "may simply have nothing to do with one another" (p. 11). Relevant pairs of cognitions may be either consonant or dissonant. Consonant cognitions occur when elements of knowledge follow from one another. Dissonant cognitions occur when the obverse of one element follows from the other. For example, if a person knows that he or she is surrounded by only friends but feels afraid or threatened, a dissonant relationship between these two cognitive elements exists. This "uncomfortable feeling" motivates the individual to lessen or eliminate the dissonance. In stating his theory, Festinger wrote, "The presence of dissonance gives rise to pressures to reduce or eliminate the dissonance. The strength of the pressure to reduce the dissonance is a function of the magnitude of the dissonance" (p. 18).

What Constitutes Good and Useful Theory?

McMillan and Schumacher (2001) discussed certain criteria that must be present for a theory to be useful in the development of scientific knowledge. A theory (1) should provide a simple explanation of the observed relations relevant to a phenomenon, (2) should be consistent with both the observed relations and an already established body of knowledge, (3) is considered a tentative explanation and should provide means for verification and revision, and (4) should stimulate further research in areas that need investigation. Agnew and Pyke (1969) recommended that good theory be (1) simple, (2) testable, (3) novel, (4) supportive of other theories, (5) internally consistent, and (6) predictive. Eisner (1993), however, framed it most cogently:

> Theory attempts to satisfy the human need for scientific rationality by providing explanations that will meet that need. The adequacy of such explanations is tested not only by their appeal, their cogency, and their aesthetic quality, but by the extent to which they can be used to help us anticipate, if not control, the future. (p. vii)

A useful theory is one that tells an enlightening story about some phenomenon. It is a story that gives you new insights and broadens your understanding of the phenomenon.

Theories in the Social and Natural Sciences

According to Langenbach, Vaughn, and Aagaard (1994), the social sciences have more theories than do the natural sciences, especially theories that compete with each other (e.g., McGregor's [1960] Theory X and Theory Y). Agreeing with this notion, Alexander (1987) noted that the social sciences in contrast to the natural sciences will always be characterized by multiple theoretical orientations and will never achieve the degree of consensus about empirical referents or explanatory schemes characteristic of the natural sciences. Indeed, because the natural sciences—physics and biology, for example—have few competing theories, disconfirming one and replacing it with another is a rather momentous event, an event Kuhn (1970) has termed a "paradigm shift." In contrast, competing theories are common in the social sciences because the nature of the phenomena being studied allows for those phenomena to be viewed from multiple perspectives, or "lenses." Each perspective could provide a reasoned and sensible explanation of the phenomenon being studied.

As an example, drawn from the discipline of psychology, consider the classical theories of play. Gilmore (1971) categorized them into the following areas: surplus energy theory, relaxation theory, recapitulation theory, and pre-exercise theory. Surplus energy theory posits that humans accumulate energy that must be released. Play uses the surplus energy the body does not need. According to relaxation theory, play allows people to build up energy that can be used later for the purposes of work. Recapitulation theory states that humans pass through stages that parallel phases in the development of the human race. Essentially, play helps to transcend the primitive stages of life. Finally, pre-exercise theory avers that play prepares children for their adult roles. During play, children rehearse the skills they will use as adults. Each of the theories may be a reasoned explanation of the phenomenon; none appear to disconfirm the others. All of them may coexist, providing different perspectives on play.

Theories in social science research exist at a variety of levels. The most common levels of theories in social science research include individual theories, organizational theories, group theories, and social theories (see Yin, 1994, pp. 29–30). Individual theories focus on the individual's development, cognitive behavior, personality, learning, and interpersonal interactions. Organizational theories focus on bureaucracies, institutions, organizational structures and functions, and effectiveness or excellence in organizational performance. Group theories deal with family issues, work teams, employer-employee relations, and interpersonal networks. Finally, social theories focus on group behavior, cultural institutions, urban development, and marketplace functions. These levels cut across social science disciplines and afford a myriad of theories at each level.

In social science research, theories are generally drawn from the various disciplines (e.g., political science, economics, anthropology, sociology, psychology). These disciplines provide a plethora of lenses for examining phenomena. Neophyte researchers often confine their consideration of theory to theories they have frequently encountered. In so doing, they may fail to uncover the wealth of theories in the various disciplines that might be efficacious. If properly used, these varied perspectives can tremendously enhance research. More than this, these "disciplines interact and mutually enrich each other" (Suppes, 1974, p. 56).

With a basic understanding of what theory is and some sense of the different ways in which theory is used in research in the natural and social sciences, let us now turn our attention to looking at what we know about the role of theory (specifically the use of theoretical frameworks) in qualitative research.

A Review of the Literature on Theoretical Frameworks in Qualitative Research

Whereas there is little disagreement about the role and place of theory in quantitative research (Creswell, 1994, 2002), such is not the situation with respect to qualitative research. Indeed, there is neither consensus about its role in qualitative research, nor about what is being discussed. Much of what we credit as warranted knowledge about qualitative research comes through the relatively small, albeit growing numbers of textbooks in the field, materials widely used by teachers of research to prepare and mentor students and neophyte researchers. Examination of the most prominent of these materials for wisdom about the role of theory in qualitative research leaves the reader with one of three different understandings: first, that theory has little relationship to qualitative research (Best & Kahn, 2003; Gay & Airasian, 2003); second, that theory in qualitative research relates to the methodology the researcher chooses to use and the epistemologies underlying that methodology (Crotty, 1998; Denzin & Lincoln, 2003a, 2003b; Guba, 1990; Lincoln & Guba, 1985), and to a subset of this position, that it is related to some methodologies (Creswell, 1994, 1998, 2002; Gall, Borg, & Gall, 1996; Patton, 1990; Yin, 1993, 1994); and third, that theory in qualitative research is broader and more pervasive in its role than methodology (Bentz & Shapiro, 1998; Flinders & Mills, 1993; Garrison, 1988; Maxwell, 1996; Merriam, 1998; Miles & Huberman, 1994; Mills, 1993; Schram, 2003; Schwandt, 1993).

The categories of understandings are not exclusive, and authors may lean toward more than one position. For example, Broido and Manning (2002) situated the role of theory within methodological paradigms, yet they hinted at the notion that theory has a much wider role to play. Similarly, Merriam (2002) acknowledged the part methodology plays in the "theoretical stances" researchers take, while continuing to address what she perceived as the broader, deeper influence of theory on the research process. It is, however, these differences in emphasis about what theory refers to and is about that are a source of confusion for the student and neophyte researcher.

Theory as Nearly Invisible

In a widely used textbook, Gay and Airasian (2003) do not discuss, nor even mention, theory in relation to qualitative research, although they noted that, "Some fundamental differences in how quantitative and qualitative research are conducted reflect their different perspectives on meaning and how one can approach it" (p. 9). Best and Kahn (2003) mentioned theory, but confined their discussion to defining it as "an attempt to develop a general explanation for some phenomenon . . . primarily concerned with explanation and therefore focus[ing] on determining cause-effect relationships" (p. 9), normally the province of quantitative research.

Several other authors give short shrift to discussions of theory in qualitative research, while acknowledging its relevance to a particular methodology. Gall, Borg, and Gall (1996) relegated the role of theory to its development or testing, identifying it as a type of research. Although most of their discussion of theory used examples drawn from quantitative research, they suggested it has some role in qualitative research. "Many qualitative studies are done to discover theory. The approach sometimes is called *grounded theory* because the researcher starts by collecting data then searches for theoretical constructs, themes, and patterns that are 'grounded in the theory'" (p. 52).

Theory as Related to Methodology

In sharp contrast to these works, where theory in relation to qualitative research is nonexistent or relatively modest, there is a substantive body of work that equates theory in qualitative research with the methodologies used in the conduct of the research and the epistemologies underlying these methods. These works are well-known, and largely written about qualitative research specifically, rather than about research in general. In earlier works by Lincoln and Guba (1985) and Guba (1990), they speak about paradigms as "what we think about the world" (Lincoln & Guba, 1985, p. 15), "basic belief systems . . . that have emerged as successors to conventional positivism" (Guba, 1990, p. 9), that is, postpositivism, critical theory, and constructivism. They speak about theories emerging from naturalistic inquiry, not framing it, and methods changing in the process of theory definition. Guba (1990), in particular, called on others to support the paradigm-methodology connection (Eisner, 1990; Schwandt, 1993), and concluded, "If inquiry is not value free, is not all inquiry ideological?" (Guba, 1990, p. 11) Interestingly enough in light of later works, Lincoln and Guba (1985) argued that "naturalistic inquiry is defined not at the level of methodology but at the level of paradigm. It is not crucial that naturalistic inquiry be carried out using qualitative methods exclusively, or at all" (p. 250), clearly relating to methodology in relatively simple terms, quantitative and/or qualitative methods.

In later works, Denzin and Lincoln (2003a, 2003b) equated paradigms with theory and argued that these paradigms contain the researchers' "epistemological, ontological and methodological premises" that guide the researchers' actions (2003b, p. 33). These paradigms are identified as: positivism and postpositivism; interpretivism, constructivism, and hermeneutics; feminism(s); racialized discourses; critical theory and Marxist models; cultural studies models; and queer theory (Denzin & Lincoln, 2003a, p. 32). The way it works, according to Denzin and Lincoln (2003b), is that the researcher "approaches the world with a set of ideas, a framework (theory, ontology) that specifies a set of questions (epistemology) that he or she then examines in specific ways (methodology, analysis)" (p. 30). This is a clear linking of theory to methodologies; it also suggests, however, that the study is widely affected by the linkage. Interestingly enough, the authors advised that the qualitative researcher needs to become "bricoleur" (p. 6), taking on pieces of representations (paradigms, methods) to fit the situation. Clearly, paradigms and theories are something to be chosen by the researcher, and with those choices come guiding epistemologies.

In attempting to clarify the relationship among the elements identified by those relating methodological approaches and their genesis in and from philosophic orientations (called paradigms by Denzin and Lincoln, 2003b; theoretical traditions by Patton, 1990; theoretical stances by Merriam, 2002; and theoretical perspectives by Crotty, 1998), Crotty differentiated among epistemology, theoretical perspective, methodology, and method, although he held that they inform one another. For Crotty, theories of knowledge, or epistemologies (e.g., objectivism, constructionism, subjectivism), inform and are embedded in theoretical perspectives (e.g., positivism, interpretivism, critical inquiry, feminism, postmodernism). He claimed that "the philosophical stance inform[s] the methodology and thus provide[s] a context for the process and grounding its logic and criteria" (p. 3). Methodologies—which include a wide range of approaches, from experimental research and survey research, to ethnography, phenomenology, grounded theory, and heuristic inquiry, to action research, discourse analysis, and feminist standpoint research—constitute research designs that affect the choice of methods to be used, for example, observation, case study, statistical analysis, document analysis, and so on. In reality, Crotty framed the reader's understanding of the relationship the other way around, as he perceived that research is constructed from the methods "we propose to use," to the methodology that "governs our choice and use of methods," to the theoretical perspective that "lies behind the methodology in question," to the epistemology that "informs this theoretical perspective" (p. 2).

Yin (1994) argued that case study research, in contrast to other qualitative research designs like ethnography, requires identifying the theoretical perspective at the outset of the inquiry, since it affects the research questions, analysis, and interpretation of findings. In a sense, he argued, "the complete (case study) research design embodies a theory of what is being studied" (p. 28), drawn from the existing knowledge base. It is interesting to note that whereas Yin categorized case study as a research design on a par with ethnography and grounded theory, Crotty (1998) saw case study as a method to be used in realizing methodologies like ethnography and grounded theory.

Creswell (1994, 1998), too, posited the role of theory in qualitative research in relation to research designs (methodologies or theoretical perspectives in Crotty's categorization, 1998). In his earlier book, Creswell (1994) argued that the role of theory varies with the type of research design. In grounded theory, for example, theory is the outcome of the research. In phenomenology, "no preconceived notions, expectations or frameworks guide researchers" (p. 94). In "critical ethnographic" designs, that is, studies with "a critical theory component" (p. 94), one begins with a theory that "informs" the study, although Creswell did not specify what it informs in the study. Interestingly enough, in referring to ethnographic designs without a critical theory component (his designation), Creswell specified that theories might be drawn from "existing theories of culture" (p. 94), outside of methodological parameters, for example, social exchange theory. In referring to how these theories might inform the study, he indicated that they might "help shape the initial research questions" (p. 94). Having said this, however, Creswell argued that

> In a qualitative study, one does not begin with a theory to test or verify. Instead, consistent with the inductive model of thinking, a theory may emerge during the data collection and analysis phase . . . or be used relatively late in the research process as a basis for comparison with other theories. (pp. 94–95)

Indeed, in depicting the research process for qualitative studies, the development of a theory or comparison with other theories comes after the gathering and analysis of data.

In a later book, devoted to distinguishing among five different "research traditions" in qualitative research—biography, phenomenology, grounded theory, ethnography, and case study—Creswell (1998) acknowledged that researchers bring paradigmatic assumptions (ontological, epistemological, axiological, rhetorical, and methodological) to the design of their studies, and may, in addition, bring ideological perspectives (postmodernism, critical theory, and feminism) that "might guide a study" (p. 78). Although he did not specify how the paradigmatic assumptions or ideological perspectives affect the various research designs (traditions), Creswell spoke to "another perspective" (p. 84), social science theories, which he referred to as a theoretical lens rather than as an ideological perspective, and how this lens affects each of the research traditions. He contended that with ethnography and phenomenology, the researcher brings "a strong orienting framework" (p. 86) to the research, whereas in grounded theory, "one collects and analyzes data before using theory" (p. 86). With biography and case study, a theoretical lens might or might not play a part, depending on the nature of the study and the disposition of the researcher.

Patton (1990) posited a set of "theoretical traditions" (a mixture of theoretical perspectives and methodologies in Crotty's [1998] categorization): ethnography, phenomenology, heuristics, ethnomethodology, symbolic interactionism, ecological psychology, systems theory, chaos theory, hermeneutics, and orientational. Because these traditions derive from the social and behavioral science disciplines and the different questions central to these disciplines, Patton (1990) argued for the close link between theory and method, and perhaps more, in a clear, compelling way: "How you study the world determines what you learn about the world" (p. 67).

Theory as More

As compelling as the work relating theory in qualitative research to methodologies and their underlying epistemologies is a body of work that, although not denying the influence of methodologies and their underlying epistemologies, suggests that the role of theory in qualitative research is more pervasive and influential than suggested by those who situate it methodologically. They contend that it plays a key role in framing and conducting almost every aspect of the study.

Merriam (1998) argued that "many believe mistakenly that theory has no place in a qualitative study. Actually, it would be difficult to imagine a study *without* a theoretical or conceptual framework" (p. 45). Referring to Becker (1993), Merriam emphasized that we would not know what to do in conducting our research without some theoretical framework to guide us, whether it is made explicit or not, and calls the theoretical framework "the structure, the scaffolding, the frame of your study" (p. 45). For Merriam, the theoretical framework is derived from the "concepts, terms, definitions, models and theories of a particular literature base and disciplinary orientation" (p. 46), and affects every aspect of the study, from determining how to frame the purpose and problem, to what to look at and for, to how we make sense of the data that are collected. She argued that the entire process is "theory-laden" (p. 48), and that every study has a theoretical framework.

Echoing Merriam (1998), Miles and Huberman (1994) spoke to what they considered to be the critical role theory plays in qualitative research. While admitting that "many social anthropologists and social phenomenologists consider social processes to be too complex, too relative, too elusive or too exotic to be approached with explicit conceptual frames," they held that "any researcher, no matter how unstructured or inductive, comes to fieldwork with *some* orienting ideas" (p. 17). Without at least "some rudimentary conceptual framework" (p. 17), they argued, there would be no way to make reasoned decisions about what data to gather, about what; to determine what is important from among the welter of what is possible. The conceptual framework "can be rudimentary or elaborate, theory-driven or commonsensical, descriptive or causal" (p. 18), but it delineates the main things to be studied and the "presumed relationships among them" (p. 18). The conceptual framework is, according to Miles and Huberman, constructed from the theories and experiences the researcher brings to and draws upon in conceptualizing the study. These theories, implicit and explicit, include grand theories, like symbolic interactionism and "middle-range concepts such as culture" (p. 91), as well as "preconceptions, biases, values, frames, and rhetorical habits" (p. 91).

Maxwell (1996) saw the "conceptual context" as one of five components of the research design that connect and interact in a nonlinear, noncyclical fashion. The conceptual context contains the "goals, experiences, knowledge, assumptions, and theory you bring to the study and incorporate in the design" (p. 6). He argued that what the researcher "thinks is going on with the phenomena" (p. 4) is brought to the consideration and development of the study and influences not only the purposes of the study, but also "what literature, preliminary research and personal experience" (p. 4) the researcher draws on in conceptualizing the study.

In his book on *Conceptualizing Qualitative Research* (2003), Schram aligned the conceptual context of a study with theory, which he saw as extending "from formal explanatory axiom[s] . . . to tentative hunch[es] . . . to any general set of ideas that guide action" (p. 42). He contended that the researcher's perspective, fundamental beliefs, values, hunches, assumptions, and purposes for engaging in the study constitute "premises about the world and how it can be understood and studied" (p. 29), and play a "pervasive but subtle" role in directing the study. This role includes "how you engage with a preliminary sense of problem and purpose, how you portray your involvement with study participants, the way you define key concepts, how you address assumptions within your research questions" (p. 39), as well as "deciding which of the things you see are legitimate and important to document" (p. 29).

Similarly, whereas Bentz and Shapiro (1998) acknowledged that there are "cultures of inquiry . . . general approaches to creating knowledge in the human and social sciences, each with its own model of what counts as knowledge, what it is for, and how it is produced" (p. 9), they contended, nevertheless, that

> Research is always carried out by an individual with a life and a lifeworld . . . a personality, a social context, and various personal and practical challenges and conflicts, all of which affect the research, from the choice of a research question or topic, through the method used, to the reporting of the project's outcome. (p. 4)

Among the advocates of the position that the theoretical or conceptual framework in qualitative research is more than the methodologies and epistemologies underlying them, few are as vehement and articulate the position as cogently as Flinders and Mills (1993). In their book, *Theory and Concepts in Qualitative Research,* they addressed the issue directly. Flinders and Mills began by asserting that "Few of us now claim that we enter the field tabula rasa, unencumbered by notions of the phenomena we seek to understand" (p. xi). They argued that theory includes "any general set of ideas that guide action" (p. xii) and that theory profoundly affects the conduct of the research. "Theory is pragmatically bound up with the activities of planning a study, gaining entry into the field, recording observations, conducting interviews, sifting through documents, and writing up research" (p. xiv). Indeed, they affirmed a statement reputed to William James, "You can't pick up rocks in a field without a theory" (p. xii).

Arguing that atheoretical research is impossible, Schwandt, in Flinders and Mills (1993), contended that it is impossible to observe and describe "the way things really are, free of any prior conceptual scheme or theory . . . without some theory of what is relevant to observe, how what is to be observed is to be named, and so on" (p. 8). It is "prior theoretical commitments and conceptual schemes" (p. 9) that guide the inquiry, according to Schwandt.

Mills (1993) defined theory as an "analytical and interpretive framework that helps the researcher make sense of 'what is going on in the social setting being studied'" (p. 103), and speaks about the implicit and explicit theories underlying the case that is the focus of his chapter—the beliefs, propositions, and theoretical conceptions that framed the study and its analysis, even though the theory was purported to be "emergent." These theories, he argued, "provide the researcher with a framework for the problem and questions to be addressed in the study" (p. 114).

Where Does That Leave Us?

Although this review of the literature on the role of theory in qualitative research is hardly exhaustive, it does provide a basis for considering where we are with respect to the role theory plays in qualitative research. Qualitative research has often been criticized for not being guided by theory in its development and conduct. Clearly, that is not the view shared by those who write about and guide neophyte researchers in doing qualitative research. Theory has a place, an unavoidable place for all but one or two of the authors we have reviewed, and plays a substantive role in the research process. For those writers for whom methodologies are primarily associated with the role of theory, the epistemologies underlying these methodologies as well as the methodologies themselves serve as lenses from and through which the researcher looks at the study. It is not just the choice of a methodology that affects the study. For those writers for whom theory affects studies in more ways than that, without speaking to the matter directly, they clearly imply that methodologies and their underlying epistemologies influence and guide the study theoretically. They do not stop there, however, but suggest that there is more that the researcher brings to the study, and it is all that the researcher brings, implicitly and explicitly, that affects all aspects of the study.

Whereas those who take either position perceive that one's theoretical framework profoundly affects the study, beyond casual mention of some of the aspects of a study affected by this framework by some authors, there is no clear delineation of what in a study is affected by the theoretical framework or how it is affected. Nor is there much discussion of the effect of implicit, unexamined perspectives, biases, and assumptions; of explicit theories that are brought to bear on one's study, for example, from the social sciences; or of the interaction of these and their effect on the study. For existing texts, consideration of theory and its effect on the study is but one aspect of a larger focus of the work. Thus, they provide neither the depth of understanding nor the specificity needed to explicate the topic. If one already understands, at some deep and intimate level, the role and place of a theoretical framework, then explanations are both understandable and confirmatory. One can put the disparate pieces together and fill in the blanks in the places they may not have mentioned. None of the texts, however, provide sufficient guidance to students, neophyte researchers, or those who may not already understand its role and place, to be able to "see" how theoretical frameworks affect research or to be able to fully and appropriately identify and apply a framework to their own research.

This, then, is the purpose of this book. But before we proceed with this guidance in the use of theoretical frameworks, it is necessary to provide a clear definition of what we mean by the term theoretical framework.

A Definition of Theoretical Frameworks

We clearly situate our conception of the theoretical framework with those authors who see theory as "more than" (i.e., Flinders & Mills, 1993; Merriam, 1998; Miles & Huberman, 1994; Schram, 2003). Acknowledging that the term does not have a clear and consistent definition, we define theoretical frameworks as any empirical or quasi-empirical theory of social and/or psychological processes, at a variety of levels (e.g., grand, mid-range, and explanatory), that can be applied to the understanding of phenomena. This definition of theoretical frameworks excludes what Guba and Lincoln (1994) have called "paradigms" of social research (e.g., postpositivist, constructivist, critical, feminist). It also does not consider methodological issues or approaches to be synonymous with theoretical frameworks (e.g., narrative analysis, systems analysis, symbolic interactionism).

Examples of what we mean by theories that can be applied as "lenses" to study phenomena might include Vygotskian learning theory, micro-political theory, class reproduction theory, job choice theory, and social capital, as well as the theories employed by the researchers who have written Chapters 1 through 10 of this book. Theoretical frameworks they used include liminality (V. Turner, 1967, 1977), transformational learning theory (Merizow, 1991), the arena model of policy innovation (Mazzoni, 1991), and grief theory (Kubler-Ross, 1969), to name a few.

There are a large number and wide variety of theoretical frameworks available for qualitative researchers to consider. These frameworks originate in the many different fields of study and disciplines in the social and natural sciences. Thus, the well-read qualitative researcher is alert to theoretical frameworks in economics, sociology, political science, psychology, biology, physics, and anthropology, to name but a few. That same researcher is open to considering the applicability of these frameworks to the research problem chosen to study. It is, indeed, this diversity and richness of theoretical frameworks that allow us to see in new and different ways what seems to be ordinary and familiar.

As examples, Hoenack and Monk (1990) applied economic theory to a study of the costs and benefits of teacher evaluation systems in education. The economic aspects they addressed included production theory and efficiency, the economics of information, performance incentives, and the distributional effects of policy interventions. The use of this unusual theoretical framework in educational research allowed the authors to present a unique view of the phenomenon being studied. Pounder and Merrill (2001) used job choice theory (developed by Behling, Labovitz, & Gainer, 1968; and later adapted to an educational setting by Young, Rinehart, & Place, 1989) to examine potential candidates' perceptions and job intentions with regard to the high school principalship.

In defining theoretical frameworks, we are cognizant that any framework or theory allows the researcher to "see" and understand certain aspects of the phenomenon being studied while concealing other aspects. No theory, or theoretical framework, provides a perfect explanation of what is being studied— a point we shall return to in the concluding chapter of this book.

Organization of the Book

The chapters that follow (1 through 10) take you "behind the scenes" to examine the role of theoretical frameworks in qualitative research. They allow you to learn how these researchers found the theoretical framework they used in a particular study, and how it affected that study. The contributors take you on their journey in using the framework and in thinking about its applicability, providing sufficient detail to allow you to assess what they saw, against the published research study discussed and cited. These insights provide the reader with practical lessons drawn from real-world studies. These lessons concern not only the contributions of theory to qualitative research, but also the dilemmas and pitfalls that theory presents to researchers.

To allow the reader to compare and contrast responses across chapters, contributors were asked to address the following items (if relevant), in approximately this order:

1. an overview of the study that formed the basis for the discussion of the theoretical framework used, including its purpose, research questions, methods employed, findings, and conclusions;

2. a detailed description of the theoretical framework(s) used in the study and the discipline in which it/they originated;

3. how the researcher found the theoretical framework and what convinced him or her that this was an appropriate framework to use;

4. what effects the theoretical framework had on the research questions, the design of the study, and the analyses obtained;

5. other conceptual frameworks considered and why they were used or discarded; and

6. any additional issues the contributors wished to discuss in relation to the use of theory in their research.

The headings and subheadings in the chapters in this book correspond to the above items. As noted earlier, this structure was imposed to allow readers

Table I.1   Chapters in *Theoretical Frameworks in Qualitative Research*

Theoretical framework	Field of study/discipline	Focus of study	Chapter number
Culture (Goodenough)	Cognitive anthropology	Organizational change; culture of teachers	Chapter 1
Transformational learning and adult development (Mezirow)	Psychology	HIV-positive young adults	Chapter 2
Arena model of policy innovation (Mazzoni)	Political science	Passage of Ohio S.B. 140 in 1989—comprehensive school reform	Chapter 3
Liminality (Turner)	Anthropology	Experiences of university faculty with a college reorganization	Chapter 4
Social identity theory and self-categorization theory (Hogg, Terry & White)	Sociology/ organizational studies	Experience of university faculty with a college reorganization	Chapter 5
Chaos/complexity (Prigogine & Stengers)	Physical and biological sciences	Midlife transitions and resolution of midlife tasks for social workers	Chapter 6
Grief model (Kubler-Ross)	Psychology	Educational reform/ organizational change	Chapter 7
Typology of grid and group (Douglas)	Social anthropology	School culture	Chapter 8
Habitus/field theory (Bourdieu)	Sociology	Curriculum development	Chapter 9
Queer legal theory (Lugg)	Law	Historical analysis of schools	Chapter 10

to compare and contrast the responses of the various contributing chapter authors. Readers will note slight variations in the wording of some of the headings and subheadings, but the variations are slight and, more important, the content in each chapter addresses each of the six areas.

Table I.1 provides an overview of the theoretical frameworks used by the contributing authors, the fields from which they were taken, and the foci of the studies that employed them.

The final chapter of the book is an analysis of Chapters 1 through 10. After carefully reading and reflecting on these chapters, we offer our readers a discussion of the salient points addressed by the authors. This discussion focuses on the relationship between theory and qualitative research, and offers readers a series of lessons learned as well as issues that need our attention.

References

Agnew, N., & Pyke, S. W. (1969). *The science game.* Englewood Cliffs, NJ: Prentice Hall.

Alexander, J. C. (1987). The centrality of the classics. In A. Giddens & J. Turner (Eds.), *Social theory today* (pp. 11–57). Stanford, CA: Stanford University Press.

Argyris, C., & Schon, D. A. (1974). *Theory in practice: Increasing professional effectiveness.* San Francisco: Jossey-Bass.

Babbie, E. (1986). *The practice of social research* (4th ed.). Belmont, CA: Wadsworth.

Becker, H. S. (1993). Theory: The necessary evil. In D. J. Flinders & G. E. Mills (Eds.), *Theory and concepts in qualitative research: Perspectives from the field* (pp. 218–230). New York: Teachers College Press.

Behling, O., Labovitz, G., & Gainer, M. (1968). College recruiting: A theoretical base. *Personnel Journal, 47,* 13–19.

Bentz, V. M., & Shapiro, J. J. (1998). *Mindful inquiry in social research.* Thousand Oaks, CA: Sage.

Best, J. W., & Kahn, J. V. (2003). *Research in education* (9th ed.). Boston: Allyn & Bacon.

Broido, E. M., & Manning, K. (2002). Philosophical foundations and current theoretical perspectives in qualitative research. *Journal of College Student Development, 43*(4), 434–445.

Creswell, J. W. (1994). *Research design.* Thousand Oaks, CA: Sage.

Creswell, J. W. (1998). *Qualitative inquiry and research design.* Thousand Oaks, CA: Sage.

Creswell, J. W. (2002). *Educational research.* Upper Saddle River, NJ: Pearson Education.

Crotty, M. (1998). *The foundations of social research.* London: Sage.

Denzin, N. K., & Lincoln, Y. S. (Eds.). (2003a). *Collecting and interpreting qualitative materials* (2nd ed.). Thousand Oaks, CA: Sage.

Denzin, N. K., & Lincoln, Y. S. (2003b). *The landscape of qualitative research* (2nd ed.). Thousand Oaks, CA: Sage.

Eisner, E. W. (1990). The meaning of alternative paradigms for practice. In E. Guba (Ed.), *The paradigm dialog* (pp. 88–102). Newbury Park, CA: Sage.

Eisner, E. W. (1993). Foreword. In D. J. Flinders & G. E. Mills (Eds.), *Theory and concepts in qualitative research: Perceptions from the field* (pp. vii–ix). New York: Teachers College Press.

Festinger, L. (1957). *A theory of cognitive dissonance*. Evanston, IL: Row, Peterson, & Company.

Flinders, D. J., & Mills, G. E. (Eds.). (1993). *Theory and concepts in qualitative research: Perceptions from the field*. New York: Teachers College Press.

Gall, M. D., Borg, W. R., & Gall, J. P. (1996). *Educational research*. (6th ed.). New York: Longman.

Garrison, J. (1988). The impossibility of atheoretical science. *Journal of Educational Thought, 22*, 21–26.

Gay, L. R., & Airasian, P. (2003). *Educational research* (7th ed.). Upper Saddle River, NJ: Merrill Prentice Hall.

Gilmore, J. (1971). The effectiveness of parental counseling with other modalities in the treatment of children with learning disabilities. *Journal of Education, 154*, 74–82.

Guba, E. G. (Ed.). (1990). *The paradigm dialog*. Newbury Park, CA: Sage.

Guba, E. G., & Lincoln, Y. S. (1994). Competing paradigms in qualitative research. In N. K. Denzin & Y. S. Lincoln (Eds.), *Handbook of qualitative research* (pp. 105–117). Thousand Oaks, CA: Sage.

Hoenack, S. A., & Monk, D. H. (1990). Economic aspects of teacher evaluation. In J. Millman & L. Darling-Hammond (Eds.), *The new handbook of teacher evaluation* (pp. 390–402). Newbury Park, CA: Sage.

Kerlinger, F. N. (1986). *Foundations of behavioral research* (3rd ed.). New York: Holt, Rinehart & Winston.

Kubler-Ross, E. (1969). *On death and dying*. New York: Touchstone.

Kuhn, T. (1970). *The structure of scientific revolutions* (2nd ed.). Chicago: University of Chicago Press.

Langenbach, M., Vaughn, C., & Aagaard, L. (1994). *An introduction to educational research*. Boston: Allyn & Bacon.

LeCompte, M. D., & Preissle, J. (1993). *Ethnography and qualitative design in educational research* (2nd ed.). San Diego: Academic Press.

Lincoln, Y. S., & Guba, E. G. (1985). *Naturalistic inquiry*. Beverly Hills, CA: Sage.

Maslow, A. H. (1954). *Motivation and personality*. New York: Harper & Row.

Maxwell, J. A. (1996). *Qualitative research design*. Thousand Oaks, CA: Sage.

Mazzoni, T. (1991). Analyzing state school policy making: An arena model. *Educational Evaluation and Policy Analysis, 13*, 115–138.

McGregor, D. (1960). *The human side of enterprise*. New York: McGraw-Hill.

McMillan, J. H., & Schumacher, S. (2001). *Research in education: A conceptual introduction* (5th ed.). New York: Longman.

Merizow, J. (1991). *Transformative theory of adult learning*. San Francisco: Jossey-Bass.

Merriam, S. B. (1998). *Qualitative research and case study applications in education*. San Francisco: Jossey-Bass.

Merriam, S. B., & Associates. (2002). *Qualitative research in practice*. San Francisco: Jossey-Bass.

Miles, M. B., & Huberman, A. M. (1994). *Qualitative data analysis* (2nd ed.). Thousand Oaks, CA: Sage.

Mills, G. E. (1993). Levels of abstraction in a case study of educational change. In D. J. Flinders & G. E. Mills (Eds.), *Theory and concepts in qualitative research: Perceptions from the field* (pp. 103–116). New York: Teachers College Press.

Patton, M. Q. (1990). *Qualitative evaluation and research methods* (2nd ed.). Newbury Park, CA: Sage.

Pounder, D. G., & Merrill, R. J. (2001). Job desirability of the high school principalship: A job choice theory perspective. *Educational Administration Quarterly, 37*(1), 27–57.

Schram, T. H. (2003). *Conceptualizing qualitative inquiry.* Columbus, OH: Merrill Prentice Hall.

Schwandt, T. A. (1993). Theory for the moral sciences. In D. J. Flinders & G. E. Mills (Eds.), *Theory and concepts in qualitative research: Perceptions from the field* (pp. 5–23). New York: Teachers College Press.

Silver, P. (1983). *Educational administration: Theoretical perspectives on practice and research.* New York: Harper & Row.

Strauss, A. (1995). *Qualitative analysis for social scientists.* Cambridge, UK: Cambridge University Press.

Suppes, F. (1974). *The structure of scientific theories* (2nd ed.). Urbana: University of Illinois Press.

Turner, J. (1974). *The structure of sociological theory.* Homewood, IL: Dorsey.

Turner, V. (1967). *The forest of symbols.* Ithaca, NY: Cornell University Press.

Turner, V. (1977). Variations on a theme of liminality. In S. F. Moore & B. G. Myerhoff (Eds.), *Secular ritual* (pp. 36–52). Amsterdam: Van Gorcum.

Yin, R. K. (1993). *Applications of case study research.* Newbury Park, CA: Sage.

Yin, R. K. (1994). *Case study research* (2nd ed.). Thousand Oaks, CA: Sage.

Young, I. P., Rinehart, J. S., & Place, W. (1989). Theories for teacher selection: Objective, subjective and critical contact. *Teaching and Teacher Education, 5,* 329–336.

1

Seeking an Understanding of School Culture: Using Theory as a Framework for Observation and Analysis

Joyce L. Henstrand

Overview of the Study

Purpose

This case study of planned change at Emerson High School, a large suburban high school, was conducted to contribute to the understanding of the process of reforming secondary schools. At the time I conducted my research, most studies of reform had involved elementary schools, but the findings of these studies did not apply to the more complex high school system (Fullan, 1990; McLaughlin & Talbert, 1990). The persistent resistance of high schools to systemic change and the lack of case studies focused on improving high schools (Miles, 1986) offered the opportunity to participate in the national dialogue related to improving the nation's high schools.

After a search of studies on school reform, I decided to approach my investigation from a cultural perspective. In the previous 20 years, most investigations of change had been from a technological or a political perspective. One example of a technological approach, the concerns-based adoption model developed by Hall and Hord (1984) to offer facilitators a formula for bringing about change in schools, assumed that if a facilitator helps individuals work through a series of predictable stages, the result will be successful implementation of reform. Politically oriented studies, in contrast, focused on examining how tensions and conflicts between individuals or among groups have slowed or prevented reform. Neither the technological nor the political approaches appealed to me. The technological change models tended to reduce the change process to a formula, assuming most people will respond uniformly to the treatment being administered by the change facilitator, and the political approaches focused on the political aspects of conflict. Neither explained the way people experience change nor the interaction of an organization's internal culture with the change process.

My interest lay in the cultural perspective because my experiences as a teacher had enabled me to witness the complexities of the change process from inside the organization. I had participated in failed reform efforts and in highly successful innovations. From my perspective, teacher values, the culture of the organization, and the leadership skills of the change facilitator were the key issues in successful reform efforts. Supporting this approach in his early work on change, Michael Fullan (1982) argued, "Neglect of . . . how people actually experience change as distinct from how it might have been intended is at the heart of the spectacular lack of success of most social reforms" (p. 4). In his classic work *The Culture of the School and the Problem of Change*, Sarason (1982) attributed the high failure rate of school reform to a lack of understanding of school culture and advocated for increased descriptive studies of the process of change in the school culture. By providing a case study (as defined by Yin, 1984, p. 23) describing how people actually experience change, this study was intended to create a dialogue between those who experience change and those who want to know about change.

I began the case study without a thesis; instead, for a full school year I observed the culture of a high school as reform was attempted (Fullan, 1990; McLaughlin & Talbert, 1990). The essential question of the study was "What is going on here?"—a question Wolcott (1988) believes is suitable for ethnographic research. The result is a description and interpretation of change in the context of a specific school culture. It does not provide a prescription for carrying out future change efforts in other places, but it does provide cultural insight to those who seek to bring about change in high schools.

Methodology

Because I approached this case study from a cultural perspective, I chose the ethnographic research techniques of cultural anthropology and conducted my research from my perspective as a full-time practicing teacher in a large high school. As this position was unusual in ethnographic research, I not only studied theory related to the conduct of anthropological fieldwork, but also wrote a rationale detailing the implications of the "native" becoming a researcher. In addition, as part of the findings, I included a detailed discussion of the implications of both being a full member of the culture and conducting ethnographic research. The theory and implications surrounding this research stance will be discussed later in this chapter.

I conducted fieldwork with a repertoire of strategies that generally followed Spradley's (1980) cycles played over many times. The strategy I used at any point in time depended on "feedback from the field, redefinition of research questions as [my] understanding of the culture [deepened], and meanings that participants [attached] to things" (LeCompte & Goetz, 1984, p. 165). The individual career history required the specialized methodology of Denzin (1970), Kluckhohn (1945), Langness and Frank (1986), and Wolcott (1983). Although the sequence of use varied from situation to situation, the strategies included:

Interviewing. I used James Spradley's (1979) ethnographic interview to guide the informal interviews, which were useful during the early months of my fieldwork when I was discovering major issues. During the later stages, I added formal interviews to focus on specific topics. As a model for the formal interviews, I used the long interview as described by McCracken (1988).

Observation. My natural involvement in school activities provided access to most school events. Whenever possible, I took notes verbatim. In instances in which I could not take notes, I jotted down key comments and crucial quotes as soon after the event as possible. Every evening, I reviewed my notes and filled in gaps.

Key Informants. I followed the advice of H. Russell Bernard (1988) and Jeffrey Johnson (1990) as I chose informants.

Surveys and Questionnaires. The work of Fink and Kosecoff (1985), Bailey (1987), Worthen and Sanders (1987), and Gay (1987) guided me in the development and administration of a census survey as part of a reciprocal agreement (as defined by Wax, 1952) with the School Improvement Team.

Additional Strategies. I used unobtrusive measures (Webb, Campbell, Schwartz, & Sechrest, 1966) such as archives and physical traces to corroborate evidence found through other data gathering techniques.

Findings

The case is presented in three sections (Goodenough, 1981) that represent the culture as a whole, subgroups within the culture, and the outlook of an individual. My goal was to provide "thick description" (Geertz, 1973) to enable readers to experience and interpret the change process during an academic year at Emerson High School. Emerging from the description is a portrait of a school that appeared to outsiders to achieve its goal: *providing multiple opportunities for success for students*. That broad goal fostered multiple projects: a mentor program, a peer tutoring project, curriculum changes in language arts and social studies, and articulation of services to students at all grade levels. Although these overt accomplishments seemed to signal success, covert changes in the school culture undermined and eventually prevented the overall success of reform at Emerson High School. When the principal, George Barnes, covertly changed policies regarding student discipline, teacher support for the entire reform project eroded. Barnes, in his determination to keep students in school and in class regardless of their behavior, violated a sacred norm of the teaching staff—the belief that strong discipline support from administration both ensured a positive climate in the school and contributed positively to the education of students. The frustrations that teachers felt over what they perceived as a lack of disciplinary support and Barnes's response that he had no intention of removing students from classes for either suspensions or expulsions, ultimately affected teachers' responses to all of the reform projects that Barnes advocated.

Comments made by administrators and teachers throughout the process indicated basic differences in how administrators and teachers perceived their worlds, so neither side understood or empathized with the view of the other. Not surprisingly, communication also suffered and contributed to teacher dissatisfaction. By focusing on information about events and goals, Barnes inadvertently violated another sacred norm of the teachers: their need to have information regarding expectations, follow-up on student issues, and information that affected their careers or their daily work. The opposing perceptions by administrators and teachers of what constituted good communication and appropriate discipline for students led to serious dissatisfaction among staff and erosion of support for all of the change projects.

Descriptions of three faculty groups, the School Improvement Team, the At-Risk Steering Committee, and the department chairs, revealed further erosion in the climate of the school because Barnes's interactions with these groups increased difficulties in reaching the school goals. Barnes created the At-Risk Steering Committee to lead school reform. He appointed new teachers and others who supported, and did not question, the school goals. It quickly became obvious that this group was steering the course of reform at Emerson

High School. Veteran teachers frequently voiced their annoyance that new teachers were influencing the future of the school more than veterans.

The School Improvement Team, a mostly veteran group elected by their teaching peers, felt frustrated that Barnes had assigned the task of leading the reform to the At-Risk Steering Committee. The teachers and classified staff on the School Improvement Team had been elected by their peers to represent them in areas such as determining and planning implementation of the school goals. Although the team members were generally supportive of the school goal "to provide multiple opportunities for success" to all students, they did not agree with Barnes when it came to implementation. A prominent example was their skepticism about the program to mentor at-risk students. Responding to comments from teachers, they strongly urged that Barnes provide professional development and support on how to mentor students, but very little training occurred. Once the mentoring program began, team members tried to inform Barnes about staff frustrations related to discipline issues. They told Barnes that they did not want to abandon the program, but suggested changes that would make the program more palatable for teachers. Disagreements emerged in the meetings. Barnes grew frustrated with their questions and questioned teachers' dedication to student success. The teachers accused him of not listening, and eventually withdrew active support for the innovations. Barnes stopped going to the School Improvement Team meetings. Abandoned by the principal, the School Improvement Team found purpose for its existence by dedicating its efforts to seeking resolution to staff frustrations. The team conducted a staff survey and published results that revealed deep dissatisfaction among the majority of the staff. Barnes's refusal to change the course of action for the school led to deeper dissatisfaction and further eroded support for the reforms.

The department heads, another group of veteran teachers, were appointed by the principal to perform administrative tasks related to running their departments. Seeking to domesticate several strong critics by appointing them as department heads, Barnes reduced their open opposition because actively supporting school goals was a condition of their employment as department coordinators. Although these influential teachers were kept out of the decision-making loop, they were charged with implementing changes in curriculum and instruction within their departments. Their meetings were marked by civility and reporting on progress toward the goals. Informally, as they interacted with colleagues, they sometimes joked about issues but seldom openly opposed Barnes. In their official roles, they worked to implement the goals, but they rarely expressed enthusiastic support among their peers.

Barnes's work with the three groups promoted a phenomenon that Fullan and Stiegelbauer (1991) refer to as balkanization and Sergiovanni (1986) calls wild centers. Normally, centers in schools provide stability and are "normal and necessary for establishing social order and providing meaning"; but they can, if left unattended, become "wild centers" that "may not only contradict administrative and organizational aspirations but may conflict as well among themselves" (Sergiovanni, 1986, p. 9). By abandoning two groups of powerful teachers, Barnes encouraged them to become wild centers, undermining his own goals.

Conclusions

Emerging from this examination of a school in the process of change is the notion that responses at all levels of the organization influence the success of attempts at reform. It is no doubt important to come to an understanding of how an entire staff accepts or rejects an innovation. Equally important to understanding the change process, however, are the roles played by small groups and by individuals. In the case of Emerson High School, all the experiences of the small groups and the individuals came together to create the overall phenomenon of the organization. To fully comprehend the culture of the school, the whole must be understood in terms of the parts just as the parts must be understood in terms of the whole. My observations of the staff, the subgroups, and the individual revealed three significant issues to be considered by those working to change schools.

Issue #1: Teachers and Administrators Have Opposing Ideational Systems. Teachers and administrators tend to interpret the same phenomena in different ways. This viewpoint supports the notions of Wolcott (1977) and Rossman, Corbett, and Firestone (1988) on how to approach issues associated with making changes in an organization. Understanding, rather than berating, the norms and sacred values of others can more productively lead to solutions and thoughtful implementation of change. The key issue at Emerson High School was student discipline. As Barnes and his administrative team worked on discipline issues, they operated from the belief that they were redirecting students to more successful choices. Because the administrative approach did not involve traditional consequences such as suspension, teachers viewed each incident as a personal insult that proved lack of support from the administration. In this and all issues I observed, the subgroup of administrators tended to think in terms of the big picture and acted to move the system toward its goals. On the other hand, teachers tended to focus on the specifics of each situation and how it impacted their own classroom. This was a cultural characteristic shared by the teacher subgroups and also by the individual teacher. Barnes wondered why teachers could not see the big picture and criticized them for focusing on small issues and incidents. A comment by one teacher represented the viewpoint of her colleagues when she stated that her job demands focus on details: daily class schedules, taking attendance, tracking hundreds of grades, and filling out paperwork. She wondered how Barnes could expect teachers to shift easily to the big picture in the context of their daily reality. The conflicting interpretations were never resolved and undermined the school improvement goals.

Issue #2: Teacher Beliefs About Reforms Have More Impact Than Facts. The beliefs of members of the Culture and subgroups are ultimately more important than the facts about what actually happens. The overly broad goal at Emerson High School led to multiple interpretations of its meaning; without adequate information and direction, teachers acted on their own perceptions. Barnes did provide teachers with factual information, but he did not provide information that corresponded with what teachers desired, such as how the reforms would impact their work, including their relationships with students. After each factual communication, teachers created their own interpretations. Those vested in the planning, such as the At-Risk Steering Committee, tended to react favorably to announcements. Teachers with less or no involvement in the development of the goals created interpretations that questioned Barnes's motives and assumed the worst. Barnes's explanations after the fact rarely changed any minds; teachers clung to their own interpretations that were closely aligned with their personal belief systems. Reactions of teachers in subgroups helped to reify the interpretations of the general population.

Issue #3: School Reforms Impact the Lives of Teachers as Well as Students. In the flurry to improve schools for the benefit of students, it is easy to forget that teachers have needs, too. Seymour Sarason (1990) argues that "schools are no less for the growth of staff than for students" (p. 150) and claims that ignoring that notion has contributed to the failure of many reform efforts. The case of an individual teacher, Linda Nelson, illustrates how *not* to nourish a talented and productive teacher. Although, Nelson was publicly acknowledged for her contributions, her work was rewarded with extra responsibilities and increased committee work. She resented the lack of compensation for extra tasks, grew disillusioned, and finally left the profession to pursue a different career. Another example is the impact on teachers related to changes in disciplinary tactics. When teachers sent students to the office because of severe disciplinary infractions (such as swearing at the teacher), they expected to be supported by administration with appropriate consequences for the student. When students were returned to the classroom with no tangible consequence, the teachers felt that their authority had been undermined. Furthermore, they reinforced their interpretations in the subgroups and at informal gatherings. The reform was making life better for students, but worse for teachers. Not surprisingly, teacher support for the reform eroded.

Although the people and events of Emerson High School will not be exactly replicated in another organization, their story offers an insider's view of the culture of a suburban high school grappling with change. Leaders in reform should take the time to study and understand each school's culture, including the variations in the ideational systems of teacher groups and individuals. Using that knowledge, the needs of both adults and students can be addressed during the process of change.

My Use of Theory

Prior to commencing fieldwork, I studied theory in two distinct areas: (1) sociological and anthropological theory that would potentially guide both the gathering and analysis of the data, and (2) theoretical discussions by anthropologists regarding the research role of an active participant observer. In the first case, I was seeking a theoretical framework that would "guide and clarify" my observations, data collection, and analysis (Wolcott, 1995, p. 183). In the second case, I sought justification for my research role, which involved being a "native" who becomes a researcher rather than the classic stance of "stranger" seeking to understand the natives. In both areas, the theoretical stances I chose were critical in every phase of the work.

Theoretical Framework

The theoretical orientation of cognitive anthropology, and, more specifically, the work of Ward Goodenough (1981), guided my data collection and analysis. Other theoretical frameworks influenced several aspects of the study, and will be explained later in this chapter, but Goodenough's framework was the major influence. My search for a theoretical stance began when I was a doctoral student at the University of Oregon and enrolled in a course in educational anthropology offered by Harry Wolcott. I developed an interest in ethnographic research, with its emphasis on description and interpretation. Eventually, I took a class from Wolcott called "Culture Theory" and wrote a paper that explored the appropriateness of various sociological and anthropological theories in anthropological research. I found multitudes of theories and continued my reading after I completed the class. I settled on cognitive anthropologist Ward Goodenough's cultural framework for the case study of Emerson High School because it allowed me to examine the multiple roles of teachers in the school culture and explained the relation of individuals, small groups, and the whole in the process of change (Henstrand, 1993).

Cognitive anthropology "focuses on discovering how different peoples organize and use their cultures" (Tyler, 1969, p. 3) and perceives that culture resides in the minds of people rather than in the material phenomena of the system. When they study a culture, cognitive anthropologists seek to understand the organizing principles underlying behavior" (Tyler, p. 3). They ask, "What material phenomena are significant for the people" and "How do they organize these phenomena" (Tyler, p. 3). Cognitive anthropologists are also interested in both differences between cultures and differences within cultures (Tyler, 1969). Their "prime inroad" for understanding groups and their cultures is language (Agar, 1987, p. 432).

Ward Goodenough, one of the early leading scholars of cognitive anthropology, "took language as [his] point of departure for studying culture" (1963, p. iii). Culture "consists of standards for deciding what can be, standards for deciding how one feels about it, standards for deciding what to do about it, and standards for deciding how to go about doing it" (Goodenough, 1963, pp. 258–259). Culture is not the material artifacts or observed traditions; rather, it is "what is learned, . . . the things one needs to know in order to meet the standards of others" (Goodenough, 1981, p. 50). Public culture is not taken as "a given simply to be described; [he] takes it as a phenomenon to be explained" (Goodenough, 1981, p. 59). Language is the primary vehicle for learning from members of the culture pool.

Goodenough's (1981) definition of culture includes not only the Culture (with a capital C) of the entire society but also allows for subgroups and for individuals. The Culture includes the values and traditions that are known to all members of the society. Subgroups consist of smaller groups or clusters that, in addition to sharing the values and traditions of the Culture, have values, traditions, and language unique to the members of their group. Individuals have their own personal idiolect or version of the language and their own private version of the shared Culture. Further, Goodenough (1981) argued, "no two individuals have exactly the same understanding of it in all respects" (p. 97). The individual outlook that Goodenough labeled "propriospect" grows "out of his own experience [as] each individual develops his private, subjective view of the world and of its contents—his personal outlook" (p. 98). The "sum of the contents of all of the propriospects of the society's members" (p. 111) becomes the Culture pool. On the other hand, each propriospect can contain pieces from many different cultures. Thus, the concept of propriospect not only allows for differences between individuals but also accounts for an individual person being multicultural and choosing an appropriate operating culture at will.

Goodenough's (1981) model of culture accounts for gradual change (culture drift), rapid change, innovation, and response to change. Culture drift occurs as younger individuals shift their ideas, beliefs, values, recipes, or traditions away from those taught to them by their elders and toward other influences. Faster change can occur when members of the Culture reevaluate and accept change in ideas, beliefs, values, recipes, or traditions. If the changes cause dissonance between the public culture and peoples' beliefs, a crisis may develop with turmoil among members. Some customs may acquire such deep commitment from the members of the Culture that

> People demand of one another that they acquire the knowledge and skills needed to perform these routines. They demand cooperation of one another in their performance, and they prohibit behavior that interferes with them or that jeopardizes the arrangements and stockpiles on which performance of these customary routines depends, investing them with moral rightness and even sanctity. (Goodenough, 1981, p. 90)

Individuals may withdraw from the changes or change may be blocked in the Culture.

Making Goodenough's (1981) model of culture the organizing framework for my study was a relatively simple choice for me. I had spent over a year (Henstrand, 1993) investigating multiple anthropological and sociological theories of culture. Although they offered insights that expanded my knowledge and influenced my work in small ways, I had not "connected" with any of them. Structural and functional theories tended to concentrate on the phenomenal world by looking at social structure and function. They were more concerned with the relationship of structure and function than with the belief systems of the members. Most analyses focused on a unit of measure. For instance, Durkheim was more interested in societal forces than in the individual, and Radcliff-Brown analyzed change in terms of the whole social structure. In contrast, Weber and Malinowski focused on individuals as their unit of analysis. In addition to the limitations of their unit of analysis, structural and functional theories lacked constructs for talking about change. Functionalism, in particular, focused on explaining continuity of culture rather than change. Because I was studying planned change, structuralism and functionalism seemed limited in usefulness for my work.

In contrast to the limitations of the structural and functional theories, Goodenough's (1981) model provided a means to understand the complexities of the social system I found in the high school. His model included a framework for analyzing the total group, smaller clusters within the group, and individuals. I was not forced to place individuals in a single category but could identify overlapping roles and relationships. In addition, Goodenough offered a framework for understanding change in a social system.

Goodenough's (1981) concept of "propriospect" also offered a valuable tool for analysis. According to Harry Wolcott (1987, 1991), propriospect draws our attention "to the individual acquisition of cultural competencies in which each of us is engaged throughout the course of a lifetime" (1987, p. 51).

Propriospect avoids taking an evaluative stance because the interest of the researcher is on the *contents* of the propriospect. Finally, propriospect "draws attention to the idea that multiculturalism is exhibited in normal human experience" (1987, p. 32). Because every propriospect contains a different combination of pieces from the operating culture and from other cultures, diversity is a natural state.

One additional theoretical approach, interpretive anthropology, also affected my study. Interpretive anthropology includes both culture theory and the practice of studying culture. Rooted in phenomenology, structuralism, structural linguistics, semiotics, and hermeneutics, interpretive anthropologists avoid creating categories like the functionalists and refuse to identify universal truths. The only reality that they claim is their own interpretation of their text. In fact, discussion of the texts themselves is an important characteristic of the movement. A major representative of interpretive anthropology, Clifford Geertz, takes a semiotic view of culture. He agreed with Max Weber "that man is an animal suspended in webs of significance he himself has spun" and he took "culture to be those webs, and the analysis of it to be therefore not an experimental science in search of law but an interpretive one in search of meaning" (Geertz, 1987, p. 5). Ethnography was not to be defined by its methods such as seeking an informant or keeping a diary; rather it is a "kind of intellectual effort . . . an elaborate venture in . . . 'thick description'" (Geertz, 1987, p. 6). The ethnographer develops an interpretation or constructs meaning from the descriptions of even minor aspects of the culture. Though this may appear on the surface to be similar to Goodenough's (1981) framework, Geertz specifically separates himself from Goodenough. Goodenough believed culture is manifested in the mind. In contrast, Geertz believes "culture is public because meaning is" (Geertz, 1973, p. 12). Furthermore, Geertz argues that the cognitive anthropologists' belief that mental phenomena can be analyzed by formal methods such as mathematics and logic "is as destructive of an effective use of the concept as are the behaviorist and idealist fallacies to which it is a misdrawn correction" (Geertz, 1973, p. 12). Geertz does not expect that there will ever develop "a perfection of consensus" but instead a "refinement of debate" (Geertz, 1973, p. 29). The "vocation" of anthropology is "not to answer our deepest questions, but to make available to us answers that others, guarding other sheep in other valleys, have given, and thus to include them in the consultable record of what man has said" (Geertz, 1973, p. 30). Despite Geertz's adamant argument separating cognitive and interpretive anthropology, more recently cognitive anthropologists have come closer to interpretive anthropology by seeing culture as public and symbolic (Dougherty, 1985).

Effects of Using a Theoretical Framework

When I originally set out to discover a theory or theories, my goal was to find theories that would guide my data collection and analysis, clarify my ideas, unify my work, and justify my research role as participant observer. As a novice researcher, I knew that tackling a year of ethnographic research in a high school involved observing and analyzing a myriad of events and relationships. I wondered, "How can I make sense of it all, or, for that matter, any of it?" Because my goal was to discover what was going on in a comprehensive high school that was attempting major change, I needed a lens that would help me filter the input and develop a defensible interpretation. Theory provided me with that lens and influenced nearly every aspect of my work. Goodenough's (1981) model of culture and change guided my data analysis, and organization of the written case. Geertz (1973, 1987) and interpretive anthropology influenced me on a holistic level by guiding my thinking about interpretation and description. Both aided me in defending my research role.

Goodenough's *Culture, Language, and Society* (1981) provided the basis of the organization of the case study into three major categories: the social group as a whole, smaller subgroups of teachers, and one teacher operating within the larger group. When I reviewed the research on teacher culture, I discovered that most work discussed teachers as a single culture. For example, Wolcott's *Teachers Versus Technocrats* (1977) represents school culture as a moiety system with teachers represented as one half of the moiety. Lortie's *Schoolteacher: A Sociological Study* (1975) provides an analysis of teachers as a type, and Sarason's *The Culture of the School and the Problem of Change* (1982) treats teachers as a group. Because of my long-term experience working in schools, I knew that subtle differences exist among teachers, and I wanted my study to expose the variations in teachers at the same time as I described the commonalities of teacher culture. Goodenough's (1981) concept of Culture, culture pool, and propriospect provided the framework for looking at both the big picture and the subtleties.

When I entered the field to live as a full participant observer for a year, I worked to ensure that I was able to collect data that represented all three major categories. I had not yet chosen the individual teacher who would be the representative for one propriospect, but she revealed herself to me rather quickly. A leader on the School Improvement Team, she enjoyed the respect of the principal, teaching colleagues, and students. Early in the year, she supported the concept of the reform, and she was always candid about her opinions even as they shifted. She readily accepted my proposal to be the subject of a major section of the study, and, unlike other teachers, she was not afraid of possible consequences when she voiced her opinions. Moreover, she provided an opportunity to test Goodenough's (1981) hypothesis that each propriospect shares characteristics with the Culture and with subgroups to which it belongs, and also possesses characteristics from outside the group that are unique to itself.

The subgroups emerged quickly as well, perhaps because, as a full participant, I was familiar with the working teachers committees and their roles. As I gathered data, I was careful to ensure that I observed each group in situations in which the group was intact. As I observed each group, I asked, "What characteristics do the members of this group share with the Culture?" and "What characteristics are common to members of this group, but not present in all others in the Culture?" I also asked, "What unique functions did the members of this group serve in the reform efforts?"

Finally, I gathered data that would reveal characteristics common to all teachers. This was done primarily by observing the teachers in large groups and by partnering with the School Improvement Team to conduct a census survey that enjoyed a 100 percent response rate. My guiding questions were also derived directly from Goodenough's (1981) theory. I sought to discover, primarily through examination of both written and oral language, the common understandings that constituted membership in the Culture. This included, "standards for deciding what can be, standards for deciding how one feels about it, standards for deciding what to do about it, and standards for deciding how to go about doing it" (Goodenough, p. 62). These were standards that cut across all subgroups and were present in individual propriospects. One section of the study, "A Year at Emerson High School," describes the culture pool, and the conclusions for the study focus on the standards that are understood by members of the culture pool.

The concept of *propriospect* was, in particular, valuable to observation, analysis, and description in the case study. Because I operated in the role of full participant observer, I was keenly aware of issues of objectivity. Using the concept of propriospect, I was able to analyze the operating culture of individuals without being evaluative of the world view. Propriospect was a tool for understanding the partial overlap of viewpoints of teachers and administrators without contradicting the discussions of their different cultural orientations. Because propriospect is a collection of all experiences, teachers and administrators did share a number of experiences; their propriospects, however, were not identical because they each had experiences unique to their roles in the school. In addition, propriospect was an aid in understanding teachers' individual and collective response to change. As explained earlier, most teachers responded strongly to the changes in discipline implemented by the principal. The change in disciplinary practices no longer aligned with the belief systems of teachers, resulting in turmoil. According to Goodenough, some customs are so deeply held that "they prohibit behavior that interferes with them ... and ... [invests] them with moral rightness and even sanctity" (1981, p. 90). Teachers talked about the changes as being morally incorrect, and, as frustration increased, the teachers' sense of being morally correct increased. Informal conversations revealed an expectation that all teachers would share the same view. Goodenough's theory helped develop my insight into how conflicts between public culture and personal beliefs can result in the upheaval and resistance that I observed at Emerson High School.

Geertz's (1973, 1987) writing appealed to me at a more intuitive level, which is not surprising when considering my academic background. Like Geertz, I studied literature as an undergraduate, and I was drawn to his emphasis on description of the public aspects of the culture. As both a student and teacher of literature, I had been schooled in the idea that no reality is the same for all people; the only reality I can claim is that of my own personal interpretation. Despite Geertz's statements drawing a line between cognitive and interpretive anthropology, my personal interpretation found the approaches to be complementary rather than contradictory. Reading that cognitive anthropologists were moving closer to Geertz's view of culture as public helped justify my blending of the two. Although Goodenough influenced my organization, Geertz's concept of thick description influenced the way I collected data and what I included in the written case. When I was taking field notes, I was always conscious of recording sufficient detail to ensure that my writing would be rich with description. As I observed social situations or conducted interviews, I recorded words verbatim. When that was not possible, I recorded key phrases and returned to the text later on the same day to complete the dialogue and add description. When I was present at key meetings, I was particularly conscious of taking detailed notes of the conversation and of the reactions of participants. Because I carried a small notebook with me at all times, I was able to describe informal situations and record conversations. In the final report of the case, I presented most of the information as a narrative, a story of the year at Emerson High School, with an emphasis on dialogue. Consciously working to provide "thick description" so that my interpretation would be clearly supported, I also wanted to provide enough description for my readers to be able to form independent interpretations. Also, like Geertz, I fully acknowledged that the account is a personal interpretation. In fact, in the last paragraph of the study I stated that "I cannot promise this represents anyone's truth except my own" (Henstrand, 1991). To tie the description back into my use of cognitive anthropology in my organization and analysis, I concluded with a reference to Goodenough's (1981) concept of propriospect to support my research role and description as one "propriospect in the culture pool of Emerson High School" (Henstrand,

1991, p. 270). In my own mind, at least, I synthesized the two approaches in my interpretation and conclusion.

Theory and My Research Role

Theory not only contributed to the design, data gathering, and analysis of my study, but also, quite unexpectedly, was critical in supporting my decision to take on the role of complete participant observer and in managing several problems that arose as a consequence of that role. Before I chose the subject of my study, I had assumed that I would follow the advice and practice of traditional anthropologists and sociologists who advocated that researchers engaging in participant observation should be outsiders to the culture being studied. Becoming too involved with the "natives" was considered a major breach of the research role because it generally involved losing the analytical perspective of the researcher (Agar, 1980; Becker, 1958; Goetz & LeCompte, 1984; Lofland & Lofland, 1984; Wax, 1971). My assumptions changed when I had the opportunity to return to my work as a teacher and, simultaneously, conduct ethnographic research for a case study of planned change. In other words, I planned to be a "native" who would take on the role of participant observer. I returned to the literature to seek justification and support for becoming a complete participant observer.

I found that researchers had begun to support the position that full membership in the social system can be advantageous (Adler & Adler, 1987; Jorgensen, 1989; Peshkin, 1988; Wolcott, 1988). Bronislaw Malinowski (1984, 1987) was one of the first anthropologists to conduct his fieldwork as a participant observer. He claimed that living with the natives enabled him to develop a better understanding of their thinking and lifestyle. In the 1920s, a group of sociologists known as the Chicago School also adopted participant observation to study subgroups of American culture, such as medical students or drug addicts; however, they also advocated the traditional stance by warning against over-involvement with the subjects (Lofland & Lofland, 1984; Wax, 1971). More recently, existential sociologists have broken from the traditional stance of researcher as stranger. Researchers within the theoretical school of existential sociology believe that people often act on the basis of emotions. The job of the researcher, therefore, is to penetrate the surface to discover insights into the emotions of the humans they study. This necessarily leads to the involvement of the researcher with the subjects. Not troubled by the possible subjectivity of the researcher, existential sociologists believe that the ability to engage in self-reflection is more important than seeking objective detachment: "They reject the claim that over familiarity leads researchers to assume the self deception of the members. Self deception is not caused by involvement per se, but by deep-rooted emotional conflicts within the individual" (Adler & Adler, 1987, p. 23).

Proponents of ethnomethodology also advocate for the involvement of the researcher with the group being studied. In order to understand contextual meanings and avoid distorting the vision of the world, ethnomethodologists believe they must participate "to the fullest degree" (Adler & Adler, 1987, p. 32). For them, "going native is the solution rather than the problem" (p. 32). They do not worry about the possibility of researchers altering the setting because "good faith members will only alter settings in ways similar to other members, so their actions are condoned" (p. 32). Armed with the support of at least two theoretical approaches and of contemporary researchers such as Adler and Adler and Peshkin, I decided to go into the field as a complete participant observer.

During my fieldwork, I followed Alan Peshkin's advice: I did not try "to exorcise my subjectivity" but rather to "enable myself to manage it—to preclude it from being unwittingly burdensome—as I progressed through collecting, analyzing, and writing up my data" (Peshkin, 1988, p. 17). At first, I used research strategies and personal reflection to manage the subjectivity. I chose an overt stance so that everyone would know what I was doing. Using Peshkin's subjective I's, I continuously monitored my own interactions to maintain the same membership role I had before I began fieldwork; and I took verbatim notes whenever possible. As I progressed into the year, however, I found that my conflicts of conscience required more than simple solutions. Taking on a theoretical perspective helped me manage those conflicts.

The personal conflicts started when I realized that the reform was not going well, and I observed conflicts between teachers and administrators. Divisive behavior nearly became a norm in the organization. Despite the fact that colleagues knew I was conducting field research, I worried about publishing negative behaviors in my study. I worried when I memorized key phrases from informal conversations and ran back to my office to record what I had heard. I also worried about being disloyal to colleagues and wondered if they felt they were being exploited. Referring to theory was my chief means of coping with these issues.

The theoretical frameworks of Goodenough (1981) and Geertz (1973, 1987) helped me to manage the subjectivity of my research role, including numerous conflicts with my conscience as I recorded unflattering behavior by members of the school. For example, as a teacher in the building, I found that I shared many of the frustrations of my colleagues related to the changes in the discipline system. Many of my colleagues made inflammatory comments that actually reflected my own feelings when I was in my teacher role. I struggled with recording their negative comments even though they were said in public.

On the other hand, I had a good working relationship with the principal. I worried about recording behaviors and words that might bring criticism his way.

To manage my subjectivity, I consciously retreated from my role as teacher and stepped into my role as researcher by applying the theoretical model to the situation. If, for example, I observed colleagues at the lunch table commenting energetically about the lack of discipline in the school, if I stayed in my role as teacher I would tend to fully engage emotionally. During the fieldwork, however, I consciously moved into the role of researcher. For example, I would apply Goodenough's model for culture to the situation by looking for the operating standards that were being revealed by the participants. In committee meetings, instead of becoming emotional over the conflict I saw, I consciously worked to understand which standards the groups shared with the Culture and what impact the groups had on the Culture. I was, therefore, able to step back from seeing the people as friends and colleagues and consciously assume the research role.

Using theory also presented challenges. A commitment to the use of theory required that I develop knowledge of various anthropological and sociological theories and read examples of the theory being used well. This required time and I had to cope with the comments, made by several of my fellow PhD candidates, urging me to do something simple so I could finish the degree. Because the PhD program was more about learning than jumping a hurdle to my next job, I spent a full year reading research theory before I gained enough knowledge to choose a theory and start fieldwork. Once I announced that I would use theory, I was accountable to apply the theory appropriately. Not only did I frame my data collection and analysis around Goodenough's theory of culture, but I also had to ensure that my analysis of the high school's Culture, culture pool, and individual propriospects remained consistent with the theory's framework. At one point, Harry Wolcott suggested that my use of propriospect was rather superficial. Because Wolcott's (1987) article on propriospect had initiated my inquiry into Goodenough's theory, I returned to *Culture, Language, and Society* (Goodenough, 1981) to increase my understanding, and then I added clarification to my writing. I continued to return periodically to Goodenough's texts to renew my understanding and reflect on the application to my research.

Conclusion: A Professional and Personal Reflection

Despite the challenges of time and accountability, using theory benefited both the process of doing the research and the product that emerged. The initial research for culture theory and the review I wrote clarified my thinking and provided the groundwork for the design and completion of the study. Before I discovered a theory that helped me to frame my understanding of the culture at Emerson High School, I was unable to start the study. The school appeared to be a chaotic collection of actions and voices; I did not know how to look at the situation or how to interpret what I saw. The application of Goodenough's (1981) theory of culture provided a lens through which I could observe and record. In addition, using theory enabled me to manage the subjectivity involved in the full participant observer role I assumed as the researcher.

The importance of using theory in qualitative research goes beyond the benefits I experienced in doing the study. Conscious and consistent use of theory by researchers should improve the stature of qualitative research in education. Researchers have long debated the relative worth of qualitative and quantitative research; qualitative research is often criticized for its subjectivity and lack of precise measurements. A leading cultural anthropologist, Clifford Geertz (1973) argues in favor of developing and using strong theory because theory helps elevate anthropology to the level of a science: "There is no reason why the conceptual structure of a cultural interpretation should be any less formulable, and thus less susceptible to explicit canons of appraisal, than that of, say, a biological observation or a physical experiment" (p. 24). Similarly, Goetz and LeCompte (1984) support the establishment of a theoretical framework for qualitative research, especially ethnographic studies. The use of theory, they believe, increases rigor and makes qualitative research more understandable when read in other disciplines. By using theory to frame and justify my work, I hope I have contributed to elevating qualitative research to the level of a science.

The discovery and use of Goodenough's (1981) theory of culture also benefited me on a personal level. In my career as a public school administrator, I have been principal of two large high schools and director of instruction for a medium-sized school district. All of my positions have involved leading the organization through large-scale change. Those who have led organizational change know only too well the struggles that occur in organizations. Despite paying attention to change models and attempting to work systematically through the change, leaders of change report resistance, blockage, and unintended consequences for many actions. Goodenough's theory of culture has given me the tools to understand the variations in behavior of the large group from smaller groups or individuals. When I think of applying a large-scale plan for change, I frame it in terms of Culture, and I devise activities and professional development based on the large group, but I have come to realize that this large-scale planning is not enough. After seeing reforms fail, I have been conscious of the roles of subgroups, not only for their official purpose, but also for the beliefs of their members. I work to understand their jointly held and individual views and to maintain communication that addresses issues of importance to them. Perhaps most important, I seek a partnership with members of the organization in the planning process so that implementation of reform respects the sacred values and needs of teachers and other staff. These efforts, in my experience, contribute to successful change over time because they attend to the individual propriospects present in the organization.

Attending to theory in research design and implementation in the field of education still tends to be relatively rare, perhaps because of the time involved in developing an understanding and the accountability that comes with applying theory during the process of research and analysis. In particular, doctoral students who intend to pursue careers as practitioners might view the use of theory as an exercise that will not yield personal benefit. On the surface, I would not have expected my exploration and application of theory to go beyond its usefulness in the completion of my dissertation. I hope this essay has illustrated that the benefits of using theory can go far beyond research applications and that knowledge of theory has relevance in the real world of teaching and administering schools. Wolcott (1995) has listed a number of benefits of using theory for the researcher, and I found several to be particularly applicable to myself. The use of theory enabled me to "join [my] work to some larger issues or accumulation of data" (Wolcott, 1995, p. 189). My study was moved from simply an account of what happened in one school to a more comprehensive generalization and understanding of culture and culture change. Moreover, as a researcher who returned to the role of educational practitioner, the use of theory has deepened my understanding of the culture in which I operate.

References

Adler, P. A., & Alder, P. (1987). *Membership roles in field research.* Beverly Hills, CA: Sage.

Agar, M. H. (1980). *The professional stranger: An informal introduction to ethnography.* New York: Academic Press.

Agar, M. H. (1987). Whatever happened to cognitive anthropology: A partial review. In H. Applebaum (Ed.), *Perspectives in cultural anthropology* (pp. 425–433). Albany: State University of New York Press.

Bailey, K. D. (1987). *Methods of social research* (3rd ed.). New York: Free Press.

Becker, H. S. (1958). Problems of inference and proof in participant observation. *American Sociological Review, 23,* 652–660.

Bernard, H. R. (1988). *Research methods in cultural anthropology.* Newbury Park, CA: Sage.

Denzin, N. (1970). *The research act*. Chicago: Aldine.

Dougherty, J. W. (Ed.). (1985). *Directions in cognitive anthropology*. Urbana: University of Illinois Press.

Fink, A., & Kosecoff, J. (1985). *How to conduct surveys: A step-by-step guide*. Beverly Hills, CA: Sage.

Fullan, M. (1982). *The meaning of educational change*. New York: Teachers College Press.

Fullan, M. (1990). Change processes in secondary schools: Toward a more fundamental agenda. In M. W. McLaughlin, J. E. Talbert, & N. Bascia (Eds.), *The contexts of teaching in secondary schools: Teachers' realities* (pp. 224–255). New York: Teachers College Press.

Fullan, M., & Stiegelbauer, S. (1991). *The new meaning of educational change*. New York: Teachers College Press.

Gay, L. R. (1987). *Educational research: Competencies for analysis and application*. Columbus, OH: Merrill.

Geertz, C. (1973). Thick description: Toward an interpretive theory of culture. In C. Geertz (Ed.), *The interpretation of cultures* (pp. 3–30). New York: Basic Books.

Geertz, C. (1987). Interpretive anthropology. In H. Applebaum (Ed.). *Perspectives in cultural anthropology* (pp. 520–524). Albany: State University of New York Press.

Goetz, J. P., & LeCompte, M. D. (1984). *Ethnography and qualitative design in educational research*. New York: Academic Press.

Goodenough, W. H. (1963). *Cooperation in change*. New York: Russell Sage.

Goodenough, W. H. (1981). *Culture, language, and society*. Menlo Park, CA: Benjamin/Cummings.

Hall, G. E., & Hord, S. M. (1984). *Change in schools: Facilitating the process*. Albany: State University of New York Press.

Henstrand, J. L. (1991). *Teacher culture from the inside: A case study of planned change from the perspective of active participant observer*. Unpublished doctoral dissertation, University of Oregon, Eugene.

Henstrand, J. L. (1993). Theory as research guide: A qualitative look at qualitative inquiry. In D. F. Flinders & G. E. Mills (Eds.), *Theory and concepts in qualitative research* (pp. 83–102). New York: Teachers College Press.

Johnson, J. C. (1990). *Selecting ethnographic informants*. Newbury Park, CA: Sage.

Jorgensen, D. L. (1989). *Participant observation: A methodology for human studies*. Newbury Park, CA: Sage.

Kluckhohn, C. (1945). The personal document in anthropological science. In A. Gottschalk (Ed.), *The use of personal documents in history, anthropology, and sociology* (pp. 79–173). New York: Social Science Research Council.

Langness, L. L., & Frank, G. (1986). *Lives: An anthropological approach to biography*. Novato, CA: Chandler & Sharp.

LeCompte, M., & Goetz, J. (1984). *Ethnography and qualitative design in educational research*. New York: Academic Press.

Lofland, J., & Lofland, L. (1984). *Analyzing social settings: A guide to qualitative observation and analysis* (2nd ed.). Belmont, CA: Wadsworth.

Lortie, D. C. (1975). *Schoolteacher: A sociological study.* Chicago: University of Chicago Press.

Malinowski, B. (1984). *Argonauts of the western Pacific.* Prospect Heights, IL: Waveland. (Original work published 1922)

Malinowski, B. (1987). The group and individual in functional analysis. In H. Applebaum (Ed.), *Perspectives in cultural anthropology* (pp. 116–120). Albany: State University of New York Press. (Original work published 1939)

McCracken, G. (1988). *The long interview.* Beverly Hills, CA: Sage.

McLaughlin, M. W., & Talbert, J. E. (1990). The contexts in question: The secondary school workplace. In M. W. McLaughlin, J. E. Talbert, & N. Bascia (Eds.), *The contexts of teaching in secondary schools: Teachers' realities* (pp. 1–11). New York: Teachers College Press.

Miles, M. B. (1986, April). *Improving the urban high school: Some preliminary news from 5 cases.* Paper presented at the meeting of the American Educational Research Association, San Francisco.

Peshkin, A. (1988). In search of subjectivity: One's own. *Educational Researcher, 17*(7), 17–22.

Rossman, G. B., Corbett, H. D., & Firestone, W. A. (1988). *Change and effectiveness in schools: A cultural perspective.* Albany: State University of New York Press.

Sarason, S. B. (1982). *The culture of the school and the problem of change* (2nd ed.). Boston: Allyn & Bacon.

Sarason, S. B. (1990). *The predictable failure of educational reform: Can we change course before it's too late?* San Francisco: Jossey-Bass.

Sergiovanni, T. J. (1986). Culture and competing perspectives in administrative theory and practice. In T. J. Sergiovanni & J. E. Corbally (Eds.), *Leadership and organizational culture: New perspectives on administrative theory and practice* (pp. 1–11). Chicago: University of Illinois Press.

Spradley, J. (1979). *The ethnographic interview.* New York: Holt, Rinehart & Winston.

Spradley, J. (1980). *Participant observation.* New York: Holt, Rinehart & Winston.

Tyler, S. (1969). *Cognitive anthropology.* New York: Holt, Rinehart & Winston.

Wax, R. H. (1952). Field methods and techniques: Reciprocity as a field technique. *Human Organization, 11*(1), 34–37.

Wax, R. H. (1971). *Doing fieldwork: Warnings and advice.* Chicago: University of Chicago Press.

Webb, E. J., Campbell, D. T., Schwartz, R. D., & Sechrest, L. (1966). *Unobtrusive measures.* Chicago: Rand McNally.

Wolcott, H. F. (1977). *Teachers versus technocrats: An educational innovation in anthropological perspective.* Eugene, OR: Center for Educational Policy and Management.

Wolcott, H. F. (1983). Adequate schools and inadequate education: The life story of a sneaky kid. *Anthropology & Education Quarterly, 14*(1), 3–32.

Wolcott, H. F. (1987). The acquisition of propriospect. Unpublished manuscript, University of Oregon, Eugene.

Wolcott, H. F. (1988). Ethnographic research in education. In R. M. Jaeger (Ed.), *Complementary methods for research in education* (pp. 185–250). Washington, DC: American Educational Research Association.

Wolcott, H. F. (1991). Propriospect and the acquisition of culture. *Anthropology & Education Quarterly, 22*(3), 250–272.

Wolcott, H. F. (1995). *The art of fieldwork*. Walnut Creek, CA: AltaMira.

Worthen, B. R., & Sanders, J. R. (1987). *Educational evaluation: Alternative approaches and practical guidelines*. New York: Longman.

Yin, R. K. (1984). *Case study research: Design and methods*. Beverly Hills, CA: Sage.

2

Transformational Learning and HIV-Positive Young Adults

Sharan B. Merriam

T he place of a theoretical framework in a research study can be compared to the construction of a new building. There is a foundation upon which the underlying skeletal structure is built. Once the building is framed, certain materials such as outer sheathing, walls, insulation, flooring, and so on are added to the framing; so, too, in the building of a research study. The foundation is the disciplinary base out of which the theoretical framework emerges. The theoretical framework of a study is anchored in a particular disciplinary base and its literature; it is in this literature that particular concepts, models, or theories that structure the study are found. This structure, or theoretical framework, then determines the problem to be investigated, the specific research questions asked, the particular data that will be collected to address the questions, and, of key importance, how these data are analyzed/interpreted. In the developing of a research study, the theoretical framework forms the underlying structure.

In this chapter, I demonstrate how in the field of adult education, the literature of adult learning and adult development were used to structure research with HIV-positive young adults. All components of the research—the concepts used, the particular literature and previous research consulted, the data collection and analysis strategies employed—were derived from the theoretical framework.

Overview of the Studies

The first study of HIV-positive young adults was conducted in the mid-1990s (Courtenay, Merriam, & Reeves, 1998). The purpose of the study was to understand how meaning is constructed in the lives of those diagnosed as HIV-positive. In-depth interviews were conducted with a sample of 18 HIV-positive men and women. Using the constant comparative method, an inductive analysis of the data revealed a process of meaning-making that involved a period of initial reaction to the diagnosis, a catalytic experience that sets into motion the meaning-making process, and three distinct yet interrelated phases of reflection and activity. The findings not only provided a clearly delineated description of the meaning-making process, they also revealed unique contributions that underscore the centrality of meaning-making in transformational learning.

Two years after the original study, my colleagues and I located 14 of the original 18 participants and interviewed them as to whether they had maintained their change in perspective uncovered in the original study. In other words, we were interested in whether a perspective transformation is sustained over time. With the advent of protease inhibitors in the 2 years between the studies, we wondered whether, with the threat of imminent death removed, participants would revert to previously held, self-oriented, and materialistic views of the world. Through an inductive analysis of the interview data we found that for all 14 participants, the perspective transformations that they had undergone 2 years earlier had held. Second, there were changes in meaning schemes that included the adoption of a future-oriented perspective, greater attention to care of the self, and an integration of the HIV-positive status into their self-definition (Courtenay, Merriam, Reeves, & Baumgartner, 2000).

The Theoretical Framework

Our theoretical framework lay at the intersection of adult learning theory, in particular transformational learning, and adult development theory. Transformational learning theory as presented by its chief architect, Jack Mezirow (1991, 2000), posits that significant learning in our lives involves meaning-making that can lead to a transformation of our personality or worldview. This type of learning is developmental in that it involves "movement toward more developmentally progressive meaning perspectives" (Mezirow, 1991, p. 192). Mezirow has proposed a 10-step process, beginning with a disorienting dilemma that sets in motion a self-examination of one's underlying assumptions, followed by sharing these thoughts with others, which leads to exploring new roles, relationships, and actions, a trying on of new roles, and finally "a reintegration into one's life on the basis of conditions dictated by one's new perspective" (1991, p. 169).

Though popular and much referenced in the field of adult education, Mezirow's (1991) theory of transformational learning had been little tested when we began our study in the mid-1990s. We were indeed intrigued by the theory's capacity to explain how adults make meaning of their life experiences, and how this meaning-making can bring about powerful changes or transformations in their view of themselves and their world. This type of learning "produces more far-reaching changes in the learners than does learning in general, and . . . these changes have a significant impact on the learner's subsequent experiences. In short, transformational learning *shapes* people; they are different afterward, in ways both they and others can recognize" (Clark, 1993, p. 47).

Two years after the completion of the first study (Courtenay et al., 1998), using the same theoretical framework of transformational learning and adult development, we conducted a follow-up study of the original participants. In our first study, we found that all of our participants had undergone a transformation in their perspective, as we would have predicted from Mezirow's (1991) theory. Also part of his theory, but untested, was that such changes in perspective are permanent. He is quite clear about this, saying that "the transformative learning process is irreversible. . . . We do not regress to levels of less understanding" (1991, p. 152). Other developmental theorists concur. Kegan (1994), for example, says of cognitive development that "each successive principle subsumes or encompasses the prior principle. . . . The new principle is a higher order principle (more complex, more inclusive) that makes the prior principle into an element or tool of its system" (p. 33). We wanted to examine the permanency of the perspective transformations after a 2-year period. Also, in the intervening 2 years protease inhibitors (PIs) had become widely used, causing remission/suppression of HIV. Thus, we wondered if the changes in perspective seen in the first study held, or, given a new lease on life through PIs, whether participants reverted back to old perspectives.

Our theoretical framework of transformational learning and development also led to a second question, that of ongoing changes in meaning schemes and perspectives. The literature suggests that meaning-making is an ongoing process and that although "at any one point in time, a meaning has to be fixed," it is "not the only meaning possible for all time" (Usher, 1993, p. 170). Mezirow (1990) proposes that changes in meaning schemes (specific beliefs, assumptions, values, feelings, and concepts) are quite common in dealing with everyday experience. It is the "accretion of such transformed meaning schemes" (Mezirow, 1990, p. 13) that can lead to changes in the larger perspective. We were thus interested not only in whether their perspective transformations had held, but also about the nature of ongoing meaning-making. We wondered, for example, if the introduction of protease inhibitors (PIs) may have served as a "disorienting dilemma" effecting yet another perspective transformation.

The Disciplinary Base of the Theoretical Framework

Transformational learning theory is firmly situated in the literature of adult learning theory and adult development. It focuses on how adults make meaning of their life situation and, in turn, how this meaning-making impacts development. The theory has its roots in constructivism, which maintains that learning is a process of constructing meaning; it is how people make sense of their experience. Mezirow's (1990) version of transformational learning in particular also draws from the German philosopher Jürgen Habermas, who proposes three types of learning, one of which is emancipatory and involves rational discourse. In Mezirow's model, the key to transformational learning is critically examining underlying assumptions and engaging in "a special form of dialogue" where we "do our best to be open and objective in presenting and assessing reasons and reviewing the evidence and arguments for and against the problematic assertion to arrive at a consensus" (1995, p. 53).

The Theoretical Framework and the Design of the Study

Our interest in the theoretical framework of transformational learning drove all aspects of our study from identifying the focus of our investigation, to sample selection, to interpretation of our data. Our central research question centered on uncovering the *process* of meaning-making, that is, we wanted to know how meaning is restructured such that one's sense of self, one's worldview or perspective becomes transformed. We thus needed to select a situation where we could be fairly certain that one's perspective would have been disrupted and challenged. We reasoned that being diagnosed with a terminal illness would constitute a "disorienting dilemma" of such great magnitude that one would be propelled into a struggle to make meaning or sense out of the diagnosis. Further, it was believed that this meaning-making would assume a particular urgency if the diagnosis meant that one's life might end at an unnaturally early age. Hence, our *sample selection* was guided by our research question about the process of meaning-making that was directly derived from the theoretical framework of transformational learning. We chose young adults under the age of 45 who had been diagnosed HIV-positive and whose T-cell count was 500 or less, indicating a compromised immune system. The interviews were conducted in late 1995 and early 1996 before the advent of protease inhibitors; an HIV-positive diagnosis at that time constituted a death sentence.

The theoretical framework also drove *data collection*. Having selected a sample of HIV-positive young adults, we wanted to explore *how* they made sense of this catastrophic news; that is, how does a young adult make meaning of this threat to his or her existence? In-depth interviews were the only way we could access their meaning-making process. The 10-step process that Mezirow (1991, 1995) outlined informed our interviews, but only to the extent that his process gave us a starting point. We wanted each participant to tell us his or her story for making meaning of the diagnosis.

Data analysis proceeded simultaneously with data collection as is recommended in qualitative research designs. As mentioned above, although the meaning-making process delineated by Mezirow (1990) informed us, we remained open to hearing about our participants' experiences. Our findings confirmed some aspects of Mezirow's process, but expanded others. For example, whereas Mezirow posits that a period of self-examination follows the disorienting dilemma, we found there was first an initial reaction characterized by cognitive, affective, and behavioral responses. Sam remembered thinking, "My life's only a fourth over. So suddenly that window on the future came slamming shut, shades drawn, black curtains" (Courtenay et al., 1998, p. 70)! Upon hearing the diagnosis, Tracy entered a crowded metropolitan area "and I was just thinking of how was I going to do this [suicide], was I going to jump in front of a bus or the train or a car" (p. 70)?

This initial reaction period lasted from 6 months to 5 years. Becoming dislodged from this initial reaction period involved some catalytic event initiated externally by family, friends, or a support group, or internally by realizing that to not get on with life meant self-destruction. Jamie talked about a friend who came to his house and yanked him out of bed:

> And she said, "Do you want to die? Just lay there and I'll kick you to death right now, and if you don't want to die then get up and live." . . . And it just clicked and I said, "That's right; you know that's the answer." That was the real turning point for me, when I realized that death was easy and anybody can do it. . . . And so I just made up my mind that day that living life well is what I wanted to do. (Courtenay et al., 1998, p. 71)

The initial reaction and the catalytic event uncovered in our study are two important components of the process not present, or if present, not explicated in Mezirow's (1991, 1995) theoretical framework. In his model, a self-examination and critical assessment of assumptions underlying one's worldview follow the disorienting dilemma.

Our findings with regard to the *process* of meaning-making served to underscore some of the weaknesses of using Mezirow's (1991, 1995) model of transformational learning as the theoretical framework. First, Mezirow's model is overly rational (Taylor, 2000); indeed, we found, not unexpectedly given our participants' diagnoses, that there was a highly emotional, affective, and spiritual component to their meaning-making. Second, Mezirow has been criticized for describing perspective transformation as happening in isolation, separated from other aspects of the individual's life context. Our data showed that even the initial reaction to the diagnosis was affected by whether or not the individuals suspected that they might be HIV-positive, by their lifestyles, or by supportive others in their lives. Context shaped the entire meaning-making process.

Despite these shortcomings, the framework overall did help us to understand the meaning-making process and the resultant change in perspective that each of our participants exhibited. Being diagnosed HIV-positive brought about self-examination of their purpose in life. Participants reported recognizing the importance of all life, and of their need to make a meaningful contribution through service to others. Characterized by empathy and altruism, their new perspectives included but went beyond Mezirow's (1991) description of the outcome of a perspective transformation (an empowered sense of self, more critical understanding, and more functional strategies for taking action).

In order to address these questions, it was necessary to interview the same participants as in our initial study (Courtenay et al., 1998). We were able to locate 14 of the original 18 participants. In preparation for the interviews, we re-read, studied, and discussed the original interviews. This

> reacquainted us with each respondent's particular story and the nature of his or her perspective transformation; second, phrases or statements were occasionally read back to the participants during the second interviews as memory prompts, or for their comments. The interview schedule contained open-ended questions regarding how participants were making sense of their lives today, the impact of protease inhibitors, current physical and emotional health, the extent to which they were still involved in service-oriented activities . . . and so on. (Courtenay et al., 2000, p. 106)

Two major findings emerged from this follow-up study. First, as we speculated, the perspective transformation proved irreversible. People continued to make meaningful contributions manifested through numerous service activities largely related to HIV/AIDS education, and to appreciate their lives and the lives of others. They maintained the more integrated, inclusive, and discriminating perspective that they had attained earlier. Interestingly, they themselves recognized the irreversibility of their perspective transformation. Joe, for example, had been an avid comic book collector until he was diagnosed HIV-positive. Once he began taking protease inhibitors and realized he might "be around another 20 years to enjoy this" [collecting comic books], he "indulged" in it again.

> But I'd changed too much. . . . Ultimately, I realized these are just things. If I'm collecting it to have just number 1 through 20 or something, you know, why am I doing it? It didn't have the same meaning anymore . . . it was one of those unimportant things, ultimately. (Courtenay et al., 2000, p. 110)

With regard to our second question of ongoing meaning-making, there were changes in meaning schemes. The dramatic changes in health brought about by PIs resulted in the adoption of a more future-oriented perspective on life. Jamie, who, for example, had lived life in "2-year increments" prior to PIs, commented that "now, suddenly, things are different. . . . I mean, it's much easier to plan to die than it is to plan to live." He realized that "knowing you might live. . . . You've got to consider consequences way down the road" (Courtenay et al., 2000, p. 112). Other meaning scheme changes were manifested by paying greater attention to issues pertaining to care of the self, and integration of one's HIV-positive status into self-definition (Courtenay et al., 2000).

Thus, the theoretical perspective of transformational learning and adult development structured both of these research studies. The questions asked (What is the process of meaning-making and how stable is a perspective transformation?) were directly derived from transformational learning theory as proposed by Mezirow (1991, 1995). To best answer these questions, we chose a sample (HIV-positive young adults) that would be driven to meaning-making and we explored this process through a qualitative research design that involved in-depth interviews with this purposefully selected sample. We used concepts from the framework in analyzing and interpreting our data and then tied our findings back into the literature derived from the theoretical framework.

Related Theoretical Frameworks and HIV-Positive Young Adults

Transformational learning theory is developmental in that changes in one's perspective occur, changes that are "more developmentally progressive"

(Mezirow, 1991, p. 192). But in addition to developmental changes in perspective, there were a number of developmental issues inherent in the design of the study and in the particular selection of participants. Our over-arching theoretical framework of adult learning and development was based on several assumptions. First, life experiences in conjunction with the individ-ual and social contexts in which they occur provide the potential for learning and development. Second, although development refers to systematic change over time, we assumed that the desired direction of development was toward positive, growth-enhancing, mature responses, a position Bee and Bjorklund (2004, p. 14) label *"developmental progress."* We saw this research as an opportunity to address several of these related developmental questions. In particular, we asked questions about the development of coping mechanisms, faith/spiritual development, and psychosocial development. We saw each of these three areas as subcomponents of the overall theoretical framework of adult development.

The Development of Coping Mechanisms

Coping with the stress of being diagnosed HIV-positive was one of the developmental issues we investigated with this same sample of 18 HIV-positive young adults (Reeves, Merriam, & Courtenay, 1999). Using an ego psychological approach that is developmental in nature, it is posited that some defense mechanisms are more mature than others. Vaillant's (1977, 1993) model presents a hierarchy of defense mechanisms with more mature ones being, for example, humor or altruism, and less mature ones being for example, repression and denial. Prior to our study, research on coping with life-threatening illness, including HIV, focused on either identifying specific coping mechanisms or plotting the relationship between coping and psy-chological stress (Reeves et al., 1999). We were interested in a *developmental* focus, that is, how coping strategies evolved over time.

In our interviews with the 18 HIV-positive young men and women, we included questions about their coping with the diagnosis and ultimately, the disease. We asked about their initial coping mechanisms and how those may or may not have changed over time. From the data, we evolved a model rep-resenting "a developmental progression over time, from coping strategies that are more reactive, evidence less control, and are more self-centered to those that are more proactive, evidence more control, and are more other-centered" (Reeves et al., 1999, p. 350).

Immediately after diagnosis, participants reported affective coping mechanisms ranging from complete denial to intense anger. Behavioral coping included self-destructive behaviors such as "excessive use of drugs and alcohol, sexual acting out, and 'automatic pilot' reactions" (Reeves et al., 1999, p. 351); less destructive behaviors involved keeping busy as they had before diagnosis, learning about treatments, and so on.

After varying periods of time, participants came to realize that their initial coping mechanisms were not effective in dealing with this life-threatening disease. This realization initiated a transition period in which participants squarely confronted their HIV-status, began taking control and responsibility, and began getting involved in activities such as joining a support group. Finally, more mature coping mechanisms evolved for living with HIV, such as the use of humor, faith, altruism, seeking the support of others, and seeking a balance between attending to their HIV-status and other things in life.

Approaching coping mechanisms from a developmental perspective allowed us to see a "clear developmental progression—from reactive to proactive, less control to more control, and self-centered to other-centered" (Reeves et al., 1999, p. 358) not revealed in other studies. Further, the transitional period bridges the period between coping with the initial reaction to being diagnosed HIV-positive, and learning to live with HIV. Whereas our findings might be interpreted as "transformational coping" (Aldwin, 1994), which posits change in positive or negative directions, our findings are more in line with the adult development literature that popularly construes development in a positive, growth-oriented direction (Bee & Bjorklund, 2004).

Faith Development

An adult development theoretical framework posits change over time. But to be manageable, research using an adult development framework must be further delineated to focus on some specific aspect of development. In the examples above, the foci were on the cognitive process of meaning-making, and on the development of coping mechanisms. Using the same sample of HIV-positive young adults, we were also able to ask about the development of faith. As with meaning-making and coping, there are specific models of faith development that helped frame our inquiry. Reich (1992), who reviewed many of the models of faith development, concluded that some factors such as a supportive family climate or an active prayer life "favor religious development" (p. 181); a life crisis such as a life-threatening illness was not one of the factors listed. Fowler (1981), however, in his well-known model of faith development does acknowledge that "growth and development in faith also result from life crises, challenges and the kinds of disruptions that theologians call revelation. Each of these brings disequilibrium and requires changes in our ways of seeing and being in faith" (pp. 100–101). Whereas others have studied the link between a traumatic event and faith (Easley, 1987), and even HIV-status and faith development (Backlund, 1990; Marshall, 1991), these studies did not explicitly delineate the nature of this development. Our research focus then, was on *how* a particular life-threatening event, an HIV-positive diagnosis, influenced faith development.

In our interviews with the 18 HIV-positive men and women, we incorporated questions dealing with faith development by asking about the meaning of life for them, their faith, their purpose in life, and their concept of a God or higher being before diagnosis, and then how those views had changed (if they had) after diagnosis.

We found that there were three ways in which the HIV-positive diagnosis had brought about change in their religious faith. First, there is a shift from an unreflective, assimilated religious practice to a faith they have formulated and assume ownership of. As John, a former Episcopal priest said, "I probably would have continued to play this game and to me it was a game. . . . The illness made me get real about what I believed" (Courtenay, Merriam, & Reeves, 1999, p. 209). Second, their concept of God shifts from an authoritarian, punishing "bully," to a loving and caring God with whom they have a personal relationship. Finally, they reported a shift from a focus on the self to realizing their real purpose in life was to help other people, and this shift was part of their new understanding of faith. As Joe reported, "To me true faith and belief in humanity is going out and doing something that's, well, for others" (Courtenay et al., 1999, p. 212).

Tying our findings back into the theoretical framework of faith development and, in particular, Fowler's (1981) model, our study illuminated movement in Fowler's stages of faith development from stage 3, characteristic of most adults, to stages 4 and 5. Stage 3 has much more to do with the expectations of others (as was characteristic of our participants before their HIV-positive diagnosis); stage 4 is characterized by reflection and taking responsibility for one's beliefs and actions, and stage 5 is an acceptance of other worldviews and the centrality of other people, rather than self-absorption.

In summary, as with the development of coping mechanisms and more mature perspectives, a particular model of faith development informed this aspect of the research. Because we were interested in delineating a process, however, and not testing a model or hypothesis, we approached the question inductively and qualitatively. Our findings contribute to our understanding of how a life-threatening event impacts development.

Erikson's Stages of Psychosocial Development

As a final example of how one's theoretical framework permeates the research process, we refer to Erikson's (1963, 1968, 1982) eight-stage model of life span development. Social, psychological, and biological factors interact in shaping a person's development from infancy to old age. Erikson (1959, p. 52), while stating that there is a "proper rate" and a "proper sequence" of development, also agrees that his model allows for "variations in tempo and intensity" (1963, p. 272). Although each of the eight stages becomes prominent at a particular segment of the life span (trust versus mistrust in infancy or generativity versus stagnation in middle adulthood, for example), stages are not bound by chronological age; in fact, the tasks of all eight stages are present throughout life. There is a sense of developmental progression, however, as various stages "unfold" at various points in the life cycle. Erikson (1963) also posits that resolution of one stage is dependent upon successful resolution of previous stages. Successful resolution means achieving "a favorable ratio" (Erikson, 1963, p. 271) of the positive over the negative for each stage.

Although there are hundreds of studies using Erikson's model or aspects of his model as the theoretical framework, and these studies are generally supportive of the timing and nature of the eight stages, only a few studies involved terminally ill participants. Two studies involving HIV-positive individuals employed instruments to measure the amount of resolution of the eight stages (Marshall, 1991; Thomas, 1994). Ahmed (1992), however, speculated that AIDS may well interfere with the resolution of life stages, in particular the young adult and middle adult stages as 91 percent of persons with AIDS are between 20 and 49 years of age.

Rather than asking a static question about someone's stage of development as measured by an instrument, we were interested in how facing death affected the *movement* through Erikson's stages of development. Are earlier, unresolved issues revisited? Is there an accelerated movement through all the stages? Do people skip to the final stage? Do they work on multiple stages simultaneously? Our inductive, qualitative analysis of the interview data was informed by Hamachek's (1990) criteria for each of the three adulthood stages. These criteria, consisting of 10 "behavioral expressions" and 3 "implicit attitudes" for each adulthood stage, were, according to Hamachek (1990, p. 678), "logically and clinically deduced from Erikson's discussions." Although we acquainted ourselves with his criteria, we were not using them to necessarily label our participants as being in one stage or another; rather, we were interested in the *developmental* question of their engagement with and movement among the stages.

Our analysis yielded three findings with regard to how facing death affected movement through Erikson's stages of psychosocial development. First, all participants revisited Erikson's fifth stage of development—which typically manifests itself in adolescence—that of identity versus role confusion. This renegotiating of identity included coming to terms with a body that was deteriorating as a result of contracting a virus through (possibly) socially stigmatized practices, figuring out "where one is going" in terms of goals and commitments, and deciding whose approval "counted." Kenneth, a 31-year-old African American, for example, talked about "learning me. I really didn't know me [before HIV]; I'm learning about being me today." Steve no longer defined himself by his possessions and what others thought; identity now came from within, "from my identity not having to be the way I looked and what I drive and how much I make. That my identity is something else, my identity is not those appearances" (Merriam, Courtenay, & Reeves, 1997, p. 226).

Our second finding with regard to Erikson's stages was that the three adulthood stages were dealt with *simultaneously* with evidence of positive resolution for each stage for most participants. The three adulthood stages are intimacy versus isolation (dealt with in young adulthood), generativity versus stagnation (characteristic of middle age), and ego integrity versus despair (the main task of older adulthood). Because our participants were under 45 years old, we would expect they would be grappling to varying degrees with intimacy and generativity issues. Their HIV-positive status made issues of intimacy particularly poignant. Jamie, for example, thought about who he would want to be with him should he end up in a "hospital bed fixing to take my last breath." . . . and "There is still one person that I want there that I don't have yet, and that's a life partner" for that "piece of intimacy that I don't have with everybody else there [at his bedside]" (Merriam et al., 1997, p. 227). Elise, in fact, made HIV her "partner; it's closer than my physical partner, closer than my husband. It's there. It's always with me" (Merriam et al., 1997, p. 227).

With regard to generativity versus despair, even the youngest members of our sample were concerned about the world, about others, about making a contribution. Twenty-six-year-old Dawn left a promising career in Washington, D.C., to work for an AIDS education agency. The week we interviewed her, she had spoken publicly on AIDS prevention at two universities and "to a gym full of 700 ninth graders, and then an hour later, 650 eleventh graders" (Merriam et al., 1997, p. 228). She also noted the gap in services to HIV-positive women and wrote a grant that was funded to address this issue. Joe, who had left a lucrative computer company job because he "didn't want to end up dead in the middle of a board meeting somewhere talking about quality assurance," used his skills to edit and print an on-line newsletter for HIV-positive readers:

> If I know I can touch somebody in [the] rural [area of the state] somewhere and get that feedback that "you touched my life," that's a significant job to me, not

how much money I get from it, or how much fame I get from it or anything like that. Is it gonna make some kind of significant change in society that will benefit other people, even if it's just one person at a time, and it's just one guy who helps? (Courtenay et al., 2000, p. 109)

Ego integrity versus despair is Erikson's eighth and final stage of the life cycle. With the realization that death is inevitable, one reviews his or her life and comes to accept "one's one and only life cycle . . . that . . . permitted of no substitutions." Further, "the possessor of integrity is ready to defend the dignity of his own life style" (Erikson, 1963, p. 168). The "virtue" of this stage of life is wisdom. All of our participants seem to have achieved a sense of peace and acceptance. Thirty-seven-year-old Tracy recounted for us how she explained to her son why she wouldn't change anything about her life: "Listen to me," she said to her son,

Everything that I have went through in my life has brought me to the place that I am in today. I said, the only thing you're looking at is me using drugs and me being HIV positive, I said, but part of that was part of my growing, part of my learning to live, part of my healing within. If any of them pieces was missing out of that puzzle, then I wouldn't be where I'm at and I wouldn't be the person that I am. (Merriam et al., 1997, p. 229)

Our third finding is that ego development is an interactive process. In our study, grappling with intimacy and generativity enabled and supported the resolution of the tasks of identity and ego integrity. That is, as participants reached out, and connected with others (intimacy), in a caring and compassionate manner (generativity), service to others and the world became central to their self-definition (identity). "Simultaneously, they evolved a sense of integrity—they accepted who they had been and who they had become, realizing they had the 'wisdom' to be of help to others" (Merriam et al., 1997, p. 231).

In summary, Erikson's model of psychosocial development structured our inquiry by shaping our research question: how the threat of death affected movement through stages of development, and, in particular, the three adulthood stages. What we discovered was that the movement is not as linear or sequential as Erikson's theory implies. Our participants were involved in an interactive process of development that meant *simultaneously* dealing with intimacy, generativity, and ego integrity, the last of which was integrally related to identity. Whether these findings are idiosyncratic to young adults diagnosed HIV-positive at a time when such diagnosis constituted certain death, or whether other catastrophic life events would trigger the same pattern of development remains to be investigated.

Some Reflections on the Role of Theoretical Frameworks in Research

In this chapter, I have tried to demonstrate how one's theoretical framework structures all aspects of a research study. Even to ask a question about some phenomenon assumes some perspective, worldview, or disciplinary orientation. Identifying a theoretical framework not only makes that worldview explicit, but also provides the tools in terms of concepts and models for structuring the investigation. The studies reviewed here all reflect an adult developmental theoretical perspective; that is, we were interested in movement, in change, and, in particular, in the *process* of change. Because we were interested in change, we purposefully selected a sample of adults—those diagnosed HIV-positive—whose pre-HIV status would have been disrupted and challenged, thus initiating change.

The fashioning of a specific research question from the larger framework of adult development involved focusing on a particular aspect of development; this focusing process is necessary to make the inquiry manageable and coherent. Mezirow's (1991, 1995) developmental theory of transformational learning thus structured our questions about the process of perspective transformation as well as the permanency of this transformation and ongoing meaning-making. We also looked at coping mechanisms and faith changes from a developmental perspective, citing relevant models in these areas. Finally, in a sense, we "tested" Erikson's theory of psychosocial development by asking questions of our participants about the presence and movement of these stages in their lives. All of our research questions were thus derived from the theoretical framework: *how* do adults make meaning, *how* do coping mechanisms become more mature, *how* does faith develop, and *how* does one engage in psychosocial development in the face of death?

These questions determined the research methodology. They could only have been investigated through a qualitative design that allows for participants' perspectives and understandings of a phenomenon to be revealed (Merriam, 1998; Patton, 2000). Although a scale or instrument might identify a participant's present state with regard to cognitive development, coping, faith, or ego development, none would be able to access the *process* through which one moved from one state or stage to another. In-depth interviews using questions derived from our theoretical framework were used to "answer" our research questions. And how we "answered" our research questions was, in turn, driven by our theoretical framework; that is, we used the concepts and models from the literature to inform our analysis of the data. These findings were then discussed in relation to the literature from which the theoretical framework was derived.

References

Ahmed, P. I. (Ed.). (1992). *Living and dying with AIDS.* New York: Plenum.

Aldwin, C. M. (1994). *Stress, coping, and development: An integrative perspective.* New York: Guilford.

Backlund, M. A. (1990). *Faith and AIDS: Life crisis as a stimulus to faith stage transition.* Unpublished doctoral dissertation, Pacific Graduate School of Psychology, Palo Alto, CA.

Bee, H. L., & Bjorklund, B. R. (2004). *The journey of adulthood* (5th ed.). Upper Saddle River, NJ: Pearson Prentice Hall.

Clark, C. M. (1993). Transformational learning. In S. B. Merriam (Ed.), *New directions for adult and continuing education: No. 57. An update on adult learning theory* (pp. 47–56). San Francisco: Jossey-Bass.

Courtenay, B. C., Merriam, S. B., & Reeves, P. M. (1998). The centrality of meaning-making in transformational learning: How HIV-positive adults make sense of their lives. *Adult Education Quarterly, 48*(2), 65–84.

Courtenay, B. C., Merriam, S. B., & Reeves, P. M. (1999). Faith development in the lives of HIV-positive adults. *Journal of Religion & Health, 38*(3), 203–218.

Courtenay, B. C., Merriam, S. B., Reeves, P. M., & Baumgartner, L. M. (2000). Perspective transformation over time: A two-year follow-up study of HIV-positive adults. *Adult Education Quarterly, 50*(2), 102–119.

Easley, E. L. (1987). *The impact of traumatic events in religious faith: Implications for social work.* Unpublished doctoral dissertation, University of Alabama, Tuscaloosa.

Erikson, E. (1959). Identity and the life cycle. *Psychological Issues, 1,* 18–164.

Erikson, E. (1963). *Childhood and society* (2nd ed.). New York: Norton.

Erikson, E. (1968). *Identity, youth, and crisis.* New York: Norton.

Erikson, E. (1982). *The life cycle completed: A review.* New York: Norton.

Fowler, J. W. (1981). *Stages of faith: The psychology of human development and the quest for meaning.* San Francisco: Harper.

Hamachek, D. (1990). Evaluating self-concept and ego status in Erikson's last three psychosocial stages. *Journal of Counseling & Development, 68,* 677–683.

Kegan, R. (1994). *In over our heads: The mental demands of modern life.* Cambridge, MA: Harvard University Press.

Marshall, C. F. (1991). *Lifespan development, spirituality, and facing mortality: Role of HIV status and exposure to death in the spiritual and psychological development of gay men.* Unpublished doctoral dissertation, Wright Institute Graduate School of Psychology, Berkeley, CA.

Merriam, S. B. (1998). *Qualitative research and case study applications.* San Francisco: Jossey-Bass.

Merriam, S. B., Courtenay, B. C., & Reeves, P. M. (1997). Ego development in the face of death: How being HIV-positive affects movement through Erikson's adult stages of development. *Journal of Adult Development, 4*(4), 221–235.

Mezirow, J. (1990). How critical reflection triggers transformative learning. In J. Mezirow & Associates (Eds.), *Fostering critical reflection in adulthood:*

A guide to transformative and emancipatory learning (pp. 1–20). San Francisco: Jossey-Bass.

Mezirow, J. (1991). *Transformative dimensions of adult learning.* San Francisco: Jossey-Bass.

Mezirow, J. (1995). Transformation theory of adult learning. In M. R. Welton (Ed.), *In defense of the lifeworld* (pp. 39–70). Albany: State University of New York Press.

Mezirow, J., & Associates. (2000). *Learning as transformation.* San Francisco: Jossey-Bass.

Patton, M. Q. (2000). *Qualitative research and evaluation methods* (3rd ed.). Thousand Oaks, CA: Sage.

Reeves, P. M., Merriam, S. B., & Courtenay, B. C. (1999). Adaptation to HIV infection: The development of coping strategies over time. *Qualitative Health Research, 3,* 344–361.

Reich, K. H. (1992). Religious development across the life span: Conventional and cognitive developmental approaches. In D. L. Featherman, R. M. Lerner, & M. Perlmutter (Eds.), *Life-span development and behavior* (pp. 145–188). Hillsdale, NJ: Lawrence Erlbaum.

Taylor, E. (2000). Analyzing research on transformative learning theory. In J. Mezirow & Associates (Eds.), *Learning as transformation* (pp. 285–328). San Francisco: Jossey-Bass.

Thomas. M. R. (1994). The Eriksonian model as a framework for the psychosocial assessment of the HIV positive individual (Doctoral dissertation, Columbia University, 1994). *Dissertation Abstracts International, 56* (01B), 0538. (UMI No. 9516193)

Usher, R. (1993). Experiential learning or learning from experience: Does it make a difference? In D. Boud, R. Cohen, & D. Walker (Eds.), *Using experience for learning* (pp. 169–180). Bristol, PA: Open University Press.

Vaillant, G. E. (1977). *Adaptation to life.* Boston: Little, Brown.

Vaillant, G. E. (1993). *The wisdom of the ego.* Cambridge, MA: Harvard University Press.

3

Struggling With Theory: A Beginning Scholar's Experience With Mazzoni's Arena Models

Frances C. Fowler

Overview of the Study

In 1990, after successfully defending my dissertation at The University of Tennessee, Knoxville, I began to work as an assistant professor in the Department of Educational Leadership at Miami University in Oxford, Ohio. At that time, I was familiar with Tennessee and Tennessee politics, but Ohio was new territory for me. My introduction to Ohio and its education politics came during my first weeks in the state. Both my students and my colleagues talked—or, more accurately, *complained*—a great deal about Senate Bill (S.B.) 140, the Omnibus Education Reform Act passed by the Ohio General Assembly in 1989. By and large, the state's educators were extremely angry about this law, which contained a potpourri of reforms, including three forms of school choice and mandatory phonics instruction. Most claimed that it had been "railroaded" through the state legislature without any meaningful input from educators or their organizations. In my classes, the students (who were almost all practicing Ohio teachers and administrators) often referred to S.B. 140 with considerable cynicism, calling it a classic example of the arrogance of contemporary politicians, who do not believe that educators know anything important about children or schools despite their years of professional practice. One student shared with me an amateur video that someone had shot at a regional meeting of the Buckeye Association of School Administrators, the state superintendents' organization. In it, superintendent after superintendent lambasted S.B. 140 and the legislative body that had enacted it. Angry comments and bitter laughter punctuated many of the speeches.

Later during that first year, some of my students and I attended a briefing session about the law, given by a high-ranking Ohio Department of Education official. In the course of the meeting, he informed his audience that "The train is leaving the station; you can get on board or be left behind." After this meeting, I stood with a group of Miami University graduate students as they angrily dissected this official's statements. Because I was greatly intrigued by this conflict-filled situation and the theoretical questions it raised, I launched a study of the passage of S.B. 140 in January 1991. My first trip to the state capital to gather data coincided with the beginning of the first Gulf War. My overall purpose in this study was to assess the extent to which the educational community was correct in believing that the law had been rammed through the legislature with little or no input from educators.

Earlier, during the fall of 1990, I had come across Tim Mazzoni's two "arena models" of policy innovation in education. In his first model, a conference proposal that I reviewed for the Politics of Education Association, he recounted how he had developed a model for major policy changes, hypothesizing that they usually result from a shift from the "subsystem arena," which is made up of education interest groups and politicians with a special concern for education, to the "macro arena," in which the general public exerts pressure on politicians to develop new policy.

After applying this first model to his study of the passage of a Minnesota law that enacted interdistrict open enrollment, however, Mazzoni (1991) found that the changes in Minnesota's education policy had resulted largely from pressure exerted by high-ranking political figures, or the "leadership arena." For several reasons, which I will detail below, this second theoretical stance seemed ideally suited for my study. Using Mazzoni's concept of decision-making arenas and a shift from his first to second model, I developed two research questions: To what extent did the Ohio events (surrounding the passage of S.B. 140) conform to Mazzoni's first arena model? To what extent did the Ohio events conform to Mazzoni's second arena model?

I chose qualitative case study as my research method, drawing heavily on the work of Yin (1984), who defines a case study as an investigation of a contemporary social phenomenon within its real-life context, using multiple data sources. I investigated the passage of S.B. 140 by the Ohio General Assembly, situating it within the social and political context of Ohio in the late 1980s. I gathered several types of data. First, I obtained a copy of the legislation. Next, I photocopied all the newspaper articles on the topic of S.B 140 that had been published by the *Cleveland Plain Dealer* and the *Columbus Dispatch* in January 1988 (when Governor Richard Celeste had called for school reform in his State of the State Address) and from December 1988 to July 1989 (when S.B. 140 was under consideration by the legislature and eventually passed). I also photocopied relevant articles from the publications of Ohio's major education interest groups, such as the two teachers' unions and the Ohio School Boards Association, during the same time periods. In addition, I obtained the three separate legislative commission reports that had been published during the period under study as well as reports of briefing sessions about the law by the Ohio Department of Education. After I had thoroughly analyzed the documentary data, I conducted 20 in-depth, semi-structured interviews with policy actors who had been involved in the passage of the law. They included leaders of the major education interest groups in the state, such as the Ohio Education Association, the Ohio Federation of Teachers, and the Buckeye Association of School Administrators; two people who had served on legislative commissions; several members of the state legislature; and a member of Governor Celeste's staff.

My major conclusion was that Mazzoni's (1991) first arena model, which hypothesized that education policy innovations are made in response to pressure from the general public, or "macro arena," did not fit the Ohio data at all. In fact, I found that Ohio's macro arena had remained inert throughout 1988 and 1989 in spite of the governor's energetic attempts to stir it to action. Mazzoni's second arena model, however, which attributed key roles in policy innovation to high-ranking leaders, came close to describing what had happened in Ohio. Summing up my findings, I wrote in my Fowler (1994) article:

> [W]hen the policy process shifted away from the subsystem arena, it moved largely to the leadership arena. Ohio's innovative education reform was defined, initiated, formulated, and pushed through the legislature by various high-ranking state and national leaders. The players in the subsystem and macro arenas were reduced to reactive positions from which they provided relatively minor input. (p. 347)

In other words, my study revealed that the state's educators were largely correct in believing that S.B. 140 had been "rammed through" the legislature.

I also found, however, that there were some weaknesses in Mazzoni's (1991) theoretical framework. I felt that he had overestimated the independence of the commissions that legislatures often appoint before developing new legislation. I also thought that he had defined the leadership arena too narrowly; my study suggested that the top business leaders in the state as well as the top political leaders could participate in it. Finally, Mazzoni had not mentioned the importance of the national political climate in shaping what happened in Minnesota, perhaps because Minnesota has pioneered the development of numerous innovative educational policies and therefore has helped to mold the national political climate rather than being shaped by it. In Ohio, however, the national education reform movement had clearly led the state's politicians to put education reform on their agenda; in fact, the three forms of school choice included in S.B. 140 had been directly copied from Minnesota's law.

In 1992, I presented a preliminary version of my study (Fowler, 1992b) at the annual meeting of the American Educational Research Association, and in 1994 *Educational Evaluation and Policy Analysis* published an article based on it, entitled "Education Reform Comes to Ohio: An Application of Mazzoni's Arena Models." This was the same journal that had published Mazzoni's article about his arena models in 1991.

In the intervening years, since I first used Mazzoni's arena models, I have used his theoretical framework for two other studies, both quite recent (Fowler, 2002, 2005). In addition, Feir (1995) used Mazzoni's framework in his investigation of state education policy innovation. Finally, in 2004, a doctoral student who was using Mazzoni's arena models as the theoretical framework for her dissertation study of the passage of a piece of higher education legislation contacted me, seeking advice about her interview protocol.

Mazzoni's arena models are used rarely for two reasons. First, the politics of education field has shifted strongly toward research on policy rather than on the political process that produces it. Second, the field tends to be rather atheoretical, a weakness that those of us who work in the politics of education deplore. The theory itself is highly regarded, and was part of the reason that Division L of the American Educational Research Association accorded Mazzoni a lifetime achievement award when he retired in 2001.

Description of the Theoretical Framework

In order to understand Mazzoni's (1991) arena models of policy innovation, one must first understand some fundamental facts about the American political system at both the federal and state levels. The founding fathers of the United States were quite skeptical about the intellectual maturity of the general public, seeing it as susceptible to rapidly changing political fads and as more likely to be swayed by emotion than by reason. They were also suspicious of centralized power, which, because of their experience of living in a British colony, they perceived as corrupt and tyrannical. As a result, they designed a form of government that is very conservative in the sense of being very resistant to policy change. Such American institutions as the Electoral College, the bicameral legislature, the separation of powers, judicial review, the executive veto, and other such "checks and balances" were adopted primarily to achieve this effect. And when the states developed their own constitutions and governance structures, with few exceptions they followed the federal model of separated powers with numerous checks and balances. The founding fathers were quite successful in their endeavor; the American political system is, to this day, extremely resistant to change, especially when compared to the more widely used parliamentary system of government (Fowler, 2004). As a result, most change in American politics is gradual, or *incremental.* This means that American politicians typically use the strategy of passing a limited and weak version of the policy that they really want and then spend years (or even decades) gradually amending it to bring it closer to their ideal. This type of slow tinkering with policy is called *incrementalism.*

Occasionally, however, American governments do adopt policies that represent an abrupt change from the past. An example would be the New Deal administration of Franklin D. Roosevelt, which passed numerous laws setting up such radically new policies as public works programs and Social Security. Because such changes—known among political scientists as *policy innovations*—are rare, they hold a special interest for those who study politics. Mazzoni's (1991) arena models were designed to explain how policy innovations came about in education during the 1980s, a period of extensive education reform, which started out as incremental change but became more radical with the passage of time. Drawing on the political science literature, he hypothesized that policy decisions are made primarily in two different arenas: (1) a *subsystem arena,* which consists of the education committees of both houses in a legislature, the state department of education, and the representatives of the major education interest groups; and (2) a *macro arena,* which is made up of the general public, top political leaders, and the mass media. He theorized that incremental changes occur when political decision making remains within the subsystem arena but that in order for a policy innovation to occur, the conflict over the issue must expand to the macro arena (Mazzoni, 1991). In other words, he believed that popular pressure is instrumental in bringing about policy innovations in education.

Mazzoni (1991) tested his model by applying it to a real-life case—the 5-year struggle to pass an interdistrict open enrollment policy in Minnesota. His analysis of events in Minnesota revealed that in that state, political elites had been considerably more important in pressing for the adoption of a school choice law than had been the general public, or the macro arena. In fact, he wrote, "There was no public clamor in Minnesota for educational choice nor any parent movement having that as an objective" (p. 120); indeed, surveys conducted in the state indicated that a "clear majority" of Minnesota's citizens opposed school choice. Nonetheless, the legislature passed a law that put such a policy on the books. As a result of his findings, Mazzoni revised his model, adding two more arenas: a leadership arena and a commission arena. The leadership arena included "top-level government officials and . . . the private groups or individuals—if any—who control them" (Mazzoni, 1991, p. 125). The commission arena is a decision-making site created by the government when it sets up a commission, task force, or study group. In Minnesota, Mazzoni found that the Governor's Discussion Group included representatives of numerous constituencies and that it had ultimately recommended the adoption of a school choice policy. In his final version of the theory, Mazzoni argues that in order for an innovative educational policy to be adopted, the central policy debate had to shift out of the subsystem arena, but that it could shift to any of the other three arenas, or to a combination of them. He concluded by saying

> Though the revised model corrects the most obvious shortcomings in the initial model, there is much work still to be done. Other likely arenas—for example, state courts, education agencies, interest group coalitions, and private elite networks—need empirical investigation and comparative analysis for their innovative potential. (p. 132)

Origins of the Framework and Why I Chose It

In this section, I will explain where Mazzoni's arena models originated, tell how I first encountered his framework, and discuss my reasons for deciding to use his models.

Origins of Mazzoni's Models

As a professor of educational administration with a specialty in the politics of education, Mazzoni was well-read in political science and related fields. His reference section in his 1991 article lists no fewer than 43 books and articles from the political science literature; in addition, he lists 24 books and articles from the politics of education literature, 3 from organizational theory, and 2 from sociology. Mazzoni was not just a prolific reader, however; in spite of the demands that his position as department chair at the University of Minnesota placed on him, he maintained an active research agenda, publishing numerous articles on educational politics and policy making in Minnesota. Therefore, his arena models grew out of years of reading, observing, and reflecting about how changes in education policy come about. A closer analysis of the works that he specifically cites in the section of his article that describes the arena models suggests that his political science reading was especially critical in shaping his theory; all but 3 of those 17 sources are from the political science realm.

The term "arena models," however, appears to have been borrowed from a sociological piece, Hilgartner and Bosk's (1988) "The Rise and Fall of Social Problems: A Public Arena Model," published just 3 years before Mazzoni's own article. In this work, the authors present a model of how publicly recognized social problems first attract attention, grow in perceived importance, and eventually are displaced in public consciousness by other problems. In elaborating their theory, they describe how social problems compete for attention and resources in such "arenas" as the mass media. Hilgartner and Bosk define "arena" differently from Mazzoni, who specifies that by an arena he means "a middle-range term, referring to the political interactions characterizing particular decision sites through which power is exercised to initiate, formulate, and enact public policy" (1991, p. 116). Mazzoni seems to have developed his understanding of the term from such political scientists as Allison, who refers to the "apparatus of government" as "a complex arena" (1971, p. 144) and from Schattschneider, who refers to "the arena of conflict where political alternatives are determined" (cited in Cobb & Elder, 1983, p. 5).

As I read through other sources cited by Mazzoni (1991), I was able to find additional clear influences on his thinking. For example, Allison (1971) organizes his book about decision making during the Cuban missile crisis of 1962 around three "conceptual frameworks" or "lenses," which he calls "models." Bardach (1972) uses the term "subsystem," and Cobb and Elder's (1983) description of the "expansion" of a political issue resembles Mazzoni's description of what happens when a shift from the subsystem arena to the macro arena occurs. The closest parallel, though, comes from Cobb, Ross, and Ross's (1976) models of agenda building. (In political science, "agenda building" is the process by which specific social issues attract the attention of the government and are placed on the list, or "agenda," of issues that the government seeks to address through its policy making [Fowler, 2004].) Cobb et al. propose three models of agenda building. Under the "outside initiative" model, groups or individuals who do not work in the government succeed in calling enough attention to a problem to cause the government to place it on its agenda for action. This model seems to involve what Mazzoni calls the *macro arena*. Alternatively, an issue may be identified *within* the government itself, but politicians and government workers mobilize the general public to become interested in it and to push for action. This model is reminiscent of Mazzoni's arena shift from the subsystem arena to the macro arena. Cobb et al.'s final model is one in which an issue is identified within the government, but politicians and government workers never bring it before the general public; instead, they seek to resolve it without public involvement. This model resembles Mazzoni's description of incremental policy making within the subsystem arena.

One question that particularly interested me as I reviewed Mazzoni's sources was: Why did Mazzoni initially develop a model that did not accommodate the possibility of policy innovations imposed by a leadership elite? Having cut my own political teeth in a Southern county where an entrenched "good old boys'" network constantly tried to impose its will on everyone else, I found this hard to understand. One possible explanation, of course, is that Mazzoni is an idealist who believes that in a democracy all decisions are made democratically. Another is that Minnesota politics are more open and more democratic than policy making in some other states. In fact, this is probably true since Minnesota's political culture resembles that of New England, which is known for the town meeting and unusually "clean" politics. In contrast, Southern politics is characterized by the heavy influence of elites (Fowler, 2004). My review of Mazzoni's sources, however, suggested another reason. Many of the books that he drew on were written during the 1960s or 1970s when some of the major policy innovations in American life were brought about by the civil rights movement. As a result, the authors he used had firmly in their minds the spectacle of huge masses of citizens mobilizing to march, demonstrate, conduct sit-ins, and in other ways pressure the government to break with the racially discriminatory past. In other words, they had in mind the mobilization of a vast macro arena to bring about civil rights reforms. Therefore, they may have tended to overestimate the extent to which the general public mobilizes around innovative policy issues, and this overestimation may have affected Mazzoni's perspective as he developed his arena models.

My First Encounter With Mazzoni's Arena Models

During my first 2 years as an assistant professor at Miami University, I was the program chair of the Politics of Education Association, then a special interest group of the American Educational Research Association. Therefore, early in the fall of 1990 I received about 25 conference proposals, which I scanned for appropriateness and then sent out for review. One of these was a paper proposed by Tim Mazzoni, then a professor of educational leadership at the University of Minnesota and a well-known scholar in the politics of education. As I read the summary of his research on the adoption of school choice policies in Minnesota and his description of his arena models of policy innovation, I became very excited. His work fit in well with the intellectual journey on which I had recently embarked and, because S.B. 140 had included three forms of school choice patterned on the Minnesota legislation, which Mazzoni had studied, I believed that I had found a conceptual framework that I could use to study the passage of S.B. 140 in Ohio.

Why I Chose Mazzoni's Theoretical Framework

I encountered Mazzoni's (1991) theoretical framework at a time when I was wrestling with some of the great theoretical issues in my field. My dissertation had been a historical policy analysis of government aid to private schools in France between 1959 and 1984. At that time, the dean of my college insisted that dissertations presented in partial fulfillment of the requirements for the PhD be based on an established social theory (EdD dissertations, in contrast, could be atheoretical). Because I was in the PhD program, one of my key challenges during the early development of my dissertation study had been finding an appropriate political science theory to use. I can still remember the sense of relief that I felt when, after months of scanning various political science works, I read two books by Robert Dahl: *Dilemmas of Pluralist Democracy* (1982) and *A Preface to Economic Democracy* (1985). Based on what I already knew about the development and implementation of the French policy, I could see how Dahl's pluralist theory could illuminate my research and facilitate my interpretation of the French data. What I did not know at the time was that pluralist theory— which posits that in democratic societies policies grow out of compromises between competing political pressure groups—is controversial and that many political scientists have seriously challenged its validity. The theory worked reasonably well for my dissertation; I even entitled my study *One Approach to a Pluralist Dilemma: Private School Aid Policy in France, 1959–1985.* Even before I reached my defense, however, I was aware of some of its shortcomings. In particular, because France has a much stronger central government than does the United States, its politics is not as pluralistic as American politics is. So I realized that some of the events that had occurred in France could not be fully explained by pluralist theory. My awareness of its shortcomings, however, was painfully intensified by several critical comments made during my dissertation defense by the sole political science professor on my committee. After recovering from my anger at him, I faced the fact that before I attempted to write any articles based on my dissertation, I needed to resolve some of the theoretical issues raised by pluralism.

Moreover, while doing my dissertation research, I had also become familiar with another social theory that is prevalent in contemporary political science. This was rational choice theory, which I encountered while doing my literature review. This review covered most of the literature on the debate over school choice in the United States, and I found that many American proponents of school choice based their position on rational choice theory. Basically, rational choice theorists believe that most social and political phenomena can be understood as activities that play out in competitive markets. If individuals in those markets simply make decisions based on their own self-interest, an "invisible hand" will guide society to the best outcome possible. Thus, in advocating school choice these proponents argued that parents should be able to choose their children's schools because education is just another market commodity like food or automobiles. If people were allowed to choose schools based on their own self-interest, the result would be greatly improved education. For philosophical and religious reasons, I strongly disagree. When reading such arguments, I often became so angry that I just skimmed over the articles that contained them so that I could go on to more congenial reading. Finally, realizing what I was doing and how unscholarly it was, I forced myself to go back and read every word of the articles based on rational choice theory! I emerged from this experience convinced that rational choice theory was far more problematic than pluralist theory, but I wanted to have a stronger reason than my emotional reaction for rejecting it, especially since it was—and still is—one of the dominant theories in political science. In short, I realized more than ever that I needed to have a well-thought-out theory to base my own work on.

My theoretical struggles were complicated after I accepted my position at Miami University in February 1990. At that time, I began to read the works of two of my future colleagues, Henry Giroux (1981) and Peter McLaren (1980), who wrote within the tradition of critical theory, a form of Marxism. I found their work and the Marxist frameworks they used intriguing. Their descriptions of social injustice in capitalist societies were insightful and contained a great deal of truth. I also thought that Giroux and McLaren were right to emphasize the importance of thinking through the influence of the structure of the economic system on social and cultural phenomena. Critical theory and other forms of Marxism, however, also posed some serious theoretical problems for me. I was prepared to believe that the economy was important, but not that it determined everything else in society as most Marxists do. I did not believe that the historical evidence supported this position. In addition, I was troubled by the fact that Giroux, McLaren, and other Marxists diagnose the ills of American society brilliantly, but offer few concrete ideas about how to bring about positive changes. Moreover, they seemed rather naively ignorant of practical politics, and therefore I did not see how they could bring about reforms even if they had concrete ideas about what reforms were needed. Thus, though interested in their work, I was not convinced that Marxism offered an adequate explanation of political phenomena.

By the fall of 1990, then, I was struggling with some major theoretical questions. With the old adage of "publish or perish" in mind, I wanted to base some articles on my dissertation and I knew that I needed a more solid theoretical grounding to do so. At that point, I was also preparing to teach my first politics of education class, and Miami University students were relatively sophisticated theoretically. It was imperative, therefore, that I decide which of the grand social theories available in academia was the truest and learn more about it so that I could use it to shape my own work.

Therefore, during my first year as an assistant professor, I launched a program of intense reading. First, I explored a more recent work by Robert Dahl (1989) and also discovered an important book by another pluralist, Charles Lindblom (1977). Much to my gratification, I learned that they had revised their original theory to respond to the criticism that they tended to overlook the disproportionate power of business in the politics of capitalist countries. Their revised theory, which they called "neopluralism," recognized that business groups essentially trump all other groups in capitalist democracies and therefore have a greater influence on policy than any others. Since this revamped version of the theory seemed to address many of the weaknesses of pluralism that had concerned me, I based an article on it, using neopluralistic theory and the French experience with school choice to argue that, contrary to the claims of rational choice theorists, school choice could only succeed in the United States if it was carefully regulated (Fowler, 1992a).

Meanwhile, as I prepared to teach the politics of education for the first time, I encountered two more social theories. The first was a political theory called "elite theory," originally developed by two Europeans of the late 19th and early 20th centuries: the Italian political scientist Gaetano Mosca (1939) and the German sociologist Robert Michels (1966). They argued that in any group or society a small elite rises to the top and rules, making most of the important decisions. Searching for contemporary American representatives of this perspective, I found the works of Thomas Dye (1976, 1990) and G. William Domhoff (1983, 1990). They argue that a small number of wealthy Americans who control several interlocking institutions run the country. Finally, I encountered the theories of the German sociologist Max Weber (1964). While recognizing the importance of the economy and economic leaders, especially in capitalist countries, Weber also insists that other forces, such as the government, the military, and widely believed ideologies significantly influence what happens in society. The most convincing modern presentation of Weber's ideas I found in Michael Mann's *The Sources of Social Power* (1986). In this book, the author draws on the sweep of Western history from prehistoric times to 1760 to build his argument that

> A general account of societies, their structure, and their history can best be given in terms of the interrelations of what I will call the four sources of social power: ideological, economic, military, and political relationships. These are overlapping networks of social interaction, not dimensions, levels, or factors of a single social totality. . . . They are also organizations, institutional means of attaining human goals. (p. 2)

Looking back after 15 years, then, I can see why Mazzoni's (1991) theoretical framework appealed to me. It was not a *grand* social theory; that is, it did not seek to explain everything in society as rational choice theory, Marxism, or Weberian theory do. It was a middle-range political theory that was more limited even than pluralism or elite theory because it sought only to explain how policy innovations come about in education. It was, however, potentially compatible with pluralism, neopluralism, elite theory, Weberian theory, or even Marxism. In fact, it actually provided a way for me to begin to test all of these theories against the concrete data of a particular case, for one of Mazzoni's models hypothesized that the macro arena (read "political pressure groups") was instrumental in bringing about policy innovation whereas the other attributed the major role to leaders (read "elites"), who might even be business leaders, as Marxists and Weberians would predict. I shaped my article as a test of Mazzoni's arena models, but it was also a personal test of the various theories with which I was then grappling.

Having described the theoretical struggles of my early academic career in some depth, it seems only fair to tell the rest of the story. My study of the passage of S.B. 140 indicated that elite figures were far more instrumental in the passage of the bill than were pressure groups, and I found that this elite group included both political and business leaders. This study, in conjunction with other studies and much additional reading, led me to conclude that the most accurate grand social theory is Weberian theory. I also concluded that elites do run all societies, but that societies vary in the degree to which these elites can be both influenced and replaced through democratic processes. One of the problems faced by every democratic society is how best to devise structures that make it possible for the macro arena to challenge policy elites when truly fundamental change is needed.

Effects of the Framework on My Study

Using Mazzoni's (1991) models as my theoretical framework shaped my study in four ways. It helped me focus my research, develop my research questions, plan my data collection, and structure my data analysis. I will discuss each of these effects in turn.

Focusing the Study

Unless a scholar is doing a qualitative project based in grounded theory, he or she is well advised to use a theoretical framework not only because it situates the author within a scholarly conversation but also because it helps to focus the study. I well remember how I felt about my dissertation project before I had identified pluralism as a suitable theory for framing it. Over a period of 4 years, I had gathered a huge amount of data; I had several books, numerous articles, copies of the French legislation and the accompanying rules and regulations, and hundreds of pages of parliamentary debate, arranged in folders and stacked all over my spare bedroom. Frankly, I felt overwhelmed and did not know where to begin to narrow the subject down so that I could reduce this project to a manageable size. As soon as I read Dahl's two books (1982, 1985) and began to apply pluralistic theory to my data, an amazing thing happened. The theory acted as a giant sieve; most of my data simply fell through it like sand, leaving behind a number of solid rocks that I could analyze from the perspective of pluralism. Clearly, I could—and should—ignore the sand and focus my attention on the rocks as I continued data collection and framed my research questions.

This was one of the reasons that I was so determined to find a suitable theoretical framework for my study of the passage of S.B. 140. It was the first study that I undertook after obtaining my PhD, and I knew that having a theoretical framework would enable me to narrow the subject and focus on only those aspects of it that were truly relevant to my theory. I must confess, however, that I did not completely let the framework do its task of sifting my data. In one of my interviews, a female respondent made some insightful comments about the fact that most of the educational practitioners on the commission on which she had served were women and suggested that because they were women they were silenced and marginalized by the male business leaders who served with them. These comments had nothing to do with Mazzoni's (1991) arena models, but I believed that they made an interesting contribution to what might be called the micropolitics of commissions. Therefore, my initial conference paper about my study (Fowler, 1992b) and the first draft of the manuscript that I submitted to *Educational Evaluation and Policy Analysis* (Fowler, 1994) included a page or two that presented these comments and discussed them. Not surprisingly, one of the blind reviewers of the article pointed out that that section was superfluous; and the editor asked me to omit it in my revised version. In other words, the theoretical framework so clearly focused my study that even other people could easily distinguish relevant from irrelevant material! I should point out, however, what this means. A theoretical framework both illuminates and conceals. This is why it can be helpful to apply more than one framework to a set of data.

Developing the Research Questions

Another advantage of using a theoretical model is that it facilitates the development of research questions. Those questions should always be firmly grounded in the framework, and any questions that might be interesting but do not relate to the framework should be eliminated. In the case of my study of the passage of S.B. 140, I conceptualized my project as a test or application of Mazzoni's (1991) arena models. Therefore, my two questions were rather obvious. I asked to what extent each of the two models accurately described what had happened in Ohio. With these two questions and the qualifying words "to what extent," I could only reach three possible conclusions. Either the Ohio data would conform to the first or the second arena model or would not conform to either. Thus, I would either accept one of the models or reject Mazzoni's framework as not fitting the Ohio data at all. Reaching the latter conclusion would imply that the framework had extremely serious weaknesses as a model of policy innovation.

In retrospect, I probably should have used more than two research questions, basing the additional questions on each of the arenas. This is, in fact, the approach that I used in my two more recent, and as yet unpublished, studies using the theoretical framework. Such questions would have focused my attention more clearly on what was happening in each arena and might have led to a more sophisticated analysis of my data. I was a novice, however, and my two questions functioned adequately.

Planning Data Collection

My theoretical framework was enormously helpful in planning data collection. It provided me with four distinct areas to explore: the activities of the legislative subsystem, the commissions (if any), the macro arena, and the leaders. Therefore, in identifying the data I would need, I simply asked myself who would be active in each arena and where they would have left usable documents to attest to their activity. This strategy permitted me to rather rapidly find such obvious documents as the legislation, the legislative history, and the publications of the interest groups that had been involved. Once I had used these sources to develop a time line, I knew which of the state's newspapers I most needed to consult and the relevant time frame within which I had to search for articles. This was crucially important because in the early 1990s it was much more difficult to search newspapers than it is today! The

Internet, search engines, and such tools as LexisNexis either did not yet exist or were not widely accessible. As a result, I had to visually scan microfilms of all the issues of the two newspapers that were published during the relevant time periods. This effort, however, was well worth the time and eyestrain involved. The newspaper coverage was not only helpful in permitting me to identify what the top leaders had done and what had happened (or, rather, *not* happened) in the macro arena, but it also alerted me to the fact that there had been a commission arena, something I had not realized until then. Indeed, three commissions, each representing a different faction of the legislature, had met and each had produced a report. I therefore proceeded to procure copies of the commission reports.

The second stage of my data collection consisted of 20 semi-structured interviews. Using my documentary data, I identified a number of people I might interview, including members of the legislature, people who had served on commissions, leaders in education interest groups, and members of the governor's staff. In planning my interviews, I also used my theoretical framework, for I deliberately chose to interview members of the subsystem arena first. My rationale was that they would be more accessible to me, who as a professor of education in a public university was relatively close to them in background and interests. I also believed that their recommendations could help me select the best people to interview from the other arenas and help me obtain access to them. As it turned out, my rationale was correct; my first set of interviewees identified several key people from the other arenas whose names had not emerged in the documentary data—such as the chief of staff for the Republican Caucus in the legislature—and helped me set up interviews with them.

Guiding Data Analysis

Finally, the theoretical framework guided my data analysis. In planning the data analysis, I relied heavily on Miles and Huberman's (1984) *Qualitative Data Analysis*. One of their suggested techniques was to compare and contrast data from different "sites." Mazzoni's (1991) arena models provided me with four obvious sites: the subsystem arena, the macro arena, the leadership arena, and the commission arena. Therefore, in analyzing the data I identified who the major players had been in each arena and listed them. I also identified all the events that had happened in each as well as which stages of the policy process had occurred there. Two themes cut across all four arenas. The first was the great lack of confidence in professional educators manifested by political leaders from both parties. They saw professional educators, from the classroom on up to the superintendent's office, as bumblers who were out of touch with the real world. Not surprisingly, the other theme was that the educators felt betrayed. It seemed to them that the rules had changed in the middle of the game and that they had suddenly become the state government's whipping boys. These themes illuminated the arena shift, suggesting why it had occurred. In the final stage of analysis, I asked myself the key questions: Did an arena shift occur? If so, what was the nature of the shift? My finding, of course, was that the policy process had indeed shifted away from the subsystem arena. It had not, however, shifted to the macro arena, but to the leadership arena.

Other Theoretical Frameworks Considered

Earlier in this chapter, I discussed the various theories that I encountered and struggled with during my years as an advanced doctoral student and a beginning assistant professor. As I searched for a theoretical framework for my study of the passage of S.B. 140, I considered and rejected three of them. My reasons for rejecting them were both intellectual and pragmatic.

First, I considered using Dahl's (1982, 1985) theory of pluralism, a framework that is widely used among political scientists who study the policy process and one with which I had grown very familiar during the writing of my dissertation. My experience conducting my dissertation research, however, and the biting comments of the political science professor on my committee led me to hold grave reservations about using it. These reservations were intensified because I already knew enough about how S.B. 140 had been passed to suspect that pluralist theory would not work well for my case study. As I understood the situation, the basic belief that lay behind the complaints of my students and colleagues about the way the law had been passed was precisely their conviction that some sort of pluralistic process that gave considerable weight to the views of educators' organizations should have been followed. Obviously, it had not been. Therefore, I doubted that pluralist theory would illuminate what had actually happened in Ohio.

Two other theories that had some appeal to me were elite theory and Marxism. Unlike pluralist theory, both of these theories included a definite role for leaders, especially business leaders. I could not, however, visualize how I could conduct a qualitative case study using either of these theories. I suspected that if a highly elite group, such as a few prominent CEOs, had been behind the passage of S.B. 140, they probably had kept a low profile. Therefore, it might not be easy to identify them; even if I were able to learn their names, I feared it would be difficult to obtain access to them for interviews. Moreover, phrasing an interview protocol in such a way that it got at the deeper issues behind elite and Marxist theory also seemed problematic.

I could not imagine asking people lower down in the political hierarchy than the elite or capitalist leaders questions like, "What capitalists (or corporate leaders, or political elites) were active behind the scenes in pushing for S.B. 140?" In my opinion, it is no accident that people who do scholarship in these traditions rarely do qualitative case studies. Elite theorists usually do documentary or computer research to identify top leaders in various institutions and trace their interconnections, whereas Marxists typically study broad social trends, such as privatization or the de-skilling of teachers as revealed in curriculum materials.

To be frank, another issue was completely pragmatic. I was a beginning assistant professor who knew that she would go up for a third-year review in 2 years and a tenure and promotion review in 5 years. Both reviews would involve external reviewers from my field. As I perused the top-tier journals in which I hoped to publish, such as *Educational Evaluation and Policy Analysis, Education Policy,* and *Educational Administration Quarterly,* I became aware that none of their articles were based on either elite theory or Marxist theory. In fact, with the exception of Laurence Iannaccone and Frank Lutz's (1970) dissatisfaction theory, I know of no scholars in my field who have ever used elite theory, and at the time only one person seemed to be working in critical theory. Actually, much of what is published in my field— both then and now—is atheoretical, although various versions of systems theory are frequently used. Therefore, I feared that these journals would not publish articles based on those two theoretical traditions and decided that Mazzoni's middle-range theory of arena models, which could easily be seen as compatible with systems theory, was more likely to be publishable. On the other hand, my perusal of possible publishing outlets suggested that those journals most likely to publish a study based on elite or Marxist theory probably would not be interested in a piece about the passage of a law—in general, they are interested in broader, more general analyses.

Using Multiple Frameworks

It is not uncommon for qualitative studies to be based on more than one theoretical framework, as researchers often find that no single framework adequately explains all their data. My study of the passage of S.B. 140, however, was, for the most part, based just on Mazzoni's (1991) arena models. I employed multiple frameworks only in the sense that I used both versions of his arena model. I chose to do so because I was interested in testing both models and also because doing so permitted me to highlight my central finding: the extremely important role played by government and business leaders

1. Issue definition

2. Agenda setting

3. Policy formulation

4. Policy adoption

5. Implementation

6. Evaluation

Figure 3.1   The stage model of the policy process

in the passage of Ohio's S.B. 140. I should also point out that in conducting my data analysis, I employed a framework called the "stage model of the policy process." This is a schematic, six-stage heuristic framework that is commonly used in political science texts and courses (See Figure 3.1).

I applied it to all four policy arenas because it simplified my determination of which political processes had played out in each. As a heuristic model, it merely describes political phenomena; it does not seek to explain them.

Refining the Framework

As a beginning scholar, I did not fully understand how theoretical frameworks are used in qualitative research. Since I was a neophyte and Mazzoni was approaching the end of a distinguished career, I accepted his models as being indisputably valid and authoritative, even though in his own article he had written, as I quoted above: "Though the revised model corrects the most obvious shortcomings in the initial model, there is much work still to be done" (1991, p. 132). Many years later, I am not sure what I thought that statement meant, or even if I noticed it at the time. Regardless of what Mazzoni himself had said, I approached my data analysis with the implicit assumption that *one* of Mazzoni's models had to fit the Ohio data, or there would be something seriously wrong with my study. I did not approach the data with the idea that my study might contribute to the refinement and further development of Mazzoni's arena models.

As a result, when I wrote the first draft of the article (Fowler, 1994) that I submitted to *Educational Evaluation and Policy Analysis*, I exaggerated the extent to which Mazzoni's (1991) second model fit my findings. Although there were obvious discrepancies between my findings and the second model, I did not acknowledge this in the article. Instead, I claimed that my study confirmed the accuracy of Mazzoni's second model. Much to my surprise, one of the blind reviewers pointed out several of these discrepancies and suggested that instead of asserting that my study supported Mazzoni's second model unequivocally, I should raise some questions about his model and suggest possible revisions of it. With a reviewer and an editor's recommendations to give me courage, I did indeed critique the second model and suggest ways that it might be refined. Later, I learned through one of Mazzoni's former doctoral students that he had actually appreciated my critique!

As a more mature scholar, I now realize that theory develops through just such thoughtful critique and refinement as I carried out in the revision of my article. No single researcher can apply a given theory to every conceivable case. The development of useful theoretical frameworks depends on numerous researchers using them in various contexts and suggesting further elaboration or refinement. If enough scholars contribute to this process, a sophisticated body of theory can be developed, laying a solid foundation for the growth of a field of knowledge.

References

Allison, G. (1971). *Essence of decision*. Boston: Little, Brown.

Bardach, E. (1972). *The skill factor in politics*. Berkeley: University of California Press.

Cobb, R. W., & Elder, C. D. (1983). *Participation in American politics* (2nd ed.). Baltimore: Johns Hopkins University Press.

Cobb, R. W., Ross, J. K., & Ross, M. H. (1976). Agenda building as a comparative political process. *American Political Science Review, 70,* 126–138.

Dahl, R. A. (1982). *Dilemmas of pluralist democracy: Autonomy vs. control.* New Haven, CT: Yale University Press.

Dahl, R. A. (1985). *A preface to economic democracy.* Berkeley: University of California Press.

Dahl, R. A. (1989). *Democracy and its critics.* New Haven, CT: Yale University Press.

Domhoff, G. W. (1983). *Who rules America now?* Englewood Cliffs, NJ: Prentice Hall.

Domhoff, G. W. (1990). *The power elite and the state.* New York: Aldine.

Dye, T. R. (1976). *Who's running America? Institutional leadership in the United States.* Englewood Cliffs, NJ: Prentice Hall.

Dye, T. R. (1990). *Who's running America? The Bush era.* Englewood Cliffs, NJ: Prentice Hall.

Feir, R. E. (1995). *National patterns of state education policy innovation and three deviant cases.* Eugene, OR: Clearinghouse on Educational Management. (ERIC Document Reproduction Service No. ED385927)

Fowler, F. C. (1990). *One approach to a pluralist dilemma: Private school aid policy in France, 1959–1985.* Unpublished doctoral dissertation, The University of Tennessee, Knoxville.

Fowler, F. C. (1992a). American theory and French practice: A theoretical rationale for regulating school choice. *Educational Administration Quarterly, 28,* 452–472.

Fowler, F. C. (1992b). *An application of Mazzoni's arena models to the passage of Ohio's S.B. 140: A preliminary study.* Paper presented at the annual meeting of the American Educational Research Association, San Francisco. (ERIC Document Reproduction Service No. ED350662)

Fowler, F. C. (1994). Education reform comes to Ohio: An application of Mazzoni's arena models. *Educational Evaluation and Policy Analysis, 16,* 335–350.

Fowler, F. C. (2002, April). *The struggle to pass Ohio's charter school legislation.* Presented at the annual meeting of the American Educational Research Association, New Orleans, LA.

Fowler, F. C. (2004). *Policy studies for educational leaders: An introduction* (2nd ed.). Upper Saddle River, NJ: Merrill.

Fowler, F. C. (2005, October). *Swallowing camels and straining at gnats: The politics behind Ohio's voucher and charter school programs.* Paper presented at the annual meeting of the Mid-Western Educational Research Association, Columbus, OH.

Giroux, H. A. (1981). *Ideology culture & the process of schooling.* Philadelphia: Temple University Press.

Hilgartner, S., & Bosk, C. (1988). The rise and fall of social problems: A public arena model. *American Journal of Sociology, 94,* 53–78.

Iannaccone, L., & Lutz, F. W. (1970). *Politics, power and policy: The governing of local school districts.* Columbus, OH: Merrill.

Lindblom, C. E. (1977). *Politics and markets.* New York: Basic Books.

Mann, M. (1986). *The sources of social power: Vol. 1. A history of power from the beginning to AD 1760.* Cambridge, UK: Cambridge University Press.

Mazzoni, T. (1991). Analyzing state school policy making: An arena model. *Educational Evaluation and Policy Analysis, 13,* 115–138.

McLaren, P. (1980). *Cries from the corridor.* Toronto, ON: Methuen.

Michels, R. (1966). *Political parties: A sociological study of the oligarchical tendencies of modern democracy.* New York: Free Press.

Miles, M. B., & Huberman, A. M. (1984). *Qualitative data analysis.* Beverly Hills, CA: Sage.

Mosca, G. (1939). *The ruling class.* New York: McGraw-Hill.

Weber, M. (1964). *Basic concepts in sociology.* New York: Citadel.

Yin, R. (1984). *Case study research.* Beverly Hills, CA: Sage.

4

Liminality and the Study of a Changing Academic Landscape

Pamela J. Bettis
Michael R. Mills

Introduction

This chapter and the one that follows (Chapters 4 and 5) are companion pieces. They both are the result of the same study of a college of education that was reorganizing its departmental structure and, in particular, of faculty's understandings of their professional identities in a new academic department. We have produced two papers (Bettis, Mills, Miller, & Nolan, 2005; Mills, Bettis, Miller, & Nolan, 2005) from the study, and the two papers employ two different theoretical frameworks that we found useful in understanding how faculty made sense of the reorganization.

Generally speaking, both papers (Bettis et al., 2005; Mills et al., 2005) focus on social construction and sensemaking as the process by which people create their social worlds and their identities. This broad theoretical orientation, along with a more specific interest in identity, is what guided our early formulations of the project, the research questions, and data collection. As the project proceeded, we refined and focused our conceptualization of the research by referencing more specific theoretical formulations from our varying academic backgrounds to explain our data and findings.

Study Overview: Who Am I in This New Organizational Unit?

Like many qualitative research studies, this study was not necessarily planned. Rather, it emerged out of the changes that were taking place in our daily work lives. The two of us were colleagues in two different departments in a college that undertook a major reorganization, which resulted in us being colleagues in the same newly created department. Although the reorganization of departments, colleges, and entire universities is a common practice found in the academic landscape, very few faculty members have formally studied these changes. Michael, however, thought that our circumstance created an excellent opportunity to examine how faculty members made sense of these changes and how they constructed new forms of identity in their new organizational home. This is the origin of our study.

First, Michael put together a team of five faculty members, one from each of the former departments that contributed members to the new unit. Thus, our research team was born. The guiding research questions were then created for the study:

1. How did university faculty members experience and make sense of their professional lives, identities, and work during a major reorganization in their college of education?

2. What contributed to or distracted from faculty members' identity construction and organizational identification as faculty members from different academic programs came together in a newly organized academic department?

Michael asked that all five of us maintain a journal about matters surrounding the reorganization during its first year. Further, he provided specific prompts during the academic year to focus some of our journal entries such as, "How has your former department manifested itself in the workings of the department, college, and work life?" and "Compare your role in the current structure to your prior role within your former department." Research team members responded to these prompts and wrote journal entries that described different facets of their work lives, which included college, school and departmental meetings, the status of their research endeavors, and their yearly evaluations. The text of the journals became the study's major data source, along with various documents (memos, e-mails, committee reports, etc.).

During the second academic year of the reorganization, we began the analysis phase of the project. All four of us (by now one member had dropped out due to time constraints but allowed us to include his data) coded the journal and document texts, and analyzed the text fragments to establish connections and contrasts. Next, we came together and compiled our individual initial list of codes into one list, which consisted of 178 codes. As a group, we then narrowed the codes to a set that would encompass all of the selected text sections in order to be as comprehensive and inclusive of the journal topics as possible; that collapsed list consisted of 48 agreed-upon codes. These 48 codes included such descriptors as: faculty governance, gender, emotional demands, decision making, redundancy/inefficiency of meeting, paradigm wars, collegiality, and values of professional life. The two of us then used these 48 codes to recode the entire 150 pages of single-spaced journal entries and assorted documents using HyperRESEARCH. The research team met biweekly for a semester, and through group discussions and shared written summaries of our conversations, we conducted iterative analyses of the data to develop our interpretations. These discussions resulted in a list of 12 descriptive categories that included a general sense of anxiety and uncertainty over what work was to be valued in the new department and leadership issues.

Our findings highlight the changing nature of our work during the reorganization as well as the fragmentation, anxiety, and lack of trust within the unit. We describe the uncertainty in which faculty members worked as the organizational expectations changed, the contradictions that faculty faced in terms of attempting to collaborate with new colleagues who were trained in very different ways, and the withdrawal of faculty members from a commitment to the new unit.

Like most researchers, we did not want to merely describe the reality of academic reorganization and faculty identity. We hoped to describe and, more important, explain why faculty held particular perceptions of reorganization and their professional identities. We wanted to contribute to the scholarly literature on faculty life during reorganizational activity as well as the understanding of our own lives as academics.

Liminality: Theoretical Framework and Explanation

Pam used the concept of liminality (Turner, 1967, 1977; Zukin, 1991) as a theoretical vehicle to make sense of the dynamic interaction between individual faculty members' responses to changes in their work lives and identities and the changing political, economic, and social landscape of higher education. Liminality provided a way to embed the day-to-day, micro context of university life within that of the wider macro, social, and economic changes taking place.

The origins of the term liminality are associated with Victor Turner (1967, 1977), an anthropologist whose work explores ritual and symbols in traditional African tribes. Turner's definition of liminality described a transitional period and status during rites of passage. Turner argued that the liminal period was an "interstructural stage" in which individuals or groups gave up one social state but had yet to enter the new prescribed social state with accompanying responsibilities and perspective. Thus, the individuals were "betwixt and between" social statuses. Examples of the liminal stage included times during girls' and boys' puberty rites when they were no longer children but had yet to acquire the status of adulthood or when before the marriage ceremony, the bride is neither single nor married. Although these rites of passage and accompanying liminal statuses were found in all societies, Turner maintained that they were expressed more fully in societies that were bound to biological or astronomical events as signs of change rather than to technological innovations.

Turner (1967) found that the symbolism surrounding people in liminal states was often complex. The initiates were treated as both living and dead and neither living nor dead; therefore, symbols used to represent liminal people incorporated both images of life and death. For example, a waxing and waning moon, a snake shedding its skin, and a hibernating bear all symbolize life and death and something other than these discrete categories. Therefore, the social category of these liminal or transitional individuals was paradoxical. "This coincidence of opposite processes and notions in a single representation characterizes the peculiar unity of the liminal: that which is neither this nor that, but both" (Turner, 1967, p. 99).

Turner (1967) also found that the relationships among liminal individuals were of extreme equality. Within the period of liminality, individuals often assumed what Turner called "structural invisibility" (p. 99). They had no status, property, kinship rank, or any marker that would distinguish them from their fellow liminal individuals. There was no hierarchy within the group, and, in fact, members often made lifetime friendships during the liminal period. Liminal people did not have to act out any social or political part, and everyone was in flux in terms of their individual identity. Turner found, however, that typically there were guides who helped individuals negotiate this undefined status or liminal state and prepared them for the transition to their new status, such as married womanhood or adulthood. Thus, there was some stability offered to these individuals embarking on a journey to the unknown.

Later on in his academic career, Turner (1977) revisited the concept of liminality with another anthropologist, Colin Turnbull (1990), and argued that he had missed the transformative possibilities embedded in the liminal state, one in which individuals can try on new ways of being. The lack of social status and fixed identity offered opportunities to explore new identities and ways of being that were not allowed in the society at large.

Since Turner's (1967) use of the term, the concept of liminality has been expanded and applied to other "betwixt and between" conditions. Educational sociologists Kathleen deMarrais and Margaret LeCompte (1999) applied the term to the entire time period of adolescence in industrialized societies. This age group is seen as neither children nor adults and occupies a precarious position in modern society, at times vulnerable, privileged, and often segregated from the rest of society. Sharon Zukin (1991), a critical urban sociologist, used liminality to describe the current historical, social, political, and economic context. Drawing from Schumpteter's notion (as cited in Zukin, 1991) that an essential fact of capitalism is its constant ability to reinvent itself, Zukin saw the landscape of advanced industrial societies as one that was always varied and changing due to this continual process of creative destruction. Specifically, she argued that neither the language of deindustrialization nor postindustrialism "captures the simultaneous advance and decline of economic forms, or the sense that as the ground shifts under our feet, taller buildings continue to rise" (Zukin, 1991, p. 5). Zukin used Turner's anthroplogical concept of liminality to make sense of the current transitional social and economic landscape of industrialized nations:

> In the abstract, economic restructuring can be thought of as a process of liminality. It socially reorganizes space and time, reformulates economic roles, and revalues cultures of production and consumption. What is always new about these processes is their mutual impact on specific groups. Once it is culturally mediated, the experiences of relative gains and losses inflict a general consciousness of change. (Zukin, 1991, pp. 28–29)

Just as Turner (1967) saw liminality as representing neither this nor that but both and more, Zukin argued that neither deindustrialization nor postindustrialism explained the current dynamic economic and social changes and that these changes were more than either of these explanations combined. Further, Zukin explored how the characteristics of both modernism and postmodernism were in evidence simultaneously in this liminal space.

This notion of liminality—articulated by Zukin (1991) as a transitional social and economic period between industrialism and postindustrialism, and modernism and postmodernism—provided a conceptual framework for explaining the macro intellectual and economic changes in all of higher education. Although Zukin is referring to the creative destruction inherent in a capitalist economy and the implications of this in terms of American culture writ large, her argument makes sense when applied to universities in their current context. The university in which the five of us worked is a part of the global economic restructuring taking place along with all of its incumbent social changes as well. At the same time, we drew from the original meaning of liminality and its anthropological roots, which explore individuals in societal transition. These two understandings helped us make sense of our data and our lives as faculty members.

Locating the Theoretical Framework

Since the two of us have been trained in different subfields of education, we have been immersed in different theoretical orientations. Therefore, it should come as no surprise that when we came to read deeply in the literature, make journal entries, and finally to make sense of the data, we did so in somewhat different but overlapping ways. Pam's training in the social foundations of education exposed her to the disciplines of anthropology and sociology as they relate to education and encouraged her to embed all of her research, particularly her qualitative endeavors, in the wider political, social, and economic context. For both published papers (Bettis et al., 2005; Mills et al., 2005), the theoretical framework came from the discipline orientation of the lead author.

Although Pam did not enter the study with the expressed purpose of drawing from the conceptual vehicle of liminality, there were several factors that made its infusion and ultimately explicit use not surprising. First, Pam had used the concept of liminality, in its micro and macro forms, in her dissertation, which explored urban high school students' understandings of their lives and futures amid a rust belt city that was deindustrializing (Bettis, 1994). Thus, she carried a heightened sensitivity from her dissertation review of the literature concerning the transitional status of the U.S. economy, and in fact all industrialized economies. Further, she was attentive to any group of individuals living between two social worlds, and she had begun to notice that being adrift between two world views and/or contexts was not limited to adolescents.

After Pam had thoroughly coded and recoded her dissertation data and completed the best preliminary analysis she could without a strong theoretical explanation of what she had found, she "sat" on the data, read new material, and reread books that she thought were significant. One of these was Sharon Zukin's (1991) *Landscapes of Power: From Detroit to Disney World*, which explores the changing political economy of cities and uses the concept of liminality to describe that changing landscape. This had been a useful concept in considering how cities were changing and what impact that might have on how urban students understood their lives. Most of Zukin's work, however, remained at the macro level and did not move into the micro or everyday lives of urban inhabitants, and this is what Pam wanted to do. When she was rereading Zukin and considering the liminal economy, she traced Zukin's use of the term to a footnote where Zukin cited the work of Victor Turner, whose work she then read. Turner's discussion helped to explain what the kids were saying and doing in her data; it provided the micro understanding that Pam needed.

Therefore, Pam had the background knowledge of the liminality concept when she began this study with Michael. Its use, however, was not triggered fully until she began reading Stanley Aronowitz's *The Knowledge Factory* (2000), which explores the changing political and economic landscape of higher education. Reading Aronowitz while coding the data led her to consider the data and their relationship to the macro political, economic, and social changes taking place throughout universities across the nation. Thus, the direct applicability of the multiple meanings of liminality came into play fairly early in the analysis phase of the project. The similarities in social disruption and shifting identities that described transitioning adolescents, the socioeconomic conditions of late capitalism, and the changing organization of our college drew us to this line of explanation. Furthermore, whereas the administrators championing the reorganization did not clearly articulate their motives in terms of the pressures on the modern university in a postmodern era, it did not take much of a leap of logic to frame the reorganization in those terms.

Effects of the Theoretical Framework on the Research

Although liminality was not explicitly named as the theoretical framework that Pam would employ in the beginning of this study, you can see her heightened sensitivity to how the individual negotiates the liminal period as well as an awareness of the changing macro contexts even in the study's early stages. In fact, various understandings of liminality can be seen throughout Pam's early thinking and writing about the research project. Obviously, part of the reason for that was her explicit familiarity with the concept. Part of its use, such as attention to the macro political economic context of higher education, however, emanates from her doctoral training and subsequent reading. Therefore, Aronowitz's arguments in *The Knowledge Factory* (2000) easily fit into her awareness and understanding of the larger global economic shifts. All of these sensitivities led Pam to notice and write about issues regarding the status of colleges and universities in American society, the external pressures they face, and how those get translated into the work and daily lives of faculty members amid the organizational shift we were experiencing. This even became an explicit focus at times in her journal writing, as these two passages, written on September 8, 1998, exemplify. The first is a reflection on our first faculty meeting of the newly created department:

> When the HRD (Human Resource Development) woman started the meeting, she had an overhead that could be read several different ways. Her point was the multiplicity of our perspectives . . . you know the kind of thing I taught to my 9th graders in 1984 in rural Arkansas. And here we are in 1998 amidst a whirlwind of economic, social, and political changes and the university is dynamically connected to them all. How obsolete can we be? Perhaps, this reorganization and its incumbent changes point to our inherent anachronism. Perhaps, Lyotard is right in saying that the Professoriate is dead and that the university can no longer be viable in a postmodern, postindustrial era. This meeting made that point to me clearly.

This second journal entry frames the everyday mundane administrative tasks as political in nature:

> Sometimes I feel like Giroux's "clerk of the empire" and it is very discombobulating. I teach with passion about schools being the last public institutions besides malls where democratic possibilities exist. But I don't feel that way in my own institution. Democracy can flounder when participants are overwhelmed with minutiae and detail; when the big decisions are lost in the everyday administrivia.

Although most of Pam's journal entries were much more descriptive in nature and less explicitly analytical, the point is that her training and reading were already evident in how she made sense of her everyday life in the newly formed academic unit.

Pam's sensitivity to the broader social, economic, and political changes that were playing out in universities across the nation could also be found in her literature review, which was an ongoing process throughout the entire research endeavor. Although all of the research team members read broadly in the area of higher education and the contemporary changes in which it was embedded, Pam was drawn to particular literatures, which she explored more deeply. For example, she read more deeply on the impact of the crisis of knowledge within university life in terms of the blurring of disciplinary boundaries, the challenges to rationality, and the history of universities. Further, she read about how these changes were manifested in university life— such as the university's greater technical and/or vocational thrust; a decline in the importance of the humanities and challenges to the Western canon; a loss of the university's role in preserving democracy and civic discourses; an exponential increase of knowledge; a heightened managerialism in the operation of institutions; a decrease in public funding and increased reliance on corporate and private monies; and changing roles for faculty members and their demoralization (Aronowitz, 2000; Bender, 1997; Bloland, 1995; Davies, 1999; Giroux, 1999; Lueddeke, 1999; Manicas, 1998; Paden, 1987; Popkewitz, 1998; Tierney & Rhoads, 1993; Ward, 2003; Welch, 1998). These kinds of readings provided her with the macro landscape in which to embed the actions and everyday understandings of faculty members who live within them, the data of this study.

So far, the heightened awareness of liminality and its characteristics could be found in Pam's journaling and her literature review. Its most explicit use, however, could be found in the analysis phase of the project. As was mentioned earlier in the study overview, after the 178 initial codes were collapsed into 48 and the entire data set was recoded by both of us, we then collapsed these 48 codes into 12 categories based on the similarity or relatedness of the topics. These 12 groupings consisted of (1) a general sense of anxiety; (2) uncertainty over what work is to be valued in the new department; (3) getting to know each other in the new department; (4) how and why participation in the new unit is difficult; (5) external pressures on the university; (6) nine programs or a coherent unit? (7) leadership issues; (8) the difficulties of curricular integration due to paradigm differences; (9) how faculty will be evaluated; (10) weak organization and administration support; (11) the discouraging of governance activities; and (12) evaluation. Then, all of the quotes for each group were printed as a set, and each set became the focus of a meeting to interpret, derive themes and differences, and apply theoretical formulations based on the content of the text units. Michael produced a written summary of the conversations, along with the relevant textual fragments, which became the subject of further conversation, sorting and recombining the interpretations within and among the original code groupings. The resulting discussions of these 12 larger descriptive categories resulted in three analytic themes that the group characterized as central to the data: (1) the changing context of higher education; (2) the dysfunctionalities and contradictions of the reorganization and the resulting new academic unit; and (3) the changes in faculty identity. Pam made sense of these three analytic themes through applying the concept of liminality. It helped explain the changing context of higher education and the anxiety and uncertainty that individual faculty expressed regarding their professional identities, and the dual understandings of liminality provided by Turner (1967, 1977) and Zukin (1991) linked these two analytic themes.

Faculty members are not mere puppets of the macro economic and social changes that Zukin (1991) and Aronowitz (2000) describe. They live within and amidst them, are shaped by them and, in turn, their own thoughts and actions reshape the university in which they live. This is where Turner's understanding of liminality came into play. Turner (1967) maintained that when individuals entered the liminal period, they shed previous roles but did not yet take on new ones. Thus, liminal individuals experience a type of paradox in which they let go of their previous roles and responsibilities but have not transitioned to the new social state and its accompanying social roles and responsibilities. This understanding of liminality helped explain why faculty members were so confused and anxious as they negotiated the contradictions of their professional lives. Liminality mediates the world of macro economic and social changes with that of the daily lives of faculty. It is a synergistic concept in that characteristics of the macro world and micro world play off of each other. Turner's notion of liminality and the multilayered conceptualization prompted by Zukin's formulation are helpful in understanding how faculty negotiate the changes brought about by a college of education's reorganization and the larger context of higher education.

Further, the concept of liminality provided a way to frame our suggestions for approaching change and alternative futures for higher education. Turner (1967) and another anthropologist, Turnbull (1990), both revisited their initial understandings of the liminal period and recognized the missed opportunity of seeing this betwixt and between time as one of possibilities, of trying on different identities and embracing play. They argued that the transformational facets of the liminal period were just as important as the uncertainty it engendered. We took their second reading of the liminal period as a way to wish for and dream about "doing" higher education differently in a rapidly changing social and economic landscape, and offered that discussion as the conclusion of our paper.

Critique of the Theoretical Framework

The purpose of a theoretical framework is to make sense of the data, to provide some coherent explanation for why people are doing or saying what they are doing or saying. It is meant to move the research project beyond the realm of the descriptive into the realm of the explanatory. It is not meant, however, to be a straitjacket into which the data is stuffed and bound. Liminality was a very helpful conceptual tool in considering how faculty members negotiate an academic reorganization. It was not a perfect fit for our data, however, nor did it explain everything in a neat and tidy manner, and we have several examples of this.

First, Turner (1967, 1977) studied mostly adolescents in their transitional period from childhood to adulthood. Our focus was on adults whose transition was situated around professional and career changes in identity. Second, Turner found that liminal individuals were typically guided with help from those appointed to shepherd them through this interstructural stage so that they could begin to learn about their new way of life. There were clearly no guides to help faculty negotiate the changes wrought by the reorganization of their professional lives. In fact, we argued in our paper that administrators were in the same liminal state as faculty without much guidance. Further, Turner's use of the term liminal is individual and related to role, so the transformation refers more to personal identity than to social change. The adolescents he studied know they are returning to the same culture they came from and, in addition, their transition is to be guided by the familiar adults of the village. The rules and roles of their new status are established within the culture and known by their guides, who pass their knowledge on to the adolescents during their transition.

It is Zukin's (1991) shift of the term to an economic and cultural sphere that emphasizes the social and organizational elements of the change and alters its character in important ways. Here, the transformation is in not only individual role but also in culture. Things will be different (even if there is likely to be some continuity of arrangements), and past experience does not provide a clear picture of what a new order will hold. There are no knowledgeable guides, or an established culture to look forward to, or any firm sense of how the future will shake out.

Another way in which Turner's (1967, 1977) conceptualization of a liminal transitional process did not match what was taking place in our college of education reorganization was that there was not a clear demarcation between the old and new roles and responsibilities of the liminal individuals. The roles and responsibilities of the old culture continued to be part of faculty members' lives, which existed simultaneously with the effort to develop new roles and culture. Thus, faculty members were expected to maintain some of their previous professional habits as well as to construct and adapt to the rules and habits of a new culture without a guide to what was coming. The demands of these two worlds weighed heavily on all five faculty members' professional lives.

Finally, Turner (1967, 1977) argued that liminal individuals experienced a sense of equity since past statuses and privileges dropped away. In line with this, one stated goal of the reorganization was to standardize and make faculty workloads more equitable in the college. Our journal entries, however, revealed mistrust and unease with attempts at reworking the new departmental culture and the college through collaboration. In fact, one of the final three themes focused on the dysfunctionalities and contradictions of the reorganization and the resulting new academic unit. This included the inability of faculty to collaborate, for example, which is the opposite of what Turner described in his liminal groups. In fact, the lack of rules and fixed institutional culture did not facilitate new and different ways to imagine our work and our interactions with colleagues. Certainly, it did not engender many new friendships, much less lifetime friendships, among faculty members.

The above are examples of how the concept of liminality did not "fit" our data exactly. The purpose of a theoretical framework, however, is not to provide comfortable clothing for data. As Michael discusses in the companion chapter that follows, a theoretical framework offers a vehicle to make generalizations to other contexts and provide an explanation for why people do and say what they do and say.

References

Aronowitz, S. (2000). *The knowledge factory.* Boston: Beacon.

Bender, T. (1997). Politics, intellect, and the American university, In T. Bender & C. Schorske (Eds.), *American academic culture in transition* (pp. 17–54). Princeton, NJ: Princeton University Press.

Bettis, P. J. (1994). *Constructing futures on fault lines: Urban working high school students' perceptions of school, work, and the future in a post-industrial city.* Unpublished doctoral dissertation, University of Toledo, Ohio.

Bettis, P. J., Mills, M., Miller, J., & Nolan, R. (2005). Faculty in a liminal landscape: A case study of a college reorganization. *Journal of Leadership and Organizational Studies, 11*(3), 47–61.

Bloland, H. (1995). Postmodernism and higher education. *Journal of Higher Education, 66*(5), 521–559.

Davies, J. (1999). Postmodernism and the sociological study of the university. *The Review of Higher Education, 22*(3), 315–330.

DeMarrias, K., & LeCompte, M. (1999). *The way schools work.* White Plains, NY: Longman.

Giroux, H. (1999). Vocationalizing higher education: Schooling and the politics of corporate culture. *College Literature, 26*(3), 147–161.

Lueddeke, G. R. (1999). Toward a constructivist framework for guiding change and innovation in higher education. *Journal of Higher Education, 70*(3), 235.

Manicas, P. (1998). The radical restructuring of higher education. *Futures, 30*(7), 651–656.

Mills, M., Bettis, P. J., Miller, J., & Nolan, R. (2005). Experiences of academic unit reorganization: Organizational identity and identification in organizational change. *Review of Higher Education, 28*(4), 597–619.

Paden, R. (1987). Lyotard, postmodernism, and the crisis of higher education. *International Studies in Philosophy, 19*, 53–58.

Popkewitz, T. (1998). The culture of redemption and the administration of freedom as research. *Review of Educational Research, 68*(1), 1–34.

Tierney, W. G., & Rhoads, R. (1993). Postmodernism and critical theory in higher education: Implications for research and practice. In J. C. Smart (Ed.), *Higher education: Handbook of theory and research* (Vol. 10, pp. 308–343). New York: Agathon.

Turnbull, C. (1990). Liminality: A synthesis of subjective and objective experience. In R. Schechner & W. Appel (Eds.), *By means of performance: Intercultural studies of theatre and ritual* (pp. 50–81). New York: Cambridge University Press.

Turner, V. (1967). *The forest of symbols*. Ithaca, NY: Cornell University Press.

Turner, V. (1977). Variations on a theme of liminality. In S. F. Moore & B. G. Myerhoff (Eds.), *Secular ritual* (pp. 36–52). Amsterdam: Van Gorcum.

Ward, K. (2003). *Faculty service roles and the scholarship of engagement*. San Francisco: Jossey-Bass.

Welch, A. (1998). The end of certainty? The academic profession and the challenge of change. *Comparative Education Review, 42*(1), 1–14.

Zukin, S. (1991). *Landscapes of power: From Detroit to Disney World*. Berkeley: University of California Press.

5

Organizational Identity
and Identification During a
Departmental Reorganization

Michael R. Mills
Pamela J. Bettis

A s noted in the previous chapter, Chapters 4 and 5 are companion pieces. This chapter shifts the focus to a second article (Mills, Bettis, Miller, & Nolan, 2005) produced from our research project on faculty members' reactions to a reorganization of their academic department. Here, the focus is on organizational identity and organizational identification as exemplified in the new academic unit.

Study Overview

The origins of the research project and the methods used are presented in the previous chapter and are not repeated here. In the article that is the focus of this chapter (Mills et al., 2005), the findings and analyses highlight the dysfunctional interaction patterns of the new department, referred to as the Department of Educational Studies (DES), as indicated by the mode of debate, lack of trust, and fragmentation within the unit. We describe a departmental faculty that had substantial difficulty working together toward important collective decisions regarding matters like curricular consolidation and promotion and tenure guidelines. Themes in our analyses include truncated communications, conflict avoidance, dysfunctional decision-making processes, and our own withdrawal from participation in the unit.

Under these conditions, the department became a weak unit within which to develop an organizational identity and identification. Given the lack of mutual processing of issues, faculty members were impeded in their ability to negotiate an agreement on the identity of the unit. This inhibited sensemaking, which, in turn, hampered our identification with the new department.

Theoretical Framework: Organizational Identity and Identification

We started the study with the notion that the new unit would have to create a new organizational culture and become home to people who had not previously shared an organization. In effect, culture is the internal and symbolic context for organizational identity. Thus, the same processes of social construction and sensemaking are involved in developing and perpetuating both organizational culture and organizational identity. As such, both constructs become susceptible to reinterpretation and shifting meanings as the context for identity is reframed. Much as recent conceptions of culture have moved beyond an integrationist view to emphasize the internal variation and fragmentation (Martin, 1992), the conception of organizational identity has also moved beyond something that people take to be central, distinctive, and enduring about an organization (Albert & Whetten, 1985) to thinking about identity as a social construction susceptible to change and incoherence (Gioia, 1998).

Organizational culture and identity, in turn, become prime considerations in organizational identification. In effect, the affiliations that we use to define ourselves are often the organizations in which we participate (Pratt, 1998). Organizational culture sets the context for organizational identity, which, in turn, says a lot about who organization members are and how they would like to think about themselves. Through organizational identification, organization members get psychological needs such as safety, affiliation, self-enhancement, and self-actualization fulfilled while the organization gets members who are more likely to act in ways congruent with organizational goals and needs. The process of identification is complicated, however, because neither the individual nor the organization has a singular identity or even consistency among multiple aspects of identities.

Alvesson and Willmott (2002) suggest that we have not moved much beyond these recognitions to more fully grasp the identity constitution processes in organizations. They attempt to address that shortcoming in the interpretive literature, and they provide an overview of four ways individuals' identities are influenced and changed in organizations. The interactions within organizations serve to define (1) the employee by directly defining characteristics; (2) action orientations by defining appropriate work through motives, morals, and abilities; (3) social relations by defining belongingness and differentiation; and (4) fit with the social, organizational, and economic terrain.

In addition to this general framework, the paper (Mills et al., 2005) used more specific theories focused on Alvesson and Willmott's (2002) third item, explanations of identity formation via belongingness known as social identity theory (SIT) and self-categorization theory (SCT). These formulations focus on how group norms, stereotypes, and individual prototypes serve to define identities and influence identification with groups, and examine factors such as groups' homogeneity, prestige, distinctiveness, and permeability. These theories have been more formally derived and tested in broad sociological contexts, and a body of literature has grown out of attempts to extend the insights of SIT and SCT (see Hogg, Terry, & White, 1995, for an overview of the theories and literature) to the identities of organizations (Ashforth & Mael, 1989; Gioia, 1998) and identification within organizations (Pratt, 1998). Working from these theories, researchers hypothesize that clear and distinct differences between groups, a high salience for organizational categories in accounting for differences between groups, and membership in an attractive or prestigious group will enhance identification with a social group and organization (Hogg & Terry, 2001; Pratt, 1998). Conversely, identification with an organization is likely to be more difficult if members are highly heterogeneous or if they are too much like members of other organizations, and the theories incorporate notions of ambivalent identification or disidentification.

Of particular interest for our study, these theories have also been used in research on mergers in organizations. Mergers are problematic because the social foundations for prior identifications usually remain intact, reducing the need for individuals to develop commitment to a new group identity. Instead, "employees of merged organizations tend to act on the basis of their premerger identity . . . rather than on the basis of the identity implied by the merger" (Van Knippenberg & Van Leeuwen, 2001, p. 251). This literature suggests that, for example, issues of in-group and out-group membership and status differentials will cause problems for organizational identification among members of the "out" or lower-status organization. Success in organizational mergers has been connected to conditions that promote interaction, such as equal status, intergroup cooperation, egalitarian orientation, and personal acquaintance. Given these conceptual foundations, this paper focused on the organizational factors that promote identity formation and identification within organizations and how those were manifest in a new department created by the college reorganization.

Locating the Theoretical Frameworks

The theories of organizational identity and identification have developed within the field of organizational studies, which was a major component in Michael's degree program and is the focus of his teaching in higher education administration. Much of his past research revolves around the concept of social construction of reality and sensemaking in organizations. Identity is directly involved in these processes, and the view of identity in organizational studies parallels the development of the concept of identity as a social construction in other social sciences. In this sense, the focus on organizational identity in this study does not stem from a theory in the specific sense of a formal model of relationships between variables or constructs. Rather, it is better thought of as a framework within which the topic is being discussed in the academic literature. It is this interest in questions of organizational identity and their association with organizational culture and sensemaking that preceded and motivated the entire research project.

In an edited book, Whetten and Godfrey (1998) chronicled the development of approaches to identify in the field. The chapters in that book helped shape our initial steps in applying the concepts in our study. It helped us bring together the postmodern formulation of identity and how it applies to organizational identity and the concept of identification. We continued our review of related literature as the research project progressed and, in the interest of being comprehensive and responsive to the literature, further investigated the notion of organizational identification and the more formal theoretical formulations of SIT and SCT in organizational studies. The theories specifically were the subject of a review article (Hogg et al., 1995) and an edited book (Hogg & Terry, 2001), which included good summaries of the literature. Several directions within that literature, including the application in instances of organizational mergers and the development of a notion of "disidentification," led to optimism about the theories' applicability to our project. As discussed later in this chapter, however, that optimism later dimmed in the analysis phase of the project, when it became clear that the theories were not rich enough to explain some aspects of our findings.

In sum, locating the framework arose from Michael's prior knowledge of the literature in the field. Further, the location of a couple of extensive literature reviews helped to summarize specific theoretical formulations and to pinpoint sets of literature for deeper review.

Effects of the Theoretical Framework on the Research

As indicated previously, the focus of the research from the beginning was on questions of identity and identification in a shifting organizational context, so we conceived of ourselves as the subjects of our research project. This made journaling appear to be the natural choice for our data gathering technique. We also wanted to avoid a situation in which the research project would significantly alter the course of the department's development. Thus, we made a deliberate attempt to keep the research project, other than the journaling, as low impact an activity as possible during the year of data collection. This meant that another data gathering technique, such as constituting ourselves as some version of a focus group at various points during the year, seemed to invite too much influence on the events we were studying. In fact, we only met as a group twice during the year, and while we did discuss substantive issues (They were hard to avoid!), the main focus was to encourage continued attention to the journaling task. We also responded to a set of common questions in our journals, as described further below.

Clearly, we had the broad framework of social construction and identity from the beginning of the study. Our specific instructions in data collection were to write about the issues the department faced and the interactions we had with faculty in formal (for example, committee meetings) and informal (hallway conversations) occasions as well as our own reactions and feelings about what we experienced.

The concern for organizational identity and identification focused journal entries on instances of interaction when members of the department were discussing issues and negotiating new understandings and expectations for their department and themselves (or finding ways not to do so). Our journaling often focused on work issues in which there were explicit discussions of the values and norms the department would embody. These instances related to both the meaning of membership in the department and how members defined their identification with DES. We also used our journals to discuss how we were feeling about the events we experienced and whether they engendered our own association with the department or people in it. Typically, the reorganization work was either tedious or acrimonious, so the journals included expressions of our disengagement with DES.

For example, Michael—in a journal entry written December 14, 1997—portrayed a faculty meeting in which committee members prepared briefing papers on issues to be resolved while drafting promotion and tenure (P&T) guidelines.

> The P&T committee members kept quiet unless prompted by the faculty to discuss a topic. Even then, they seemed reluctant to speak and did not say much to help the conversation. Predictably, we spent a lot of time on the first few items and the later items got little attention at the meeting. The result is that we sometimes voted on questions that we may not have fully understood or appreciated the complexity of, and we did not always have the benefit of a full discussion to inform our vote. Thus, this exercise in pseudo-democracy really turned out to limit our ability to have full and informed input into some important decisions. The result is that I feel, and I have heard others express, that we still have not had sufficient time to discuss and deal with the issues that the P&T document raises. This also served to limit the value of the vote and conversation for the members of the committee, since they now have to interpret written votes on paper, and they do not have the "rich media" of face-to-face conversations to inform them of how the faculty thinks about an issue.

It is easy to see how the attention to certain events and the way they are framed in the journals reflect the theoretical framework for the study, as the journal entry itself noted the missed chances at interaction that could have promoted a greater sense of shared participation in the department.

One aspect of our journaling that we adopted was that, at five points during the year, Michael asked the group members to respond to specific questions in the journals. The questions were meant to prompt some reflection on common subject matters in the journals, and the effects of the theoretical frames are evident in the questions themselves. We were asked to comment on topics such as changes we were experiencing in our professional identities, our perceived influence on our academic program and the new department, and the continuing role of our former departmental affiliations.

In the analysis phase, the specific theoretical frameworks also played explicit roles in the project direction. The analysis process began with members of the research group reading their own and another full journal and coding sections of text with a term that characterized the main idea being expressed. As a group, we then narrowed the list of codes to a set that would encompass all of the selected text sections in order to be as comprehensive and inclusive of the journal topics as possible. We then applied those codes to all the journal entries. Thus, this inductive and inclusive form of coding allowed the influence of the theoretical frame on the data collection process to roll through to the coding and sorting of the textual fragments. The codes selected focused on the (1) topical areas that promoted interaction in the department (promotion and tenure guidelines, selection of a chair, curricular integration), (2) modes of participation and communication among former and new colleagues, (3) roles in the new department, (4) our professional identities, (5) the view of DES from inside and outside, and (6) the status and relations of the degree programs that constituted the department. All of these issues highlight aspects of building an organizational identity for the department and our identification with it.

As the next step in the analysis process, we gathered the codes into 12 groupings based on the similarity or relatedness of the topics. Then, each set became the focus of a group meeting to interpret, derive themes and differences, and apply theoretical formulations based on the content of the text units. Michael produced a written summary of the conversations, which became the subject of further conversation, sorting and recombining the interpretations within and among the original code groupings. Eventually, the focus on interaction and sensemaking in the process of identity formation led the analysis to focus on how difficult it was to interact and create a new identity for the department. We were also led to stress missed opportunities for (and even avoidance of) communication and interaction to build a departmental identity and the retreat of faculty into the separate programs that constituted the department. Thus, in the analysis of our journals, the themes and concepts of the theoretical frameworks took on greater and more direct relevance to the data and our modes of understanding them.

Critique of the Frameworks

The events in DES reinforce the SIT/SCT position that mergers encourage the airing of differences and separation within a new unit because they heighten attention to the differences and tensions between subgroups. In addition, the general connection between the permeability of subgroups and the success of mergers is supported by negative example, since, in this unsuccessful merger, the unit quickly becomes characterized as a collection of separate programs rather than a coherent department. The role of prestige factors in this case, however, is more complicated than the SIT/SCT literature suggests. For example, the literature says that low-prestige groups would emphasize alternative characteristics related to their identity that would de-emphasize characteristics on which they were relatively weaker. In this case, research orientation and productivity—elements of academic prestige—were central issues in the conflict over promotion and tenure standards. Both high- and low-prestige programs within the department, however, opposed including stricter standards in the criteria language, opting instead to emphasize values of autonomy, collegiality, and egalitarianism—also highly prized among academics—in order to reinforce the independence of the various programs in the department. Thus, in this context, prestige was less of a factor in members' orientation to and identification with the new unit than these theories suggest, and egalitarianism promoted subgroup autonomy rather than group permeability.

Ultimately, the DES case urges us to think beyond the models and hypotheses of SIT/SCT approaches to organizational identity. Even while acknowledging the multiplicity and variability of identity in both people and organizations, SIT/SCT conceptions still focus identification upon the primacy of defining or prototypical characteristics and assume an integrationist view of a dominant organizational culture and identity. A broader and more comprehensive view of identity suggests, however, that there are inescapable multiplicities, complications, and even contradictions in identity. Furthermore, individuals have multiple sources of identity and different aspects of themselves that they apply with different salience in the contexts of each of their affiliations. Thus, in DES the multiple values and meanings must be combined in ways that an integrationist theory of identity would overlook.

Alvesson and Willmott's (2002) list of identification modes presented previously suggests some of the value, environmental, and contextual dimensions that are part of the identity development process and thus represents a broader viewpoint for thinking about the identity construction and identification processes in DES. This theoretical formulation led us to highlight the lack of engagement in the department and to locate the problem in the constricted communication that curtailed sensemaking and, therefore, the formation of organizational culture and identity. The framework that acknowledged the multiplicity and ambiguity of identity, without also making it an inherent problem, allowed us to look beyond differences as the source of disidentification and to suggest that the problems of interaction chronicled in our journals limited the faculty's ability to build organizational identity while still accepting differences and contradictions within the organizational culture.

Possible Alternative Theoretical Frameworks

Various frameworks for the notion of organizational culture would have clear applicability to this case, as the close association of culture and identity discussed above makes apparent. From early in the study, however, we considered the unit of analysis to be us—the five journal keepers—rather than the department or college as a culture. Although we did comment and interpret aspects of the units and the faculty as a whole, thus approaching a cultural analysis, the real focus was our perspectives and experiences of the new unit and their effect on our organizational identification.

We also could have used frameworks and theories from leadership and/or organizational change literatures. In fact, presentation and article reviewers have questioned why we have not made fuller use of theories from these sources. From the beginning, however, our attention was focused on the questions of faculty members' identity and how it was tied to and affected by the organizational change we were experiencing. Regarding the questions about leadership, for example, our response has been to focus on the faculty's own responsibility for developing the identity of the department and our own failures in accomplishing this, rather than on the shortcomings of the administrators involved in the organizational changes.

The Use of Multiple Theoretical Frameworks

As discussed previously, we used different theoretical frameworks in two articles from our project (see the previous chapter). Although they describe the conditions in the new department in very consistent terms, the different theoretical frameworks pushed the articles to focus on different aspects of the case and produced notable differences in the conclusions of the papers. The notion of liminality applied in the first paper (Bettis, Mills, Miller, & Nolan, 2005) directed the focus to the social, political, and economic contexts of the departmental change and to an externally derived definition of faculty work. The focus on organizational identity and identification in the second paper produced an emphasis on the internal construction of values, expectations, and belonging that resulted in greater attention to the formation of internal agreements such as the debate over the department's promotion and tenure policies.

Weick (1995) and Chapter 4 make the point that there are really two different types of problems during sensemaking in organizations—one when there are not enough interpretations for members to work with and the other when there are too many interpretations floating around. In our department, we experienced both problems, and the two different theoretical frameworks each highlight one of the problem types. The article on liminality (Bettis et al., 2005) showed that the faculty was constrained, in part, by the fact that there were only two characterizations of the faculty job that we were stuck between—the modernist searcher for Truth and the postmodern laborer in the knowledge factory. The article concludes by discussing the need to develop more interpretations of what the faculty job can be, something we were not successful at accomplishing during the reorganization. The paper on organizational identity and identification (Mills et al., 2005) showed that the new department's faculty had many different perceptions and values to bring to discussions about promotion and tenure, curriculum, and other internal matters. That article concluded that we needed to have better conditions for communication in order to work together to negotiate and better reconcile the different approaches to and interpretations of our organization and its purposes.

Thus, the use of different frameworks allowed us to have greater breadth in our analyses of the situation we studied. In effect, we were able to consider several of Alvesson and Willmott's (2002) different ways identities are influenced in organizations: (1) the fit with social and organizational contexts through the liminality framework, and (2) orientation through values and belongingness through organizational identity and identification. In addition, the two versions exposed how the lack of imagined alternatives in one realm limited choices for identity, whereas the wealth of alternatives and constricted interactions in another realm constrained sensemaking and identity construction.

Additional Comments

In addition to the pervasive influence theoretical frameworks have on the conduct and focus of the research, we also want to emphasize ways in which they contribute to one type of problem as well as provide a solution to another problem for qualitative research. On the one hand, the impact of theoretical frameworks on every phase of qualitative research contributes to one of the stickiest problems for the trustworthiness of qualitative research. On the other hand, theoretical frameworks provide the pathway to overcome the local, contextualized nature of data collection and to allow a form of generalization that some say qualitative research lacks.

If we are as beholden to our theoretical frameworks as the premise of this book and this chapter suggests, then we also have to be concerned that these frameworks become self-fulfilling prophecies. There is a real danger that they guide our data collection by determining where we direct our attention as well as the very terms we use to characterize what we see, and they turn the analyses toward conclusions that could be theorized before the research began. In qualitative research, our mechanisms for analytical skepticism are not as strong or explicit as those developed for quantitative research (and even in quantitative research, the mechanisms are limited and also serve to hide certain preconceptions). This places an extra obligation on qualitative researchers to question ourselves; to seek out alternative data, interpretations, and explanations; and to doubt our framings and understandings. We need to search out data that may contradict our expectations and promote change in our own understandings. Obviously, this does not mean that the theoretical framework stops directing the study. On the contrary, it suggests that the framework directs the study in two directions—both toward and away from the perceptions and concepts of the framework. Only when we do that can we push our analyses to more nuanced stages that go beyond what our frameworks provide us. And when qualitative researchers have accomplished this, we can be assured of the restored trustworthiness of our data and analyses.

Theoretical frameworks also contain the breadth that our data do not have. Theories allow our intense, specific data collection and contextualized interpretations and conclusions to speak to broader issues and conceptual formulations. As Wexler (1992) noted,

> The theory is really a 'fusion of horizons' between the elements of the analytic fields as I blended them and what the subjects of the study said and did. I let the subjects lead me to the language and understandings that could only be found on the field of perception for which I had prepared. (p. 6)

By working back and forth between the detailed data and the broader concepts of the framework, researchers and readers can highlight why research can be relevant for other contexts and social settings. Qualitative researchers often talk about the continual comparisons and multiple iterations they perform with their data during analysis, but the theoretical framework is also part of this iterative process—the part that adds greater weight to the mundane data we gather and pore over.

Another way to think about this expansive process is to consider the researcher at the conjunction of two different communities of discourse. In effect, the researcher is involved in social constructions via interactions with the participants in the study and with intellectual colleagues that have helped formulate the framework being used in the study. The study involves both making sense of the research site and the participants' meanings in the context of larger theoretical ideas as well as making sense of the larger theoretical framework in light of the specific things learned in the research. Each perspective informs the other as the researcher brings both to bear in the interpretive process, and the multiple layers of the conversation make the research context speak to issues and in terms meaningful beyond its boundaries.

References

Albert, S., & Whetten, D. (1985). Organizational identity. In L. L. Cummings & B. Staw (Eds.), *Research in organizational behavior* (Vol. 7, pp. 263–295). Greenwich, CT: JAI.

Alvesson, M., & Willmott, H. (2002). Identity regulation as organizational control: Producing the appropriate individual. *Journal of Management Studies, 39*, 619–644.

Ashforth, B. E., & Mael, F. A. (1989). Social identity theory and the organization. *Academy of Management Review, 14*(1), 20–39.

Bettis, P. J., Mills, M., Miller, J., & Nolan, R. (2005). Faculty in a liminal landscape: A case study of a college reorganization. *Journal of Leadership and Organizational Studies, 11*(3), 47–61.

Gioia, D. (1998). From individual to organizational identity. In D. Whetten & P. Godfrey (Eds.), *Identity in organizations: Building theory through conversations* (pp. 17–31). Thousand Oaks, CA: Sage.

Hogg, M., & Terry, D. (2001). Social identity theory and organizational processes. In M. Hogg & D. Terry (Eds.), *Social identity processes in organizational contexts* (pp. 1–12). Philadelphia: Psychology Press.

Hogg, M., Terry, D., & White, K. (1995). A tale of two theories: A critical comparison of identity theory with social identity theory. *Social Psychology Quarterly, 17*(1), 255–269.

Martin, J. (1992). *Cultures in organizations: Three perspectives.* New York: Oxford University Press.

Mills, M., Bettis, P. J., Miller, J., & Nolan, R. (2005). Experiences of academic unit reorganization: Organizational identity and identification in organizational change. *Review of Higher Education, 28*(4), 597–619.

Pratt, M. (1998). To be or not to be? Central questions in organizational identification. In D. Whetten & P. Godfrey (Eds.), *Identity in organizations: Building theory through conversations* (pp. 17–31). Thousand Oaks, CA: Sage.

Van Knippenberg, D., & Van Leeuwen, E. (2001). Organizational identity after a merger: Sense of continuity as the key to postmerger identification. In M. Hogg & D. Terry (Eds.), *Social identity processes in organizational contexts* (pp. 249–264). Philadelphia: Psychology Press.

Weick, K. E. (1995). *Sensemaking in organizations.* Thousand Oaks, CA: Sage.

Wexler, P. (1992). *Becoming somebody: Toward a social psychology of school.* Washington, DC: Falmer.

Whetten, D., & Godfrey, P. (1998). *Identity in organizations: Building theory through conversations.* Thousand Oaks, CA: Sage.

6

Chaos and Complexity: A Framework for Understanding Social Workers at Midlife

Irene E. Karpiak

I magine for a moment that you are a graduate student embarking on a chosen research path. You may be among those searching for ideas, methods, perhaps an approach that would set your work apart from others', some feature that would express your unique interests and aptitudes. You may be going through periods of wonder and bewilderment—do I know enough, will I know enough, will it be enough, will I ever find those precious materials? Sometimes it would surely feel like a state of chaos, of being overwhelmed, puzzled, uncertain, or overcome by the mountainous array of information. Such feelings and fears might bubble up at the most inopportune times. But above all, if you were in this space, you would be in a state of alert awareness and attentiveness to matters related to your research. Materials and ideas would crop up in the most unexpected way—an article presents itself, a comment strikes a chord, a phenomenon takes a new slant, an image or idea emerges; and suddenly a sense of order, a new confidence is born. And even this is likely to be short-lived as you find yourself in the cycle of chaos and order.

Chaos and complexity theory can be seen as akin to these experiences. Its defining features include uncertainty, unpredictability, stress, dynamism, chaos, and the emergence of a new order. It mirrors human experiences and societal happenings in ways that connect these more closely, and reveals the parallels that exist in the behaviors of individuals, society, and nature. This chapter explores chaos and complexity as a still novel, yet promising, framework for qualitative research. It begins with an illustration of its application to a study that took me into the processes of midlife adulthood, chosen for this chapter because it represents my introduction to chaos and complexity theory and the beginnings of my work with it. Whereas I have since undertaken other research projects, this study and this framework endure as having defined my scholarship as a teacher and researcher.

An Overview: An Interpretive Study of Social Workers at Midlife

Introduction and Purpose of the Study

At the time of my study (Karpiak, 2000), I was a social worker and director of a continuing education program for social workers, as well as a doctoral student in adult education. I was fascinated with the theories of adult development that had been part of my graduate studies, and, being myself a midlife adult, I was attracted to this period in the adult life course. I was curious to know the ways in which social workers traverse this developmental period, what changes they might undergo, and how these changes might be expressed in their personal lives and their professional practice. My research questions were: What happens to these professionals in their work, their personal relationships, and their sense of self during the midlife transition? How do they manage the changes and transitions during this period? Finally, for those for whom this period has ushered in major changes, what events triggered them?

Method and Analysis

Based on an initial survey that I conducted to identify social workers who had some experience of a midlife transition, 11 women and 9 men between the ages of 35 and 55 were selected for the study. They were interviewed on two occasions with the material tape-recorded and transcribed. In order to allow each individual to express in his or her own terms what the experience of the midlife transition was like for them I chose "clustering"—a unique tool developed in creative writing by Rico (1983) as an ideal technique to elicit images and feelings, and facilitate the individual's telling his or her own story. Accordingly, participants were asked to cluster around the phrase, "Me,

Myself at Midlife." They were then left to generate phrases, words, or images that came to mind. Then I asked them to "take me through the clusters," allowing them to go as deeply as they wished into the material of each cluster. These clusters, then, provided the guiding framework for the first portion of the interview, with an interview schedule of open-ended questions constituting the second part.

In studying the data, I paid close attention to the language of the participants, the areas they chose to focus upon, and the significance they attributed to particular aspects of their life experiences. Analysis consisted of searching for patterns and major themes, which were examined through a template of relevant theory composed of Jung's (1966, 1969) model of personality development; Levinson, Darrow, Klein, Levinson, and McKee's (1978) model of the midlife transition; and Prigogine and Stengers's (1984) theory of chaos and complexity. The findings were developed through this theoretical template, or theoretical "sieve."

Study Findings: The Processes of Change

My study (Karpiak, 2000) revealed that there is no single way in which midlife change occurs. Rather, change appears to come about in several rather distinct ways that relate to the nature of events that individuals experience at midlife and their responses to those events. The three processes of change, representing also the three subgroups of individuals in the study, are described in the following sections.

Change Through Transformation. Transformative change is qualitative change leading the individual to a new view of self and the world. In the study (Karpiak, 2000), 5 individuals underwent some transformation that led to a shift in their view of self, which became reflected in their personal priorities, relationships, and work. These individuals showed the most evidence of attending to the tasks of midlife and to the individuation process that Jung (1966, 1969) and Levinson et al. (1978) had identified. In their work, these social workers were exemplary, revealing a deep appreciation of their profession, a strong sense of compassion for those they served, and authenticity in their work. Significantly, they were very much aware of their own changes, voicing this awareness through such phrases as, "I am different now," or "I used to be . . . ." Finally, their language conveyed not stability nor stagnation, but rather a movement toward something. For most this was a stronger self-definition.

Change Through Self-Renewal. The second way of change was through self-renewal. In this mode, individuals, of which there were 11, when faced with challenges from within or without, behaved in ways that maintained their present state of their life and sense of self. Small adaptations served to offset or forestall the need for larger, more encompassing changes. These individuals maintained a lifestyle distinguished by stability, continuity, and control. They demonstrated less evidence of undertaking the tasks of the midlife transition than was witnessed among the 5 "transformers." For instance, in the self-renewers there was considerable focus on achievement in work and work roles (a primary task of the first half of life), and comparatively little focus on reappraisal of the self and life structure (a primary task of the second half of life).

Whereas the self-renewers appeared to live their lives in a way that is generally satisfying, this method of change had its negative aspects for 4 of the 11 individuals. This was especially the case when individuals persisted too long, trying to adapt to difficult work circumstances. They showed evidence of boredom, burnout, and even breakdown. One individual in this situation summed it up, "One person can only give so much, and I burnt myself out. I didn't know quite what I was doing."

Being on the Threshold of Becoming. Being on the threshold of becoming, the third way of change, was characterized by the presence of struggle and flux in people's lives in relation to work, relationships, and self. Things felt like they were coming apart. The fluctuations were experienced as a push and pull in relation to work, intimacy, or spiritual renewal. Four individuals experienced a sense of disengagement from work (primarily the women) and from family relationships (primarily the men). Though outwardly stable, their inner world was in a state of flux, struggle, and ambivalence. One individual expressed it thus: "All of a sudden I was quite sick of work. . . . Is it me or the nature of work?" These fluctuations, however, were met with an equally powerful push toward maintenance of the present state of affairs. One individual determined, "I'm going to be very cautious, because I could lose something." In contrast to one "transformer" who observed, "Life is change," these individuals felt that change is disruptive, negative, and potentially hazardous.

The Power of Transformative Change

The findings suggested that the most powerful means to effect transformative change is the shocking and sudden critical event, "not of one's choosing," as one woman noted, such as a sudden life-threatening illness or the death of a loved one. Individuals who underwent this kind of event felt "pushed against the wall," and overcome with their assumptions and illusions. Then new insights and new behaviors followed. An externally generated crisis, however, was not the only way for transformation to happen. Transformation came about also when inner "rumblings" and demands were felt and given attention. Choices and changes followed; and changes made in one area of life led to changes in others. One individual described it in this way: "You jump off a diving board and you don't know who you are going to become." Regardless of the precipitating event, whether external or internal, whether shocking or subtle, transformation appears to entail the following process: the experience of turmoil, then a period of self-reflection, making hard choices, and finally, an integration of that experience. Individuals emerge with some shift in their view of self and of the world.

A New Look at Change

This study (Karpiak, 2000) promoted a new look at change and at crisis events—those troublesome, chaotic moments that disturb prevailing patterns of behavior. It suggested that it is not the stable eras and the comfortable times that yield transformative change; rather, it is the shocks and sudden innovations that become the major triggers for psychological developmental. It became clear, too, however, that change at midlife is intensely difficult to make. Formidable forces operate against change, both from within and without. Defensive efforts of avoidance and distraction awaken to curtail change and maintain a stable state. On the other hand, when transformative change does occur, it can lead to a new level of consciousness, which, in turn, is expressed in work, love, and identity. Those individuals who underwent transformative change, and who experienced a shift in their sense of self, were able to look back now to a happening that was important, even essential to them—as "the worst of times and the best."

Principles and Concepts of Chaos and Complexity

"Science is a dialogue between mankind and nature, the results of which have been unpredictable" (Prigogine, 1996, p. 153). This observation by Nobel Laureate Ilya Prigogine captures the spirit of chaos and complexity theory that provided the major orientation to my study. Prigogine appropriately titles his book *The End of Certainty* (1996) to highlight his characterization of the world as following more probabilistic processes than mechanistic predictability and determinism. The framework he presents is one of dynamic openness, interconnectedness, and emergent properties. Moreover, Prigogine insists that time matters immensely. "The notion of time and what it preserves, creates, and destroys, is central to complexity. That is, that time changes a phenomenon" (Prigogine, 1996, p. 154). These ideas of a limited predictability of future events, due to events that occur in the space of time, have challenged traditional science and its assumptions concerning prediction and control (Prigogine, 1996; Williams, 2000).

Chaos and complexity is not a single theory, but rather a composition of various theoretical frameworks and concepts, variously conceptualized by theorists in several fields. "Chaos" refers to the "dynamic instability" of even simple systems and their tendency toward complex behavior that may look erratic and random (Halmi, 2003). It is a term used to describe not the absence of order, but rather a more complex relation to order. "Complexity," in turn, involves the study of living, adaptive systems; their elements and patterns of relationships; how they are maintained; and how they self-organize, evolve, and change. A more contemporary term for this theory is simply "complexity" or "the sciences of complexity." I have continued with the use of the term "chaos" to highlight the substantial way that I continue to draw on Prigogine's ideas concerning chaos, order, and transformation.

Complexity defines not only those systems that have a number of components or parts, but also where those parts relate to and depend on one another. The more interdependent and interconnected the parts of a system, the more complex the system, and the less likely that its future is predictable (Cilliers, 1998). Whereas simple systems may be represented by an element such as a grain of sand or a rock crystal, complex systems, because of the complex interrelationships of their components, are exemplified through phenomena such as a tornado, a cell, a developing embryo, a caterpillar-pupa-butterfly, a human organism, a rainforest, a town or city, a planet. Paul Cilliers (1998) outlines 10 characteristics of complexity: (1) the large number of elements in a system, (2) the dynamic interaction among elements, (3) the rich interaction among elements, (4) the interactions are nonlinear, (5) the interactions have a short range, (6) the interactions involve feedback loops, (7) the systems are open, (8) the systems operate under conditions that are far from equilibrium, (9) the systems have histories, and (10) the individual elements of the system are ignorant of the whole system.

According to the theory, living systems—from one-celled organisms to human beings, groups, and social systems—are described as "self-organizing," that is, operating according to their own internal principles of organization. These systems are called "dissipative structures" referring to their tendency to lose energy over time. At the same time, being open systems, they make up for this loss through constant response, interaction, and "dialogue" with their environment (Prigogine & Stengers, 1984). These interconnected subsystems themselves are evolving and have the capacity to transform, that is, to spontaneously reorder their structure in ways that are unexpected and unpredictable (Cilliers, 1998; Prigogine & Stengers, 1984). When faced with change they may adapt in order to maintain their self in a stable state. They may even collapse into chaos and destruction. Most strikingly, however, systems have the capacity to respond to change by evolving into a new, more complex form. Disturbed order does not necessarily lead to chaos—higher levels of organization are possible.

Whereas Prigogine and his colleague, Isabella Stengers, worked with transformation of chemical and biological systems, more recent authors have related these principles to human and social systems. Both earlier (Jantsch, 1981; Prigogine & Stengers, 1984) and contemporary (Briggs & Peat, 1999; Cilliers, 1998) scientists have identified several major properties associated with chaotic systems: self-organization, emergence, fluctuations, and sensitivity to initial conditions, bifurcation, and transformation. The following paragraphs briefly describe these concepts and principles.

Central Concepts of Chaos and Complexity Theory

Self-Organization. Self-organization or self-reference refers to the capacity of living systems to make meaning out of randomness (Montuori, 2003), to change and develop from less structured beginnings to more complex structures (Cilliers, 1998), and to create order out of chaos (Montuori, 2003; Prigogine & Stengers, 1984). As an example, the economic system of a country changes its structure in response to factors such as political changes or natural disasters; in nature birds form into flocks; tornados form funnels; and a dripping faucet develops a regular rhythm. Montuori observes that chaos theory as a field of study itself may be viewed as a self-organizing process, being "the spontaneous emergence of a coordinated and collective behavior in a population of elements (researchers), making meaning out of (apparent) randomness" (p. 242).

Emergent Properties. Ours is a world not only of systems, but also of emergent and evolving systems. Complex systems manage through the processes of interaction and accommodation to develop new properties and patterns that are more complex, more integrated, and more coherent. This means that when we look at systems of increasing complexity and ordering, from molecules to living cells to organisms to brains, we find emerging on each level of complexity properties that are inherent characteristics of *that* level of complexity and not the lower one (Cilliers, 1998).

The Critical Role of Fluctuations. Complex systems (such as the human body, or a family) are composed of subsystems that are continuously fluctuating. These systems experience numerous such fluctuations and stresses that threaten their stability. They appear to manage to avoid chaos by diffusing the fluctuations through communication and interaction among the various parts of the system (Prigogine & Stengers, 1984). On those occasions, however, when the system allows itself not to diminish but to embrace a novel, destabilizing fluctuation, the new elements may lead to a new pattern of behaviors and relations. Moreover, at times a single fluctuation adding its strength to other fluctuations may become powerful enough that the whole system reorganizes into a new pattern.

Sensitivity to Initial Conditions. In stable systems slight changes lead to slight effects. But in dynamic, unstable systems "small perturbations in the initial conditions are amplified over the course of time" (Prigogine, 1996, p. 30), so that even the smallest difference in initial starting values could lead to very different behaviors and outcomes. Moreover, small changes at crucial points anywhere in the system could result in major effects; this is sometimes referred to as the "butterfly effect," where the flapping of a wing in the Amazon may lead to storms in the United States.

Bifurcation. As a system moves further and further from equilibrium, it reaches a point of decision or "bifurcation," beyond which a new set of phenomena and several possible paths arise (Prigogine, 1996). The choices made at that moment are indeterminable and unpredictable. "As the system approaches the critical point, it 'decides' itself which way to go, and this decision will determine its evolution" (Capra, 1983, p. 288). In fact, the further the system has moved from equilibrium, the more options will be available to it (Capra, 1983). Jantsch (1981) describes these choices as "trumpet-shaped" openings, suggesting the many options that open to a system at the point of decision.

Self-Renewal Versus Transformation. Development of structures can occur in two ways: (1) through self-renewal, wherein the system, in response to fluctuations, makes an effort at error-correction, thereby increasing its complexity, while maintaining the same structure; and (2) through transformation, which occurs when the existing structure reaches a critical point, at which time the system transcends its structure and leaps to a higher level of self-organization.

Transformation: Order Out of Chaos. Transformation refers to the capacity of systems to reach out creatively beyond their boundaries and to create novel forms. Prigogine and Stengers (1984) describe transformation in the following way: When a system is *far*-from-equilibrium, that is, when it is not stable, which suggests a comparatively high level of perturbation and flux, the system is inordinately sensitive to events from within or without. A comparatively small trigger may propel the system out of its current structure and into a new order. The authors actually describe the process whereby a system, at the point of seeming chaos and imminent destruction, suddenly and *unpredictably* restructures itself into a new, now more complex whole. Prigogine and Stengers (1984) have called this type of transformation "order through fluctuations" or "order out of chaos" to emphasize the important role of disturbances in the creation of a new order.

Strengths and Limitations of This Framework

Chaos and complexity theory represent the efforts of researchers to incorporate theory and method from the natural sciences into the social sciences (Halmi, 2003). In recent years, the concepts associated with the theory have continued to be refined and other concepts and frameworks have been added, as more researchers in various disciplines turn their attention to this orientation. Halmi sums up the strength of this theory: "Chaos theory appears to provide a means for understanding and examining many of the uncertainties, non-linearities and unpredictable aspects of social systems behavior" (p. 88). Moreover, it mirrors the nature of qualitative research through its concepts of nonlinearity, interdependence, emergence, process, and transformation.

Nonlinearity expresses itself in qualitative research through the inputs and outputs of the process, which may not always be balanced or predicable (Cilliers, 1998). For instance, one comment by a participant in a study may take that study into an unanticipated direction, which, in turn, may require improvisation that may lead to even more unpredictability (Montuori, 2003). On this point, Hill (1993) points out that in the case of archival research, the effort of the researcher may not at all be reflected in the outcome, because the flow of this research may be frequently interrupted, whereby its outcomes become unpredictable. Whereas this aspect may be viewed as undesirable in traditional research, it is acknowledged as prevalent in complexity.

Chaos and complexity theory affirms the unique role and behavior of a qualitative researcher, who is frequently placed at the edge of chaos, with little to rely upon with respect to guidelines, instructions, and responsibility for the direction of the interview. The situation may demand surrendering control and embracing the unpredictable and evolving nature of the research. Further, Casti (1993) notes that because complexity research is "observer dependent," its outcomes are "extremely sensitive" to the capacities of the researcher to be aware, attuned, and perceptive, and therefore requires these qualities in the researcher. Doll (1993) maintains that the theory's emphasis on relationship, dialogue, and connectiveness reinforces the centrality of the relationship between researcher and participant and the nature of the authentic dialogue that transpires. Doll further contends that transformation of understanding is at the cornerstone of both complexity and qualitative research, whereby inquiry and dialogue may lead to heightened consciousness and an enlarged vision.

In their book, *Metaphors We Live By,* Lakoff and Johnson (1980) contend that more than 90 percent of our language and our thought processes are metaphorical. Waldrop (1992), a member of the Santa Fe Institute—specifically established to explore with mathematical rigor the science of complexity in the light of chaos theory—notes that science works less by deduction, as is generally assumed, and more by metaphor. Chaos and complexity theory has introduced a shift in metaphors, from mechanistic to biological, metaphors more akin to the growth of a plant, or the flocking of geese, or a spider-like web of relations (with each thread affected by the slightest motion of the web). More recent authors have advocated music metaphors to describe leadership, jazz metaphors to inspire improvisation in our work (Montuori, 2003), the "turbulent mirror" to highlight the irregularity and unpredictability of our world (Briggs & Peat, 1999), and "life as a river" to reflect the life task of learning to become better navigators in a world in which humans and nature interact. Thrift (1999) suggests that these metaphors of complexity may be signaling a wider cultural change toward greater openness and possibility concerning the future. Finally, Ron Padgham (1988) summarizes the power of these novel metaphors for the field of education:

> When I view the world through the lenses or images provided by these [chaos and complexity theorists], I begin to see the world in a very different perspective. This is the power of the imaginal. It provides us with new perspectives: it gets us out of the framework of the accepted and the known—that which is. When we are operating in the imaginal realm, we can act "as if." I can think about curriculum "as if" these theories were true. (p. 135)

Whereas in the past this theory's usefulness has been limited to its metaphorical applications, more and more methods have been developed that use complexity-based methodologies for research in the social sciences (Murphy, 2000). One consists of the qualitative interpretations of phenomena by applying principles of chaos and complexity to unexpected or unintended outcomes (Murphy). A second involves the application of computer simulations to study patterns and ramifications of empirically derived data around certain complexity-related concepts, such as "emergence" or "self-organization."

Halmi (2003) examines its use in modeling strategies in social work research, and Warren, Franklin, and Streeter (1998) apply it to the processes associated with human change. Finally, Walters (1999), who analyzed crime patterns through the complexity framework, observed that it provides alternatives to the positivist view and permits closer analysis of the interactive and interdependent aspects of human behavior.

One limitation of the framework arises from the nature of complexity itself—that complexity-based analysis does not lead to easy predication or timing of future events and requires a stance of the researcher that can accommodate the unpredictability and uncertainty of the findings (Murphy, 2000; Williams, 2000). Further, chaos and complexity theory is still undergoing refinement of principles and concepts; it is a theory still in the making, still being adapted by various disciplines, including the natural and social sciences and various professions, such as education, management, and psychology. No one knows yet what the full impact of the theory will be (Waldrop, 1992). Thrift (1999) notes that complexity theory has thus far enjoyed only partial success and its future as a scientific paradigm is still uncertain against the forces of reductionism. Doll (1993) has further observed that until the social sciences accept such a framework it is unlikely that education will. Much more research in this area needs to be carried out before more definitive statements can be made concerning the utility of chaos and complexity theory.

Origins and Discovery of the Framework

Although it is generally assumed that chaos and complexity theory arose from research in the physical and the natural sciences, there are actual references to this orientation in earlier philosophical works, including the writings of Spinoza, Bergson, Goethe, and Whitehead (Neuman, 2003). Prigogine (1996) himself attributes his orientation to science to the childhood influence of Henri Bergson, and he notes that nonequilibrium thermodynamics accords with the view expressed by both Bergson and Whitehead. As a product of the physical and biological sciences, chaos and complexity theory's roots date back to the loss of scientific faith in the 1900s, when certain facts could not be explained by traditional physics. Its development was furthered by Einstein's theory of relativity and Heisenberg's "uncertainty principle," as well as the second law of thermodynamics, which challenged the Newtonian view of the universe as orderly and predictable. The first chaos theorists, the scientists who set the discipline in motion, shared certain sensibilities; attended to pattern, randomness, and complexity; and questioned many of the prevailing notions of scientific reductionism and certainty.

General Systems Theory

In the late 1920s, German-Canadian biologist and philosopher Ludwig von Bertalanffy began to describe what was more than a theory, but rather an organized body of knowledge, a new perspective, a new way of doing science that some have called a new paradigm. He challenged the view that biological phenomena could be reduced to the physical domain, and resolved this concern through his formulation of the organismic system theory, which later became known as general systems theory (GST). General systems theory (Von Bertalanffy, 1968) conceived the world as a pattern of parts in relation, of open systems, of integrated wholes, and of relationships and interconnections. Bertalanffy began with a general definition of systems as a "set of elements standing in interrelations" (p. 55), noting that whereas it is important to study parts and processes in isolation, it is also necessary to consider their organization, their order, and their dynamic interaction. His theory was in effect a general science of wholeness; and the often quoted phrase "the whole is more than the sum of its parts" was to say that the characteristics of a system could not be explained by examining its isolated parts, since these characteristics appear or "emerge" out of the interactions of the various parts. In other words, something new would be added by the *relationship* of the parts. For example, the human body could not be explained solely through a description of its organs, because through their interactions new qualities would emerge.

Evolutionary Systems Theory

Sharing many of the features of general systems theory, evolutionary systems theory, which came into being in the 1970s, extended its focus beyond systems and their structural entities and onto the processes through which they evolve (Jantsch, 1981). According to Jantsch, evolutionary theory looks for commonalties in the way that all systems—simple, complex, physical, human, and social—evolve. In contrast to a static, survival-oriented, adaptive view of systems, the theory highlights "self-organization" as a feature of systems, which are always "at work," either renewing themselves or naturally evolving or transcending their own boundaries. Unlike the neo-Darwinian model that focuses on gradual adaptation, this theory focused on the "sudden innovative changes" in complex systems (Jantsch, p. 117). Evolutionary theory added to systems theory a critical dimension—that of transformation, gradual or sudden, leading to a whole new form or order. Ilya Prigogine and his colleague, Isabella Stengers, have been the central proponents of this theory, outlined in their book, *Order Out of Chaos* (1984).

Chaos and Evolutionary Systems

Prigogine and Stengers (1984), Jantsch (1981), and Capra (1983) challenged the prevailing views concerning science and the growth of knowledge. They disputed the primacy of classical science, its determinism, and its implied possibility of absolute knowledge, and they challenged the mechanistic, rational, logical world described in most of the traditional scientific literature. In contrast to a world of order, predictability, and control, these theorists depicted the world as complex, indeterminate, turbulent, open, and evolving, a world rich with probabilities, not certainties, characterized by interconnectedness, interrelatedness, and interdependence of all phenomena—cultural, biological, psychological, and sociological. Moreover, they depicted nature to be less machine-like, as viewed by traditional science, but rather, intriguingly, more human-like—unpredictable, highly sensitive to the surrounding world, and altered by even the slightest variations.

Fritjof Capra's work as a physicist, outlined in *The Turning Point* (1983), echoed the work of Bertalanffy, as biologist, and Prigogine, as chemist. Although Capra's (1983, 1988) research had been in the field of quantum physics, his writing outlined a systems view of the universe in which all phenomena are interdependent and interrelated. He urged the advancement beyond conventional disciplinary distinctions, and the use of whatever language becomes appropriate to describe different aspects of the multileveled, interrelated fabric of reality. Capra (1996) emphasized that descriptions associated with the "new sciences"—"*non*-reversibility," "*non*-determinism," "*non*-predictability," and "instability"—are all suggestive of an *opposition* to what was assumed before.

Chaos and Complexity in Other Disciplines

Chaos and complexity theory is increasingly receiving support in various disciplines. Many have written metaphorically of social chaos or have noted its presence in diverse phenomena. It has been found in organizational behavior (Wheatley, 1994), and it is noted in social work (Germain & Gitterman, 1980; Halmi, 2003), in human relations (Gordon, 2003), in aging (Schroots, 1996), in psychology (Skar, 2004), and in literature (Hayles, 1991). Doll (1993) envisioned the chaotic, transformative learning situation in which both learner and teacher are transformed. Cavanaugh and McGuire (1994) have demonstrated the usefulness of the framework to interpret life span cognitive development and lifelong learning by integrating the concepts of bifurcation and chaos. In the field of adult education, Domaingue (1988) and Karpiak (2000) have outlined new principles, practices, and perspectives arising from complexity thinking.

Finding Prigogine

I came across this work largely by chance while in graduate studies at the University of Minnesota. I had by this time been exposed to the ideas of general systems theory through a course of that name led by educator/ anthropologist Dr. Marion Dobbert. In the process of searching out various educational journals, I came upon *Theory Into Practice,* from which I plucked the article "Prigogine: A New Sense of Order, A New Curriculum," by Doll (1986). Doll heralded the changes occurring in the "new sciences," specifically in chaos theory. He interpreted Prigogine and Stengers's (1984) model of transformation, and drew on both Piaget's (1977) model of development as well Dewey's (1964) conception of experience to build and articulate his own new vision of education, the learner, and learning.

William Doll (1986) anticipated the emergence of a new curriculum from the "new order" that Prigogine and Stengers (1984) had outlined. In the self-organizing, transformative open-systems framework that Doll envisioned, every aspect of education would be affected: educational goals, the teaching/learning process, and the teacher/student relationship. Challenge and perturbation, qualities that in the traditional curriculum are assumed to be disruptive and inefficient would, in the emerging paradigm, become essential. Learning would occur not in the zone of comfort, but in the zone of confusion. Teaching would rest not on student compliance, but on student challenge. The goal of teaching would be not to transmit knowledge, but to transform it. And finally, the role of the teacher would be not to instill the known, but to inspire a desire to explore the unknown and to keep the dialogue going.

At the time of reading Doll's (1986) paper, I had already been introduced to the work of Dewey (1964), specifically his description of the process of transformation, a unique happening made possible through having *"an* experience"—one that stands out for the individual as something unique and enduring. Correspondingly, I had been reading the work of adult educator Mezirow (1981), who was proposing for adult education the theory of transformative learning, a theory and method of enlarging the learner's perspective and most specifically suited to adults and their level of cognitive and experiential development. In my view, Doll had taken the concept of transformation that Mezirow and Dewey had presented as a psychological phenomenon, and positioned it within science, or rather within nature and the natural world. Its effect was to universalize the concept of transformation to every living system—human, biological, physical, and social. This is why the article "Prigogine: A New Sense of Order, A New Curriculum" compelled me as it did.

I immediately acquired Prigogine and Stengers's *Order Out of Chaos* and devoured it. As Arthur Miller had once proclaimed on reading Henri Bergson, it was "a moving day for the soul." Prigogine and Stengers's (1984) detailing of their experiments provided me with the link that would connect chaos theory to human processes and action, and it spoke to my interest in adult learning and development and the role of crisis to promote transformative change. Doll's connection of these ideas to education affirmed the importance and value of this theory for my changing perspective and aspirations to become an educator. Attending conferences and reading authors such as Capra (1983, 1988) and Jantsch (1981) led me further into this exploration and discovery, an interest that has persisted to the present day. These authors offered a different language of education, that spoke to my sense of what was possible—a call for humanness, even the Divine. The metaphors that were guiding them were unique, being not mechanistic but biological, not static but dynamic and emergent, not adaptive but generative and transformative. Like David Suzuki (1988), a Canadian scientist, who once characterized his personal growth as a process of metamorphosis through "maggothood," these writers and their words inspired me to find avenues through which to further explore.

The writings of the authors associated with chaos and complexity became for me like twigs, connected to branches, with the promise of a base that brought these together into a coherent whole. Such joy I felt when, in reading one author, I found him or her referring to another whom I had also read. I sensed that I was on the right track. I began to feel that I had in some way appropriated these authors. They were now part of my inner circle. I felt protective and possessive of them, vigilant of their being accurately interpreted by colleagues who spoke of them. These writers became part of me, part of my writing, and in time, part of my teaching. Later, I would feel the joy of having my students voice their ideas of what was possible in education and hearing them say that these authors were reading their thoughts, too, and were speaking to them.

How Chaos and Complexity Affected My Study

What could be more affirming to a qualitative researcher than to read the following lines by scientists in a field where the hallmarks of research require quantification, measurement, and prediction?

> As scientists we are now beginning to find our way toward the complex processes forming the world in which living creatures and their societies develop. Indeed, today we are beginning to go beyond . . . "the world of quantity" into the world of "qualities" and thus of "becoming." (Prigogine & Stengers, 1984, p. 36)

These researchers are proclaiming the growing appreciation of complexity, development, qualities, process, and emergence.

Effect on the Study Design

The above-mentioned features supported both the rationale and the methodology of my study, which took an approach that was both interpretive and qualitative. The qualitative, interpretive methodology permitted an "inside view" into the subjective, complex, and varied experiences of these people. Through personal narratives, the social workers were able to share their images, give individual expression to their own stories, and describe their experiences of change and growth—of *Becoming,* a concept associated with chaos and complexity (Jantsch, 1981; Prigogine & Stengers, 1984). My study design echoed the observations of Prigogine and Stengers, above, through its focus on the qualities of peoples' lives, concerning their development, critical incidents, developmental tasks, and emergence of new qualities that found expression in their current personal and professional spheres. Accordingly, my research questions focused on three areas: the present state of midlife social workers, the precipitators and processes of their changes and transitions, and the potential outcomes of the changes and possible future directions for growth.

The interview schedule consisted of open-ended questions concerning individuals' experiences (actions, feelings, attitudes) in particular areas. One such area was the "marker event," any significant precipitator event that may or may not have been experienced as a crisis. The marker event was understood to be a "bifurcation point," a chaos and complexity concept that was to constitute a crossroads, wherein the path of the past was no longer an option and where new avenues emerged. One question concerning "stepping-stones" was expected to identify main points of development and emergence in each individual's professional career. And the question concerning "valued images" (role models) encouraged reflection on their future direction and on what they might yet become.

The chaos and complexity theoretical framework supported my use of interview methods that would allow individuals to determine the direction, content, and emotional tone of the interview. I began with the "clustering" exercise that asked them to generate feelings, images, and experiences around the phrase, "Me, Myself at Midlife." This tool enabled their self-directedness in terms of the information they provided, but it also advanced the emergent, uncontrollable, and unpredictable direction of the interview process itself. That is to say, I as the researcher would take the risk that, prompted to respond to "Me, Myself at Midlife," they could direct their attention to the unexpected, focus solely on a tangential aspect, or say little or nothing at all.

Effect on Data Analysis

I began my analysis by arranging my findings according to a theoretical "template" comprised of Jung's (1966, 1969) theory of personality development, Levinson et al.'s (1978) theory of midlife transition, and Prigogine and Stengers's (1984) chaos/complexity theory of system change. I found that Jung and Levinson's psychological theories helped me to appreciate the current state of my study participants and their concerns and issues in work and personal relationships. Chaos and complexity theory, however, provided a way to attend to the processes through which personal changes occurred—through self-renewal, through self-transcendence, or through being "on the threshold." Moreover, through this framework I gained an understanding of the features that underlay each kind of change—the fluctuations, the stresses, the "bifurcations" or crossroads, the efforts to resist or dampen change, and the experience of undergoing a perspective transformation.

As I approached the discussion section related to the experiences of the midlife transition, Prigogine and Stengers's (1984) theory of *Becoming* provided both a metaphor and a model for exploring how the stresses of midlife, how being in flux and far-from-equilibrium, could hold the potential for reordering the individual at a higher state or stage of development. Following their model, I could begin to speculate that intrapsychic stresses (fluctuations from within) and environmental stresses (fluctuations from without), touched by a comparatively small precipitating factor, could usher the individual into a higher state of development—into a self-transformation. Moreover, their description of a system as being in a continual state of change, of *Becoming*, fit with Jung's (1966) concept of individuation. Finally, Prigogine and Stengers's theory supported the view that midlife stress, so often dismissed jokingly as a "midlife crisis," a passing fancy, could actually have functional import, possibly signaling or initiating the individual's evolution toward higher stages of development.

Effect on the Findings and Interpretation

My findings revealed the three ways in which one group of social workers were traversing the midlife transition: through transformation, through self-renewal, and through being "on the threshold of becoming." From the perspective of chaos and complexity theory, the latter pattern—of being "on the threshold of becoming"—developed as the most fascinating, since these individuals, being in such a state of flux, of questioning, and exploration, intimated that their future was the most uncertain, that they were possibly the most vulnerable of any group to change, and therefore "on the threshold" of further development. Readers may recall from chaos and complexity theory

(Prigogine & Stengers, 1984) that when a system is in a state of flux, it is highly sensitive to stimuli from within and without; a small event can have major effects. It would follow that in the case of these individuals no one can predetermine or predict what events might occur and how these individuals might respond. Would they shift to become transformers or would they restabilize as self-renewers?

Were one to interpret the study findings through a traditional paradigm that values certainty, predictability, and rationality, the individuals in this study would likely be viewed perhaps in a reversed fashion from the way that they have been depicted in this chapter. In the case of the transformers, it could be said that they had suffered too much. Of the self-renewers, it could be said that they were fortunate, indeed, being blessed with stable lives. Of those "on the threshold of becoming," they might have been advised to stay put and to count their blessings. Through the chaos and complexity lens, however, those who have suffered have been privileged, their hardships being the soil for their growth; those who have been spared self-confrontation have been perhaps constrained in their own evolution or transformation; and those who are now undergoing flux and struggle have new information, clues as it were, as to who they are and who they can yet become.

Another Framework: Developmental Stage Theory

My research into the lives of social workers and how they experience and resolve the midlife transition rested on several theoretical frameworks that seemed to take, in turn, greater and lesser importance as the study proceeded. The initial literature underlying the study incorporated several theories of adult development, each providing a unique perspective on the midlife period of adulthood. Developmental stage theory, represented by Kohlberg (1981) on moral development and Kegan (1982, 1996) on cognitive development, each provided the initial theoretical framework, with their detailing of the various stages or centers of development throughout adulthood. Development was described as continuous hierarchical growth from simple to more complex forms, from lesser to greater complexity. Accordingly, each developmental stage emerged through its previous stage, added new elements, and integrated these into a more complex whole. Moving through each stage, individuals would gain greater levels of inclusiveness, complexity, and integration of personality. This theory served early to support the rationale for this study, since stage theory mapped out what was possible for psychological development throughout the human lifespan. It did not, however, illuminate the actual processes and dynamics of change, a limitation that was noted also in the research of Warren, Franklin, and Streeter (1998).

Multiple Frameworks: Jung and Levinson

Several other theoretical frameworks maintained a central place through the various phases of the study. The first was depth psychology that drew most heavily on the developmental psychology of Jung (1966, 1969). His views served this study because he outlined the course of human personality development as an individuation process, and described the possible states of further development. The second framework focused more directly on the various transitions throughout the adult life span, including the midlife transition. Daniel Levinson's pioneering work provided this material, and since his research had drawn heavily on Jung's work, many parallels existed between the two. Each of these will be examined briefly before turning to the way in which chaos and complexity theory brought fresh insights into the developmental process of this group of social workers.

Jung: The Voice of Depth Psychology

Carl Jung has been called the "father of adult development" for his insistence on the continuation of personality development throughout the adult life cycle. Being in association with theorists in the natural sciences, he was influenced by the early systems thinkers to utilize principles from physics and systems theory in his conception of energy and psychic balance (Jung, 1966). His basic concepts clearly transcended the mechanistic models of classical psychology and brought his science much closer to the conceptual framework of modern physics than any other psychological school (Capra, 1983). Jung viewed the human psyche as a self-organizing system that progressively evolves from a less complete stage of development to a more complete one. The center of the personality is the self that becomes increasingly accessible as the personality differentiates itself from the personal unconscious as well as from the collective mass, and then integrates these newly acquired perspectives. He described this process as "individuation"—the coming to selfhood.

In Jung's (1966) view, individuation did not occur simply as a natural consequence of age, but rather followed from the working through of life's problems; and more often came about through suffering, abandonment, and sudden shock. Jung believed that life's problems and shocks were not negative events to be avoided and dispelled; rather these painful struggles became the soil for growth of personality.

Jung's (1966) constructs were particularly useful when analyzing the interview data in the following ways: They helped me to appreciate the nature of the crises that individuals were experiencing and the significance of these to the tasks of the second half of adult life. Second, they helped me to understand the specific issues with which the individuals were coping—the integration of opposites, the recovery of what was lost, and the struggle for authenticity. Third, they illuminated the actual tasks of the "noon of life," that is, of the midlife transition. Finally, they provided directionality for development—the growth of personality toward individuation and selfhood.

The Life Course and the Midlife Transition

The nature and tasks of the midlife period, described earlier by Jung (1966), became concretized through the research of Levinson and his colleagues (1978). Although these researchers set out to study adulthood and the eras of adulthood, their study of 40 men, representing four diverse professional fields, surfaced an unexpected finding—the presence of a midlife transition, occurring between the ages of 40 and 45. Levinson et al. (1978) identified the midlife transition as the most critical one in the life cycle, its function being to terminate the period of early adulthood and to initiate the era of middle adulthood. Levinson et al. identified several major tasks of the midlife period: The first was to appraise one's life. The individual may ask, "What have I accomplished?" "Where am I going now?" Long-held assumptions and beliefs about self, work, and the world are reevaluated; talents and strengths are reexamined. The second task is to modify the life structure to bring it into accord with newfound values and perspectives. The individual may make major changes in family or career, or these changes may be less dramatic and internal. A gradual shift occurs from present to future and to planning for the next era. The third task is to begin the work of individuation, described earlier in the section about Jung. This involves confronting the opposite tendencies or major polarities—young/old, masculine/feminine, attachment/separation)—that coexist within each individual, and reintegrating these. The individuation process as described by Levinson et al. closely paralleled the features of Jung's individuation process. His framework served my study by delineating the features of midlife and the midlife transition, and it permitted comparison of the individuals in my study group, both to each other and to the tasks and qualities that Levinson's schema had outlined.

The Study as an Evolving Process

Like evolutionary systems theory, which views life as an evolving process, my study, too, took on an evolving quality. Initially, I had expected that the data analysis would draw most heavily on the ideas of Jung (1966, 1969) and Levinson et al. (1978), since both had focused on midlife as an important period developmentally (and since midlife was the focus of my study). As the data were collected and the analysis proceeded, however, the chaos and complexity framework became the most informative because it helped to illuminate *the nature and processes of change* that these individuals were undergoing or not undergoing. Through the lens of this theory, I could see the possibilities for human evolution that may follow from disorder, turbulence, chaos, and crisis. The hazardous event becomes an opportunity; an unfortunate happening becomes a gift; the bewildering and puzzling tensions and struggles become harbingers of the individual's *Becoming*. Chaos and complexity theory afforded insights into the ways in which changes and transformations could come about in human systems.

The End of Certainty

Readers may be familiar with the ancient rhyme

> For want of a nail, the shoe was lost;
> For want of the shoe, the horse was lost;
> For want of the horse, the rider was lost;
> For want of the rider, the battle was lost;
> For want of the battle, the kingdom was lost;
> And all for the want of a horseshoe nail.

(Lobel, 1986, p. 53)

The rhyme captures the possible and unforeseen consequence of something so inconsequential as a nail dropped from a soldier's shoe. It highlights an essential feature of chaos and complexity and that is nonlinearity—how a small occurrence can precipitate huge consequences. In our own experience, we can surely recall singular moments that altered our lives—a phone call, a chance meeting, a missed appointment, inattentiveness while working, a second of distraction while driving. At these moments, we are diverted down a path we could hardly have predicated, nor even envisioned.

The chaos and complexity perspective presents a challenge to the traditional and taken-for-granted view of the world as somehow being orderly, controllable, and predictable. It portrays a world that at one moment reveals order and in the next, chaos, and then again a new order. In one moment something appears with clarity; in the next it is blurred. In one moment, individuals with whom we interact profess their love of their career; in the next moment they have left it. This orientation allows for the instance where at the start of a research interview an individual may express feelings of disappointment and loss regarding his or her career, whereas at the end, some new insight has surfaced, and with it new hope. Chaos and complexity alerts us to the inexactitude and dynamism of our environments and the lack of certainty and assuredness of our methods. It advocates a certain level of tentativeness concerning our findings and conclusions and humility regarding our discoveries, in the knowledge that something new, something yet unknown is just around the corner, still to emerge. The following is a summary of some of the features of a chaos and complexity framework:

- It moves us to see parts as being "holons," as part of a whole;
- It reveals how everything is related to everything else;
- It suggests that seemingly insignificant events can have momentous effects;
- It encourages us to become curious about stress and flux as information;
- It demonstrates that what we do does make a difference;
- It reminds us that we cannot control nature, or much of anything;
- It encourages attention to minute detail and subtle occurrences;
- It reminds us to be humble about outcomes, since many factors come into play;
- It affirms that growth does happen; that selves can change.

Montuori (2003), who earlier introduced the concept of improvisation to complexity-based work in social science, provides a fitting closing that sums up the chaos and complexity of doing qualitative research:

Perhaps one key challenge is to find, like jazz musicians, a voice or voices, that incorporate both subjective and objective, rational and emotional, theory and experience, risk and trust. This makes the task of being a social scientist/artist also a task of self-development, of finding one's identity in dialogue with and through the world one is studying. (p. 17)

References

Briggs, J., & Peat, F. D. (1999). *Seven life lessons of chaos: Spiritual wisdom from the science of change.* New York: Harper-Perennial.

Capra, F. (1983). *The turning point.* New York: Bantam.

Capra, F. (1988). *Uncommon wisdom.* New York: Simon & Schuster.

Capra, F. (1996). *The web of life.* New York: Anchor Books.

Casti, J. (1993). *Searching for certainty: What scientists can know about the future.* London: Abacus.

Cavanaugh, J. C., & McGuire, L. C. (1994). Chaos theory as a framework for understanding adult lifespan learning. In J. D. Sinnott (Ed.), *Interdisciplinary handbook of adult lifespan learning* (pp. 3–21). Westport, CT: Greenwood.

Cilliers, P. (1998). *Complexity and postmodernism: Understanding complex systems.* New York: Routledge.

Dewey, J. (1964). Having an experience. In A. Hofstadter & R. Kuhn (Eds.), *Philosophies of art and beauty* (pp. 577–646). Chicago: University of Chicago Press.

Doll, W. E. (1986). Prigogine: A new sense of order, a new curriculum. *Theory Into Practice, 25*(1), 10–16.

Doll, W. E. (1993). *A post-modern perspective on curriculum.* New York: Teachers College Press.

Domaingue, R. (1988). Introducing metaphors of chaos to adult education. *New Horizons in Adult Education, 2*(11), 55–59.

Germain, C. B., & Gitterman, A. (1980). *The life model of social work practice.* New York: Columbia University Press.

Gordon, K. (2003). The impermanence of being: Toward a psychology of uncertainty. *Journal of Humanistic Psychology, 43*(2), 96–114.

Halmi, A. (2003). Chaos and non-linear dynamics: New methodological approaches in the social sciences and social work practice. *International Social Work, 46*(1), 83–101.

Hayles, N. K. (1991). Introduction: Complex dynamics in literature and science. In N. Katherine Hayles (Ed.), *Chaos and order: Complex dynamics in literature and science* (pp. 1–33). Chicago: University of Chicago Press.

Hill, M. R. (1993). *Archival strategies and techniques: Qualitative research methods* [Series 31: A Sage University Paper]. Thousand Oaks, CA: Sage.

Jantsch, E. (1981). Unifying principles of evolution. In E. Jantsch (Ed.), *The evolutionary vision: Toward a unifying paradigm of physical, biological, and socio-cultural evolution* (pp. 3–27). Boulder, CO: Westview.

Jung, C. G. (1966). Animus and anima. In Gerhard Adler & R. F. C. Hull (Eds. & Trans.), *Collected works of C. G. Jung: Vol. 7. Two essays in analytical psychology* (2nd ed., pp. 188–211), Princeton, NJ: Princeton University Press.

Jung, C. G. (1969). Stages of life. In Gerhard Adler & R. F. C. Hull (Eds. & Trans.), *Collected works of C. G. Jung: Vol. 8: Structure & dynamics of the psyche* (2nd ed., pp. 1–18). Princeton, NJ: Princeton University Press.

Karpiak, I. E. (2000). Evolutionary theory and the "new sciences": Rekindling our imagination for transformation. *Studies in Continuing Education, 22*(1), 29–44.

Kegan, R. (1982). *The evolving self: Problem and process in human development.* Cambridge, MA: Harvard University Press.

Kegan, R. (1996). *In over our heads: The mental demands of modern life.* Cambridge, MA: Harvard University Press.

Kohlberg, L. (1981). *The meaning and measurement of moral development.* Worcester, MA: Clark University, Werner Institute.

Lakoff, G., & Johnson, M. (1980). *Metaphors we live by.* Chicago: University of Chicago Press.

Levinson, D. J., Darrow, C. N., Klein, E. B., Levinson, M. H., & McKee, B. (1978). *The seasons of a man's life.* New York: Ballantine.

Lobel, A. (1986). *The Arnold Lobel book of Mother Goose.* New York: Knopf.

Mezirow, J. (1981). A critical theory of adult learning and education. *Adult Education, 32*(1), 3–24.

Montuori, A. (2003). The complexity of improvisation and the improvisation of complexity: Social science, art and creativity. *Human Relations, 56*(2) 237–255.

Murphy, P. (2000). Symmetry, contingency, complexity: Accommodating uncertainty in public relations theory. *Public Relations Review, 26*(4), 447–462.

Neuman, Y. (2003). *Processes and boundaries of the mind: Extending the limit line.* New York: Kluwer Academic/Plenum.

Padgham, R. E. (1988). Thoughts about the implications of archetypal psychology for curriculum theory. *Journal of Curriculum Theorizing, 8*(3), 123–145.

Piaget, J. (1977). *The development of thought.* New York: Viking.

Prigogine, I. (1986). The reenchantment of nature. In Rene Weber (Ed.), *Dialogues with scientists and sages: The search for unity* (pp. 181–197). Markham, ON: Penguin.

Prigogine, I. (1996). *The end of certainty: Time, chaos, and the new laws of nature* (O. Jacob, Trans.). New York: Free Press.

Prigogine, I., & Stengers, I. (1984). *Order out of chaos: Man's new dialogue with nature.* New York: Bantam.

Rico, G. L. (1983). *Writing the natural way.* Los Angeles: Tarcher.

Schroots, J. (1996). The fractal structure of lives. In J. E. Birren, G. M. Kenyon, J. E. Ruth, & J. F. Schroots (Eds.), *Aging and biography: Explorations in adult development* (pp. 117–130). New York: Springer.

Skar, P. (2004). Chaos and self-organization: Emergent patterns at critical life transitions. *Journal of Analytical Psychology, 49,* 243–262.

Suzuki, D. (1988). *Metamorphosis: Stages in a life.* Toronto, ON: General.

Thrift, N. (1999). The place of complexity. *Theory, Culture & Society, 16*(3), 31–69.

Von Bertalanffy, L. V. (1968). *General systems theory.* New York: George Braziller.

Waldrop, M. (1992). *Complexity: The emerging science at the edge of order and chaos.* New York: Simon & Schuster.

Walters, G. D. (1999). Crime and chaos: Applying nonlinear dynamic principles to problems in criminology. *International Journal of Offender Therapy and Comparative Criminology, 43*(2), 134–153.

Warren, K., Franklin, C., & Streeter, C. (1998). New directions in systems theory: Chaos and complexity. *Social Work, 43*(4), 357–370.

Wheatley, M. J. (1994). *Leadership and the new science: Learning about organization from an orderly universe.* San Francisco: Barrett-Koehler Publishers.

Williams, M. (2000). Sokal, chaos and the way forward. *Sociology, 34*(2), 341–346.

7

A Look Through the Kubler-Ross Theoretical Lens

Kerri S. Kearney
Adrienne E. Hyle

Overview of the Study

Impetus for the Study

This study (Kearney & Hyle, 2003), like many studies, was born of a series of what appeared to be only vaguely related experiences of Kerri Kearney that eventually collided with similar research interests of Adrienne Hyle. This "collision of common concern" ignited a series of collaborative research projects that will quite likely be ongoing well after this book has been published and found its way into the hands of aspiring researchers. The foundation for this chapter, however, is provided by the original study as it presents the best backdrop for discussion of the consideration and selection of a theoretical framework for research, as well as all of the associated consequences of that decision.

Because students often wonder where the ideas for research come from, it seems wise to start at the beginning. The original impetus for this study was a series of change management efforts made at *WorldCom*, Inc., during its merger with MCI in 1999. At that time, this was the largest corporate merger in U.S. history and, as senior corporate trainer, Kerri was charged with the development and implementation of change management training for the company's domestic locations. It was through her struggle to find something meaningful for "managing" this massive change that she realized that grief models could be very powerful tools for both the understanding and management of the individual grief with which she suddenly found herself surrounded. The suicide of one employee—who left a suicide note that mentioned the merger as a factor in the decision—certainly seemed to validate her suspicion that individual emotions were major factors in the change, and this event greatly solidified her determination to address the role of individual emotion and organizational change.

A year later, Kerri left *WorldCom* to obtain her doctorate and return to the field of education; her experiences, however, continued to fire a desire to study the relationship between individual emotion and organizational change. She soon encountered a faculty member, Adrienne, who had a similar desire, created from her work with organizational change in schools, and so began a collaboration that continues today.

Overview of the Study

Our initial expectations regarding grief and organizational change were quite similar. We expected to find grief in the educational setting just as Kerri had observed it in the for-profit world because both undergo an inordinate amount of change. Change efforts traditionally focus on rational process issues, strategic decision making, or external behaviors while avoiding the emotion that is natural to an organization of people (Fineman, 1993; Marshak, 1996; Vince & Broussine, 1996). The focus of our study was specifically on educational organizations. Although schools have attempted to change, they have not been considered successful by most (Fullan, 1999; Fullan & Hargreaves, 1996; Sarason, 1996). We speculated that the lack of success in change was based on a lack of attention to individuals and their emotional experiences during the processes of change. Therefore, our study focused on individual loss and grief for those who stay with the organization as possible key factors in the failure of educational change.

Purpose of the Study

Because the study of individual, change-related emotions in organizations is not particularly common, we decided that the use of a grief construct as a theoretical framework would be very helpful, if not critical, in finding direction for both collecting and understanding our data. Our initial intent was to use a grief construct, or model, to examine the emotional impacts of imposed organizational change on individuals as a potentially integral, yet missing, piece of most organizational change strategies. Although the decision to use an individual, change-related emotions theoretical framework to guide our study was made very early in the process, our challenge became to identify the appropriate framework. Our efforts in this area resulted in the selection of the Kubler-Ross (1969) model; the details of this selection process and its impact on all facets of our study are discussed in detail in a later section.

Although we have additional research that uses Kubler-Ross's (1969) work as a theoretical framework, the information discussed within this chapter is based upon our original study (Kearney & Hyle, 2003) of individual emotions and organization change. Two peer-reviewed articles resulted from this research. The first, "The Grief Cycle and Educational Change: The Kubler-Ross Contribution," was published in *Planning and Changing* (Kearney & Hyle, 2003). This article specifically addressed the application of the Kubler-Ross grief construct to an organization (as described in the next section) undergoing broad-ranging change. The second, "Drawing Out Emotions in Organizations: The Use of Participant-Produced Drawings in Qualitative Inquiry," was published by *Qualitative Research* (Kearney & Hyle, 2004). This second article resulted from the same original study but was a methodological article about the use of participant-produced drawings to access the types of emotional data needed for analysis using the Kubler-Ross framework. The details of this drawings methodology, and why it was used to produce data that could be analyzed by our theoretical framework, are discussed in a later section.

Study Site and Focus

One of our first steps for this study (Kearney & Hyle, 2003) was to find a site that was willing to be the subject of our inquiry. Our efforts resulted in our study being conducted at a technology training school that was part of a larger state system of technology school districts located in the southwestern part of the United States. The school district met training needs for high school students (who were concurrently enrolled at their "home" or public high school), adults, and business and industry clients.

The school was situated in a close-knit, rural community of 5,500 people, which was also home to the main campus of a 4-year, regional university. The school was overseen by a publicly elected, five-member board of education and served a district that included parts of seven counties. Training classes were both short and long term, might be ongoing during both day and evening hours, and culminated in certifications, licensures, or college credit. Funding came from a variety of sources including local and state taxes, revenues from tuition and fees, federal grants, and loans. The school had had a single superintendent with 17 years' tenure who was nearing retirement and beginning to prepare the organization for transition.

Approximately 18 months prior to this study, one of the school's "own," a man who had been raised from childhood in the area but spent 15 years "downstate," took the assistant superintendent's position at this school campus. As a possible "heir apparent" for the system, he brought new philosophies and practices that had resulted in far-reaching changes. The primary focus of this study was the impact of those changes on employees of the school; however, information provided by participants early in the study led to the addition of a secondary focus on widespread changes that had been proposed at the state level of the technology school system.

Methods

The partners in this study, the respondents, voluntarily participated in a four-phase process. Each was asked to complete a brief demographic profile that captured both personal (i.e., age, etc.) and organizational (i.e., position, etc.) information. Additionally, respondents were asked to create two drawings about their experiences of organizational change. These drawings were used as entry points to unstructured interviews and will be discussed in more detail in a later section.

Unstructured interviews began by asking each participant to explain their drawings; the researchers asked follow-up questions to further clarify this explanation, focusing specifically on the identified emotions, as well as other needed information. As an additional tool for capturing emotions-based data, interviews also incorporated the use of lists of feelings from which the participants were asked to identify those that resonated with them. Follow-up interviews were conducted for the purposes of asking clarifying questions, conducting member checks (confirming tentative interpretations with the respondents as outlined by Merriam [1988]), and addressing a separate methodological issue—the efficacy of the drawings methodology itself. The data collection was intended to address, in theory, a single point in time as it related to the overall changes. In practice, the process of data collection extended over 8 weeks.

Data Analysis Using the Kubler-Ross Lens

Because we chose to use the Kubler-Ross (1969) grief construct, which provides five stages of grief that are directly associated with specific emotions, our data were first organized by like emotional clusters. We coded interview transcripts line by line following our review of participant drawings and emotions lists. We then examined and compared the clusters to the categories provided by the Kubler-Ross grief model. This comparison process, as described by Merriam (1988), directs that the "database is scanned to determine the fit of a priori categories and then the data are sorted into the borrowed categories" (p. 137). In this way, examination of the data produced both what fit the Kubler-Ross grief cycle and what did not.

Findings

Based upon the Kubler-Ross (1969) model, grief reactions were clearly found for employees who had *experienced* organizational change as well as for those who *anticipated* organizational change at a local level. In addition, a tremendous amount of participants' energy was being absorbed in dealing with naturally occurring, change-related emotions—many of which the participants themselves were resistant to. Reactions, however, were unique to the individual and did not necessarily include all stages of the Kubler-Ross grief construct. Every participant in this study reported that most of the organizational changes at the local level were "good." Their emotional reactions lend support to Barger and Kirby's (1995) assertions that grief occurs even in response to change that is perceived to be "good."

Like the emotions reported at the local level, it appeared that emotions associated with grief were present within these participants' responses to proposed state-level change, although perhaps in early stages. These data support the idea that grief can be anticipatory, or occur prior to the actual loss itself, a premise originally reported by Kubler-Ross (1969). Again, the loss found at the state level was similar to grief descriptions for death and dying (Bowlby, 1980; Kubler-Ross, 1969), as well as grief found in other organizational change studies (Clapper, 1991; Humphrey, 1997; Massey, 1991, 1992; Perlman & Takacs, 1990; Schoolfield & Orduna, 1994; Stein, 1990a, 1990b; Triolo, Allgeier, & Schwartz, 1995).

Description of the Theoretical Framework

The Kubler-Ross (1969) model was the result of a collaborative research project by the author and students at the Chicago Theological Seminary on the experience of death. This project included a multitude of real-life interviews with dying patients on the various defense and coping mechanisms that surface during different periods of time—replacing each other or existing side by side, depending upon the individual and his or her unique perspectives. The stages discovered and identified by Kubler-Ross and her students include: denial and isolation, anger, bargaining, depression, and acceptance. Hope was also included, not as a stage in the process, but rather as an underlying feeling that threaded throughout the dying process. This process was viewed by Kubler-Ross not as a linear progression of grief but as stages that may replace each other, repeat themselves, or exist side by side.

Denial and Isolation

Denial in Kubler-Ross's (1969) death and dying arena refers to the patient's denial or refusal to accept the diagnosis of a terminal illness; this denial may lead to isolation from others. Kubler-Ross considers denial a healthy reaction. Schoolfield and Orduna (1994) carry this position over into their work in a medical organization quoting Kubler-Ross (1969), "Denial functions as a buffer after unexpected shocking news, allows the patient to collect himself and, with time, mobilize other, less radical defenses" (p. 52) and "Denial can give individuals needed time to understand that the change is going to occur and what it may mean for them" (p. 60). Barger and Kirby (1995) character ize denial as the most prevalent response to organizational loss and grieving.

Anger

In the stage of anger, Kubler-Ross (1969) includes feelings of anger, rage, envy, and resentment associated with impending death and loss. This stage can be difficult to cope with as emotions may be "displaced in all direc tions and projected onto the environment at times almost at random" (p. 64). Wherever the person looks, he or she will find reason for complaint.

Bargaining

Best described as attempts to trade one action for avoidance of death or loss, bargaining, says Kubler-Ross (1969), is only helpful for brief periods of time. This grief response stems from the temporary belief that "there is a slim chance that he may be rewarded for good behavior and be granted a wish for special services" (p. 94). In organizations, bargaining may be subtle and is often designed to weaken the proposed change so that it can more easily be condemned or sabotaged (Schoolfield & Orduna, 1994).

Depression

Depression or overt sadness signals the replacement of anger with a sense of great loss (Kubler-Ross, 1969). It occurs when the patient can no longer deny the impending outcome of an illness, grieves the losses accompanying the illness (i.e., the opera singer's loss of ability to perform), and begins to pre pare for death. Daugird and Spencer (1996) state that overt sadness is usually acknowledged and honestly expressed—but likely only to trusted friends or colleagues or to no one at all.

Acceptance

Acceptance is described by Kubler-Ross (1969) as a stage where anger and depression about "fate" have dissipated; in fact, it is described as a stage almost devoid of feelings. Those who have applied the Kubler-Ross model to those who chose to stay in the organization see this as a time that peace has been made with the change as well as a time in which creative work around the change can commence (Daugird & Spencer, 1996; Schoolfield & Orduna, 1994). In the realm of Kubler-Ross's work, death follows the state of acceptance and the grief cycle ends for the patient him- or herself. (Kubler-Ross maintained a focus on the patient's grief cycle and gave little time to the post-death grief of family and friends of the patient, although her work has since been extensively applied to the post-death grief of others.)

As mentioned previously, Kubler-Ross posits that hope is threaded throughout the grieving process. Perhaps it is during the stage of acceptance, then, that hope re-asserts itself as the primary emotion for the stayers who have experienced grief as a result of imposed organizational change.

Origins of the Theory and How It Was Selected

Our selection of Kubler-Ross (1969) resulted from a search for assistance in understanding and awareness of individuals in the change process. Because we chose to focus on individual emotions and grief that we believed were present in the organizational change process, we reviewed a broad variety of grief constructs in the field of death and dying (an obvious place to look for emotions and grief models) and other life loss, as well as those that have resulted from limited efforts to apply grief models to organizational change.

We have often been asked about the applicability of using a death and dying framework for organizational change. Woodward and Buchholz (1987) address this question very succinctly and also appropriately for our study:

> At first . . . to compare change and death seemed a little heavy. But the more we thought about it, the more we realized that the process was, indeed, very similar. In many ways, it is identical to it. . . . When loss occurs, the people who remain have to go through some basic states—denial, anger, bargaining, depression—to finally achieve acceptance. (p. 66)

Because the use of any individual grief model in an organization was, itself, not prevalent in the current research literature, we believed it was important to identify a framework that was well-researched and well-accepted as an emotions and grief model, even if it had not been used in the organizational environment. It was also important that the model selected lend itself to a practical ability to apply it as a framework for analysis. A useful theoretical framework in our opinion can be easily visualized and therefore brings guidance as to organization and approach in terms of data collection and analysis. The theoretical framework need not be linear necessarily although this helps in judging stages or progression. We believe it is essential that a framework be able to be drawn in picture form where components and their relationships can be clearly defined because we need to know how to categorize or code data according to theoretical components. Following is a brief review of our process in reviewing grief models we considered in the areas of life loss, as well as others that have been used in organizational environments.

Grief Constructs Related to Life Loss

We looked first at the also well-known work of Bowlby (1980) who attributed four stages to the process of adult grieving. Although Bowlby's work was certainly well-known and well respected, we did not believe that his model was easily operationalized for research. It did not have great enough detail to facilitate distinctions necessary for data collection and analysis. In a later comparison to the Kubler-Ross (1969) model, it seemed clear that Kubler-Ross's work, which identified a specific emotion at each stage of grief, was more practical for our specific purposes.

Although other life loss models we reviewed had certain strengths or positives that drew our attention, all had certain aspects that made them less desirable for our particular research than that of Kubler-Ross (1969). For instance, whereas we liked the nonlinear approach of the Solari-Twadell, Bunkers, Wang, and Snyder (1995) pinwheel model of grief, it was clearly not as well researched or supported as Kubler-Ross's model. Worden's (1991) work, again, did not meet our requirements for ease of operationalization.

Perlman and Takacs (1990) actually used the Kubler-Ross (1969) construct as a foundation but added five additional stages, doubling the number of stages in the original model. Although this level of detail was desirable, again the model drew most of its positive standing in the literature from the use of the original Kubler-Ross model. We believed the original model was a better, and better-supported, place for us to start.

Crosby, Gage, and Raymond's (1983) study into divorce-related grief showed that grief resolution that results from divorce is similar to the bereavement that follows death, and Trolley (1993–1994) sought to link the death-related grieving literature to a number of traumatic life events. Although both studies further affirmed our desire to apply a traditional grief model to non-death-related grief, neither of these two authors produced a working model that we believed could be successfully applied to our work.

Following this broad review of existing individual grief models, we looked to organizational change literature to determine which, if any, grief models had been applied. We then reviewed each of these studies, again looking for a grief model that was well researched, well supported, and that could be operationalized for studying individual grief in organizations.

Grief Constructs in Organizations

Most of the efforts to apply grief models to change in organizations were based upon anecdotal reports and observations (Barger & Kirby, 1995; Jeffreys, 1995; Kaplan, 1991; Owen, 1987; Perlman & Takacs, 1990; Schoolfield & Orduna, 1994). Others used varying levels and types of both qualitative and quantitative inquiry (Clapper, 1991; Humphrey, 1997; Kavanagh & Johnson, 1990; Massey, 1991, 1992; Stein, 1990a, 1990b; Triolo et al., 1995). Although some anecdotal efforts did not produce clear empirical data, the reported insights in organizational change, loss, and grief were remarkably similar to the empirically based studies. In none of these cases, however, did we find a model that met our criteria as well as did the Kubler-Ross (1969) model.

Organizational Change With the Kubler-Ross Model

It was at this point in our review that we began to feel somewhat certain that the Kubler-Ross (1969) model—although perhaps not ideal, primarily because of its tendency to be misinterpreted as a linear process—would be our best choice for a theoretical framework for our study. To confirm our thoughts, however, we conducted a review of the use of Kubler-Ross's work in the organizational setting. Although we did not expect to find many studies, a few efforts caught our attention.

Perlman and Takacs (1990) used a modified version of the Kubler-Ross construct in a medical organization, and Schoolfield and Orduna (1994) combined the Kubler-Ross model with other models for their analysis of the individual impacts of restructuring a major hospital oncology unit. We also discovered that others had used models that were incredibly similar to Kubler-Ross (Barger & Kirby, 1995, 1997; Bridges, 1991). A few researchers chose to use the Kubler-Ross model very much as it was originally developed in the death and dying literature for their work in organizational change, again, with the exception of Clapper (1991), primarily in health-related organizations (Daugird & Spencer, 1996; Kavanagh & Johnson, 1990). Our review led us to the conclusion that, whether it is used in part or in whole, the Kubler-Ross model is one of the most broadly applied models to organizational change (in addition to arguably being the most well known and well accepted in the field of life loss). This review also gave us some information about the operationalization of the model for collecting and analyzing emotional data, critical factors for our study.

Final Selection of Kubler-Ross as Our Model

It was with the review and consideration of all of the grief models, constructs, and suppositions noted above that we chose to proceed with the Kubler-Ross (1969) model. From our review, we believed it had the greatest depth and breadth of research as its foundation, as well as broad acceptance of its practical applicability. In considering the purpose of our research, to identify the emotional impacts on individuals who had experienced organizational change, this theoretical framework seemed the best choice.

Effects of the Framework on the Study's Questions, Design, Analysis, and a Critique

After selection of Kubler-Ross's model (1969) as the lens to be used for our study, we did a full review and revision of our original study questions. Instead of focusing on traditional components of change such as leadership strategies, processes, outcomes, initiation, implementation, and institutionalization, we took a very fine focus specifically on the emotions that are related to educational change as operationalized through the individual grief focus of the Kubler-Ross model. It would not make any sense to use this model to address traditional components of change because the focus of these models is institutional or organizational whereas Kubler-Ross's is individual and emotional.

Specifically, the following research tasks were addressed:

1. Describe the emotional responses of individuals impacted by imposed change.

2. Analyze these responses through the lens of the Kubler-Ross grief cycle.

3. Report other findings that may evolve from the data.

Additionally, we used knowledge gained by our review of the limited number of applications of the Kubler-Ross (1969) work to organizations to add an additional research question about the viability of the Kubler-Ross construct. Clapper's (1991) study of grief and change in the schools used the Kubler-Ross model, without additions or modifications, as a tool. Although Clapper found evidence of grief at the school site, the issue of whether the Kubler-Ross grief model was an appropriate tool for this type of work was never clearly addressed. This observation and our decision to use the Kubler-Ross construct caused us to add a fourth research task:

4. Assess the usefulness of the Kubler-Ross grief cycle for understanding change in organizations.

Impact on Methodology

The use of the Kubler-Ross (1969) framework impacted methods for this study in multiple ways. The major impacts were created because of the huge challenge of unearthing the individual emotions for which the framework could be used for analysis. We knew from both experience and research in the field that getting individuals in organizations not only to access personal emotions but also to share those emotions is extremely difficult. The ability of the individual to access, recognize, and effectively label emotions, even if they are willing, is challenging and something few are ever asked to do openly. Knowing that U.S. organizations tend to create environments in which emotions are unwelcome or devalued in terms of organizational decision making (Fineman, 1993; Vince & Broussine, 1996) heightened this challenge. This led to the addition of the use of participant-produced drawings and lists of feeling words as methods for quickly accessing individual emotions.

The drawings were deliberately placed at the beginning of the interviews in the hope that they would set a stage for emotion retrieval and discussion. The lists of feelings served to confirm and add to our understandings of individuals' emotional experiences in the change process. This list also allowed for the assumption that different people would use different words for a variety of emotions. We believed that language might be a powerful limiter and were working to find ways to bridge these limitations. The details of each of these methods are discussed below.

Use of Drawings. The ability of drawings to surface unspoken thoughts and feelings has long been accepted by art therapists who have used this tool for many decades. "Drawings offer a different kind of glimpse into human sense-making than written or spoken texts do, because they can express that which is not easily put into words: the ineffable, the elusive, the not-yet-thought-through, the subconscious" (Weber & Mitchell, 1995, p. 34). In the limited amount of research available on the use of drawings in organizations, it has also been found that drawings may be a more specific or direct route to the emotions and unconscious responses or feelings underlying behaviors during organizational change (Vince, 1995). Imagery can "bridge the gap between the apparently individual, private, subjective, and the apparently collective, social, political" (Samuels, 1993, p. 63). In his 1988 study, Zubroff found that, for clerical workers experiencing organizational change, "pictures functioned as a catalyst, helping them to articulate feelings that had been implicit and hard to define. . . . These simple drawings convey feelings that often elude verbal expression" (pp. 141–142).

We used participant-produced drawings in this study (Kearney & Hyle, 2003) for two reasons. First, both the literature (Vince, 1995; Vince & Broussine, 1996; Weber & Mitchell, 1995; Zubroff, 1988) and our previous organizational development experience suggested that drawings were a way to tap quickly into the emotional lives of participants. With the selection of the Kubler-Ross (1969) model as our study lens and our concern about the natural resistance to sharing emotions in the organizational setting, drawings appeared to be a way to access the needed data. Second, the use of drawings as a catalyst for unstructured interviews, an integral part of the study design, afforded participants every opportunity to frame their own experiences, unencumbered by our biases about people and organizational change (Kearney & Hyle, 2004).

Recognizing that both the participants' and the researchers' perspectives on the drawing methodology are culturally rule bound, we chose to include both perspectives as an important foundation for our findings. The experiences created by the use of participant-produced drawings in this study, combined with the experiences reported in the literature, led to a number of observations about the application of this methodology as it relates to both the use of the Kubler-Ross (1969) construct as well as to qualitative research in general.

1. Participant-produced drawings appear to create a path toward participant feelings and emotions, making them viable tools for researchers who seek access to this type of data.

2. The cognitive process required to draw leads to a more succinct presentation of the key elements of participants' experiences.

3. The personal experience depicted by participant-produced drawings could only be considered complete with additional interpretation of the drawing by the participant.

4. Whether the drawing activity encourages or discourages participation in the research process is dependent on individual and situational characteristics, and its impact may be unpredictable for any given study.

5. The provision of little structure in the drawing activity allows for participants' unique experiences to be communicated. This lack of boundaries helps to combat any preconceived biases of the researcher that otherwise might have been unintentionally imposed.

6. The amount of researcher-imposed structure on the drawing process is a determinant in how the drawings may be interpreted.

The demonstrated ability of drawings to create a path to participant feelings and emotions, and to lead to succinct presentations of their experiences appeared to create the opportunity for more meaningful and honest verbal reports—arguably the methodology helped respondents reveal more than what may have been captured with only the unstructured verbal interview. It was our belief that this methodology allowed as to more adequately collect the crucial emotional data that was needed for successful use of the Kubler-Ross (1969) model.

Use of Feelings Lists. In building on one of the few existing Kubler-Ross–based studies, Clapper (1991), we provided participants with a preset list of emotions and asked them to identify those that they either had experienced or were still experiencing as a result of the local change. The spontaneously produced emotions (those that did not appear on the preset list but evolved through the drawings and interviews) were also compiled from the interview data.

Impact on Data Analysis

One of the greatest challenges in qualitative research is finding a starting place for sorting the masses of data that are collected. The Kubler-Ross (1969) construct was critical to our finding a place to start with analysis as well as playing an essential role in our final understandings of individual change.

The Kubler-Ross (1969) grief model provided an initial working plan for us to follow. The stages of grief bounded our initial review of the data and afforded a scaffold from which to begin. From other work, we knew that this initial scaffold would change as we discovered additional emotional components of the change process for individuals. (As you can see from our study results [Kearney & Hyle, 2003] as published by *Planning and Changing*, we ultimately proposed modifications to the framework that we believe are important components in the development and refinement of theory and its application to organizational change.)

One difficulty in the data analysis process emerged almost immediately. We had deliberately collected emotions that were both contained within the preset lists of emotions as well as those that arose spontaneously through both the drawings and interview processes. As a result, we had a number of emotions that had not been categorized within the Kubler-Ross stages via one of the few organizational studies that used Kubler-Ross as a lens (Clapper, 1991).

We returned to the Clapper (1991) study to review how feelings had been categorized within the Kubler-Ross (1969) grief stages. This categorization had occurred through a series of field tests in a study by Michael (1984). In order to categorize the spontaneous emotions occurring in our study, a process similar to Michael's was used, although with slightly more rigor.

A regionally based review panel of 13 professionals who were both formally trained, as well as experienced in working with individuals and grief, served as a review panel. Seven of the reviewers were either counseling or clinical psychologists. Three others provided counseling services through various religious associations—one was a minister, one was a deacon and a trained Stephen minister (trained to deal with long-term care), and one was a bereavement and spiritual care coordinator with a doctoral degree in counseling. Two additional reviewers were patient liaisons in the medical field—one of those was certified for long-term care. The final reviewer was the executive director of a regional hospice unit that specializes in nursing and support care of the terminally ill and their families.

Reviewers worked independently and were asked to place each spontaneously reported emotion in the grief stage in which the emotion, from their training and experience, was most likely to be found. Reviewers were also asked to indicate those reported emotions that did not seem to fit within the categories identified by Kubler-Ross (1969). A category for "hope" was not included as a part of previous organizational research (Clapper, 1991) but, as it was presented by Kubler-Ross as "the one thing that usually persists through all these stages" (p. 148), it was added as a potential category for this set of reviewers.

Each of the final categories used by the current study included those emotions that had been placed in the same stage by 62 percent or 8 of the 13 reviewers. This requirement was intentionally higher than the Michael (1984) study, which required only 33 percent of the reviewers to agree on an emotion's placement. With the completion of this process, we were able to move forward with our data analysis using the Kubler-Ross construct.

Strengths and Weaknesses of the Theoretical Framework

As a result of our study, we found both strengths and weaknesses in applying the Kubler-Ross (1969) model to our research problem. The reality that we needed an "emotions" framework to study change in organizations and the paucity of known options in the field of organizational change caused us to look to other fields for proven models. The death and dying field may seem a strange place to go but knowing from our own experiences that loss is part of every change led us to Kubler-Ross. The strength of this model was its proven appropriateness and usefulness for understanding emotions and grief and the potential for it to be operationalized in a way that made it useful for guidance in study design, data collection, and analysis. What we did not know at the outset was its appropriateness for the specific context or situation we wanted to explore. In part, this became (as it does in all of our theoretical research) part of the research problem and findings.

In considering any theoretical framework for a particular context, some questions always remain as to whether or not it will be a perfect fit. All any responsible researcher can do is make their best effort to remove questions and design a "fit" between the problem, theoretical framework, methods, and analysis. We believed that the Kubler-Ross model would work and was the best "fit" available. We also believe we were right—it did work.

From our data, it was clear that participants reported a full spectrum of emotions that appeared to fit within the Kubler-Ross (1969) stages. Each individual's experiences, however, seemed to be as unique as the individuals themselves. This brought up the question of whether a representative "process" of grief can actually exist for humans who have such different experiences and perspectives. In some ways, this question, also set forth by Hagman (1995), Solari-Twadell et al. (1995), and Schwartzberg and Halgin (1991), is about the way that "grief models" in general have been both presented in the literature and practiced in the field.

The literature has, in some ways, attempted to simplify Kubler-Ross's (1969) work by presenting it as a process that each individual moves through and comes out at the end having processed their grief. From her original writings, it appears this is a gross oversimplification of the intent of Kubler-Ross, who said the defense mechanisms or stages "will last for different periods of time and will replace each other or exist at times side by side" (1969, p. 147). The only visual depiction of her grief stages (p. 265) depicts anger as partially crossing over with denial, elements of denial throughout anger, anger and depression sitting almost on top of one another, and so on. This mixing and meshing of emotions was certainly found to be true for this organization, although some employees did refer to the "processing" of their emotions.

Evidence of "processing" and the individuality of this process seemed to be present in some of the most reported emotions. For instance, feelings of apprehension were reported by six of the nine respondents; however, five reported that these feelings had "passed." Those who reported emotions like "peaceful" and "contented" identified them as present, not past, feelings. Eight respondents reported feelings of excitement but only in the present;

respondents had "grown into" these feelings. Six described feelings of happiness; only one reported they had been happy about the change in the past. Feelings of optimism were reported by eight respondents, four of whom said this was a recent feeling, whereas the other four said they had been optimistic throughout the change.

One respondent noted that, although there had been ongoing frustration in the process of change, it had recently gotten better. Another agreed that there had been a process of getting back to a place of comfort. Two drawings also suggested a process of grief, and this was supported by the verbal explanations of the participants who produced them.

No linear process or order of emotions, however, was clear in the data. In this organizational setting, it appeared that each change brought new and very individualized feelings. Changes came one on top of another so, even had there been a specific path for processing a particular change, it would have been highly unlikely that an individual could have fully processed one change before being hit with another. Organizational life for the individual was simply not that organized, no matter how much these employees would have preferred that. For some, the emotions became individual overall responses to ongoing and complex organizational change—change that could not be defined by one event or decision. Another respondent described anxiety as just a general feeling. So, in some ways, the usefulness of the Kubler-Ross (1969) model for individuals experiencing organizational change is very dependent on how the construct is applied—as a process or as a collection of emotions that are common in response to change.

One additional concern, as discovered during the process of categorizing spontaneously reported emotions at the local level, dealt with the difficulties of placing some emotions, such as pleased, positive, and happy, into the stages of Kubler-Ross's (1969) grief construct. These emotions were shown to occur within different stages across the model, depending on the context the emotion occurred within. This is an important consideration when using the Kubler-Ross grief model for the study of individual reactions to organizational change.

Other Theoretical Frameworks Considered

As noted in the previous discussion describing how the Kubler-Ross (1969) construct was selected, other grief frameworks were considered. None, however, had a foundation of either research or practice that we believed appropriate for use as a theoretical lens for a qualitative research study. A brief review of the other theories considered from the literature on individual grief and grief in organizations follows.

We did not believe the work of Bowlby (1980) and Worden (1991) could be easily operationalized for our research. The work of Crosby et al. (1983) and Trolley (1993–1994) affirmed our desire to use a grief model, but neither of these works produced a model that we believed could be used for our own work. Solari-Twadell et al. (1995) did produce a model but it was not based in a deep foundation of research—a criterion we believed important for our study. Studies that used grief models in organizations were primarily anecdotal and did not produce grief frameworks that would be usable for our research. Other non-anecdotal organizational research did not produce a model that appeared to better fit our work than Kubler-Ross's (1969). Other frameworks (Barger & Kirby, 1995, 1997; Bridges, 1991; Perlman & Takacs, 1990; Schoolfield & Orduna, 1994) were either extremely similar to the Kubler-Ross model or clearly stated that the framework was based upon the work of Kubler-Ross. Ultimately, none of the other frameworks had a research foundation comparable to that of the Kubler-Ross framework. Likewise, none of the other frameworks appeared to present a model that could be more easily operationalized for our work—a factor that was important for both study design and data analysis.

Free Response

Some have criticized our work for it is an a priori application of a theory within the context of qualitative research. The qualitative purists believe that notions flow only from the data and analysis is done with a completely open mind. We, however, know that each researcher brings to the research process biases, frames, beliefs, and experiences that bound and color his or her perspectives. We believe that the use of a framework affords clarity in design, data collection, and analysis that is impossible to get in any other way. For students and other less-experienced researchers, this is particularly important and helpful because a roadmap is provided for data collection and analysis. Instead of having to "blindly" come up with categories and themes emerging from data sets, these individuals have before them a clearly defined and detailed strategy for analytically viewing the data.

Another important component of the use of theoretical frameworks is the requirement to both present the data and analyze it. In this way, the thick, rich description provides information that allows the reader to determine whether transferability applies for other environments. This requires that the data be presented independently of the framework; a view through the framework lens is analytical. In this way, others may be able to apply a different framework to the same data presentation and gain great insights and transferences. It is incumbent on the researcher (student or academic) to analyze the data through their framework lens as well. Although we earlier made a convincing case that the framework guided virtually all aspects of data collection and analysis, we believe that there is nothing to support the position that only one framework is the best for analysis. Whether or not that framework was used to design the research questions or study design, other frameworks may also be applicable and provide remarkable insights. The importance of thick, rich description is paramount! Transferability comes from this essential component of any study.

References

Barger, N., & Kirby, L. (1995). *The challenge of change in organizations.* Palo Alto, CA: Davies-Black.

Barger, N. J., & Kirby, L. K. (1997). Enhancing leadership during organizational change. In C. Fitzgerald & L. K. Kirby (Eds.), *Developing leaders: Research and applications in psychological type and leadership development* (pp. 337–360). Palo Alto, CA: Davies-Black.

Bowlby, J. (1980). *Attachment and loss: Vol. 3: Loss: Sadness and depression.* New York: Basic Books.

Bridges, W. (1991). *Managing transitions: Making the most of change.* Reading, MA: Addison-Wesley.

Clapper, A. T. (1991). *Loss, gain, and grief as a result of externally imposed demands for educational change (educational reform).* Unpublished doctoral dissertation, Drake University, Des Moines, IA.

Crosby, J. F., Gage, B. A., & Raymond, M. C. (1983). The grief resolution process in divorce. *Journal of Divorce, 7*(1), 3–18.

Daugird, A., & Spencer, D. (1996). Physician reactions to the health care revolution. A grief model approach. *Archives of Family Medicine, 9*(5), 497–500.

Fineman, S. (1993). Organizations as emotional arenas. In S. Fineman (Ed.), *Emotion in organizations* (pp. 9–35). London: Sage.

Fullan, M. (1999). *Change forces: The sequel.* Philadelphia: Falmer.

Fullan, M., & Hargreaves, A. (1996). *What's worth fighting for in your school?* New York: Teachers College Press.

Hagman, G. (1995). Mourning: A review and reconsideration. *International Journal of Psycho-Analysis, 76*(Pt. 5), 909–925.

Humphrey, G. M. (1997). *A study of loss and grief with employees who remain after organizational change in a medical setting.* Unpublished doctoral dissertation, Kent State University, Kent, OH.

Jeffreys, J. S. (1995). *Coping with workplace change: Dealing with loss and grief.* Eldridge, IA: Bawden.

Kaplan, T. (1991). Death of an institution. *British Journal of Medical Psychology, 64*(Pt. 2), 97–102.

Kavanagh, K. H., & Johnson, L. D. (1990). When an institution dies. *Journal of Psychosocial Nursing and Mental Health Services, 28*(9), 11–15.

Kearney, K. S., & Hyle, A. E. (2003). The grief cycle and educational change: The Kubler-Ross contribution. *Planning and Changing, 34*(1, 2), 32–57.

Kearney, K. S., & Hyle, A. E. (2004). Drawing out emotions in organizations: The use of participant-produced drawings in qualitative inquiry. *Qualitative Research, 4*(3), 361–383.

Kubler-Ross, E. (1969). *On death and dying.* New York: Touchstone.

Marshak, D. (1996). The emotional experience of school change: Resistance, loss and grief. *NASSP Bulletin, 80*(577), 72–77.

Massey, P. (1991). Institutional loss: An examination of a bereavement reaction in 22 mental health nurses losing their institution and moving into the community. *Journal of Advanced Nursing, 16*(5), 573–583.

Massey, P. (1992). Nurses' reactions to hospital closure. *Nursing Standard, 6*(15–16), 30–32.

Merriam, S. B. (1988). *Case study research in education: A qualitative approach.* San Francisco: Jossey-Bass.

Michael, R. O. (1984). *A social psychological approach to the student of organizational change.* Unpublished doctoral dissertation, Georgia State University, Atlanta, GA.

Owen, H. (1987). Reconciliation, griefwork and leadership. In *SPIRIT: Transformation and development in organizations* (pp. 104–113). Potomac, MD: Abbott Publishing.

Perlman, D., & Takacs, G. T. (1990). The 10 states of change. *Nursing Management, 21*(4), 33–38.

Samuels, A. (1993). *The political psyche.* London: Routledge.

Sarason, S. B. (1996). *Revisiting "the culture of the school and the problem of change."* New York: Teachers College Press.

Schoolfield, M., & Orduna, A. (1994). Understanding staff nurse responses to change: Utilization of a grief-change framework to facilitate innovation. *Clinical Nurse Specialist, 8*(1), 57–62.

Schwartzberg, S. S., & Halgin, R. P. (1991). Treating grieving clients: The importance of cognitive change. *Professional Psychology: Research and Practice, 22*(3), 240–246.

Solari-Twadell, P. A., Bunkers, S. S., Wang, C. E., & Snyder, D. (1995). The pinwheel model of bereavement. *IMAGE: Journal of Nursing Scholarship, 27*(4), 323–326.

Stein, H. F. (1990a). Adapting to doom: The group psychology of an organization threatened with cultural extinction. *Political Psychology, 11*(1), 113–145.

Stein, H. F. (1990b). New bosses, old losses: A brief case study in organizational culture. *Organization Development Journal, 8*(2), 1–5.

Triolo, P. K., Allgeier, P. A., & Schwartz, C. E. (1995). Layoff survivor sickness. Minimizing the sequelae of organizational transformation. *Journal of Nursing Administration, 25*(3), 56–63.

Trolley, B. C. (1993–1994). A bridge between traumatic life events and losses by death. *Omega: Journal of Death & Dying, 28*(4), 285–300.

Vince, R. (1995). Working with emotions in the change process: Using drawings for team diagnosis and development. *Organizations & People, 2*(1), 11–17.

Vince, R., & Broussine, M. (1996). Paradox, defense and attachment: Accessing and working with emotions and relations underlying organizational change. *Organizational Studies, 17*(1), 1–23.

Weber, S., & Mitchell, C. (1995). *That's funny, you don't look like a teacher: Interrogating images and identity in popular culture.* London: Falmer.

Woodward, H., & Buchholz, S. (1987). *Aftershock: Helping people through corporate change.* New York: Wiley.

Worden, J. W. (1991). *Grief counseling and grief therapy.* New York: Springer.

Zubroff, S. (1988). *In the age of the smart machine: The future of work and power.* New York: Basic Books.

8

Mary Douglas's Typology
of Grid and Group

Edward L. Harris

Overview of the Study

In this chapter, I describe social anthropologist Mary Douglas's typology of grid and group (1982) and address various ways grid and group theory can be useful in qualitative research. I also highlight a principal resource for this chapter, "Toward a Grid and Group Interpretation of School Culture" (Harris, 1995) published in the *Journal of School Leadership,* which introduced grid and group theory to the field of educational leadership. The use of a theoretical framework has influenced significantly the depth and integration of my teaching, research, and service activities. I discuss some of those benefits and boundaries below as well as the evolution of my understanding and use of grid and group analysis in qualitative inquiry.

Purpose and Research Question

At the time of writing "Toward a Grid and Group Interpretation of School Culture" (Harris, 1995), the notion of school culture had gained popularity in educational literature. In many cases, however, culture was viewed in either homogeneous or figurative terms, and cultural comparisons were difficult to make.

The purpose of the article and research questions that guided the content was rather pragmatic. In studies conducted by various authors, grid and group theory had previously been used to explain a variety of social arrangements, including political cultures, ethnic groups, work environments, and religious contexts (Douglas & Wildavsky, 1982; Ellis, 1993; Lingenfelter, 1992; Rayner, 1984). In Harris (1995), I desired to explore the framework's utility in educational settings and determine whether grid and group theory was a viable means of explaining nuances of school culture. The purposes of the publication were to explain school culture in terms of grid and group and to determine the framework's applicability to educational settings. Central research questions included

- How can a social context be suitably interpreted, explained, and compared with other contexts?
- How effective is Douglas's typology in accomplishing those tasks?

Methods

Much data collection and analysis for the article (Harris, 1995) occurred prior to my discovering Douglas's (1982) work. For example, from 1989 to 1993, my graduate students and I conducted numerous qualitative studies concerning school culture that used either a grounded theory approach or no particular formalized theory at all.[1]

In these initial studies, data were gathered through qualitative strategies such as interviews, observations, and document analyses. From each respective school context, chief informants included teachers, students, central office administrators, and community members. For those original explorations, constant comparison methodology, as outlined in Lincoln and Guba's (1985) *Naturalistic Inquiry,* was used in data analysis.[2]

This foundational research resulted in various narrative case studies that portrayed schools and their dynamic cultures. My discovery of grid and group theory occurred in 1993, after many of these narratives had been written. Douglas's (1982) framework provided a fresh lens to examine those existing data sets and narratives.

Grid and group theory also offered a means to explore new explanations for each research setting, and, in general, was useful in revealing and comparing distinct cultural forms. Because data were collected and analyzed prior to my knowledge of Douglas's (1982) typology, application and exploration of the model's utility in Harris (1995) were a posteriori considerations.

Four fundamental cultural categories constitute Douglas's (1982) typology. As I wrote in Harris (1995), criteria describing these categories were used to select four schools from the existing databases. A collection of case studies was chosen that suitably represented Douglas's cultural prototypes. My understanding of grid and group was elementary and developing at the time. Therefore, considerations for classification were somewhat rudimentary and included

- How are rules and role expectations defined?
- How are activities and objectives directed?
- How are values and norms manifested?

Essential classification criteria, grid and group dimensions, as well as Douglas's four prototypes are explained further in the following section.

Detailed Description of the Theoretical Framework

Mary Douglas (1982) offers a typology that helps educators meet conceptual and methodological challenges inherent in cultural inquiry and educational practice. Her typology of grid and group is useful, as it

- provides a matrix to classify school contexts;
- draws specific observations about individuals' values, beliefs, and behaviors;
- is designed to take into account the total social environment as well as interrelationships among school members and their context; and
- explains how constructed contextual meanings are generated and transformed.

The theory helps bring order to experience and provides a common language to explain behaviors and interactions in a school setting. According to the typology, one may find him- or herself in one of four, and only four, distinctive cultural contexts. Two dynamic dimensions, grid and group, define each of those four prototypes.[3]

The Grid Dimension of the Structural Frame

In Douglas's (1982) frame, grid refers to the degree to which an individual's choices are constrained within a social system by imposed prescriptions such as role expectations, rules, and procedures. For instance, in some schools, autonomy is constrained by bureaucratic rules that regulate curriculum, teaching methods, and grading procedures. In other schools there are nominal regulations, and teachers have freedom of choice in most areas of the teaching and learning process.

Grid can be plotted on a continuum from strong to weak. At the strong end of the grid continuum, roles and rules dominate the environment, and

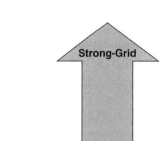

Strong-Grid

- Minimal autonomy
- Specifically defined roles, rules, and responsibilities
- Centralized power and authority

- Maximum autonomy
- Loosely defined roles, rules, and responsibilities
- Decentralized power and authority

Weak-Grid

Figure 8.1   The grid dimension of school culture.

explicit institutional classifications regulate personal interactions and restrain individual autonomy.

In strong-grid environments, teachers typically do not have the freedom to select their own curricula and textbooks, and many decisions are made at upper levels of administration. Strong-grid environments also contain many role distinctions at the teaching and staff levels with proportionately fewer distinctions farther up the organizational ladder.

For example, in a classic strong-grid school system, the superintendent is at the pinnacle of a regulated chain of command. Significant power and authority are delegated by the school board to the superintendent. In this regulated chain of command, each layer of authority in the hierarchy has specific communication and job procedures, which insulate it from other layers and positions.

At the weak end of the grid continuum, teachers experience significantly more autonomy in choosing curricula, texts, and methods. In weak-grid schools, roles are achieved rather than ascribed, and individuals are increasingly expected to negotiate their own relationships and professional choices. There are few role distinctions, few institutional rules, and individuals are valued for their skills, behaviors, and abilities. Also, value is placed on individual success in an openly competitive environment. Salient features of grid can be seen in Figure 8.1.

The Group Dimension of the Structural Frame

Group represents the degree to which people value collective relationships and the extent to which they are committed to the larger social unit. Group

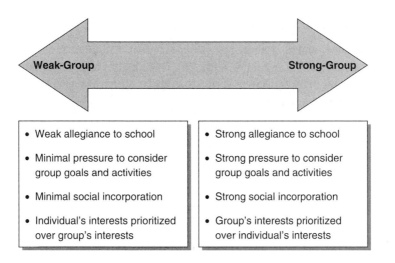

Weak-Group	Strong-Group
• Weak allegiance to school	• Strong allegiance to school
• Minimal pressure to consider group goals and activities	• Strong pressure to consider group goals and activities
• Minimal social incorporation	• Strong social incorporation
• Individual's interests prioritized over group's interests	• Group's interests prioritized over individual's interests

Figure 8.2   The group dimension of school culture.

deals with the holistic aspect of social incorporation and the extent to which people's lives are absorbed and sustained by corporate membership. Like grid, group has a continuum of strong to weak.

In strong-group environments, specific membership criteria exist, and explicit pressures influence collective relationships. The survival of the group is more important than the survival of individual members. An extreme case of strong-group strength can be seen in a monastic or communal environment. In such settings, private property is renounced upon entering, and cultural members rely on the unit for physical, emotional, and social support.

Private schools provide good illustrations of membership criteria with their explicit admission requirements. Many public schools, however, exhibit implicit, de facto criteria for group membership and allegiance through features such as elite neighborhoods and exclusive cliques or gangs. In strong-group environments, the goal of group interaction is to perpetuate the life of and allegiance to the whole school rather than its individual members.

In weak-group environments, pressure for group-focused activities and relationships is relatively low. Members of social and working subgroups tend to focus on short-term activities rather than long-term corporate objectives, and their allegiance to the larger group fluctuates. When group strength is low, people are neither constrained by, nor reliant upon, a faction of others.

The dynamic forces of grid and group are simultaneously at work in any school setting. Figure 8.2 depicts some pertinent features on the group continuum.

Schools as Ecosystems: Four Cultural Prototypes

An analogy that illustrates the symbiotic relationship between grid and group is a rain forest.[4] In a rain forest, grid is analogous to the unique "roles" and particular "rules" that govern individual plants, animals, and insects (i.e., the law of the jungle). Group is analogous to the interrelationship and holistic incorporation of these living organisms.

The dynamic interaction among the unique forces of any rain forest constitutes a unique, biological community, which is greater than the sum of its parts. Moreover, there are different categories of rain forests, which are determined by their overall make-up and location. For instance, there are cloud forests, tropical rain forests, subtropical rain forests, and temperate rain forests. Likewise, in the social realm, based on the simultaneous consideration of grid and group, Douglas (1982) identifies four distinct prototypes of social environments:

- Individualist (weak-grid and weak-group)
- Bureaucratic (strong-grid and weak-group)
- Corporate (strong-grid and strong-group)
- Collectivist (weak-grid and strong-group)

The Four Environments and Their Social Games

Although the dynamics of human life are highly variable, when grid and group coalesce over time, certain themes and dominant patterns of thought and behavior tend to define a particular setting. These patterns are referred to as prevailing mindsets or social games, which influence the entire cultural environment.[5] Knowledge of the different social games helps to

- identify roles and relationships in a school setting,
- understand how those roles and relationships are structured, and
- interpret how and why each member of the school engages in educational activities.

Figure 8.3 categorizes the four social games with their respective grid and group environments.

Individualist (Weak-Grid, Weak-Group) Environments

In individualist environments, relationships and experiences of the individual are not constrained by imposed formal rules or traditions. Role status and rewards are competitive and are contingent upon existing, temporal standards.

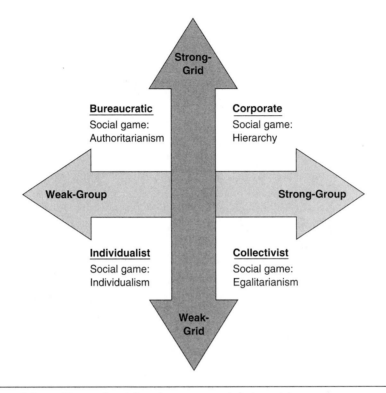

Figure 8.3   Types of social environments and their social games.

The emphasis on social distinction among individuals is submerged, there are few insider-outsider screens, and little value is placed on long-term corporate survival. The predominant social game in this environment is "individualism," which encourages members to make the most of individual opportunities, to seek risks that result in personal gain, and to be competitive and proactive in carving their future in life.

Bureaucratic (Strong-Grid, Weak-Group) Environments

Bureaucratic environments offer little individual autonomy. They are often hierarchical, and the classifying criteria focus on such factors as race, gender, family heritage, or ancestry. Individual behavior is fully defined and without ambiguity. Cultural members have meaningful relationships and life-support networks outside of the group, and little value is placed on group goals or survival.

The social game in this environment is "authoritarianism." Authoritarianism promotes limited opportunity for advancement, compliance with rules and procedures, lack of control of school goals and rewards by teachers, and autocratic rule by administrators.

Corporate (Strong-Grid, Strong-Group) Environments

In corporate contexts, social relationships and experiences are influenced by boundaries maintained by the group against outsiders. Individual identification is heavily derived from group membership. Individual behavior is subject to controls exercised in the name of the group. Roles are hierarchical; at the top of the hierarchy, roles have unique value and power (generally limited to a small number of experts).

There are many role distinctions at the middle and bottom rungs. Perpetuation of traditions and group survival are of utmost importance. The social game valued in this environment is "hierarchy," because the members understand that in a hierarchical system what is good for the corporation is good for the individual. Central office administration, site administration, teachers, students, and parents work in a cohesive, integrated system for the benefit of all involved. All share in the opportunities, risks, and future of the school.

Collectivist (Weak-Grid, Strong-Group) Environments

Collectivist contexts have few social distinctions. Role status is competitive, yet because of the strong-group influence, rules for status definitions and placement are more stable than in weak-group societies. The perpetuation of group goals and survival is highly valued.

"Egalitarianism" is valued as this environment's social game. Egalitarianism places a high value on unity, equal distribution of teaching supplies and space, suspicion of those outside the school community who may want to help, conformity to the norms of the group, as well as rejection of authoritarian leadership and hierarchy.

Disciplinary Origins of Grid and Group Analysis

Grid and group analysis originated in the field of social anthropology. Social anthropologist Mary Douglas earned a doctorate from Oxford University and conducted her early fieldwork in the Belgian Congo. Her academic career included appointments at Oxford University, University College London, University of London, Northwestern University, Princeton University, and the Russell Sage Foundation, where she served as Director for Research on

Culture. She advanced grid and group theory in three major works: first and second editions of *Natural Symbols: Explorations in Cosmology* (1970, 1973) and *In the Active Voice* (1982).[6]

In *Natural Symbols* (1970), Douglas builds on Bernstein's (1964, 1970) work on language codes, social control, and relationships. She uses Bernstein's blueprint to hypothesize that individual cosmology, the set of concepts and relationships that bring order to one's world, is largely shaped by one's experience of social control.

In the second edition of *Natural Symbols* (1973), she further develops the notion of grid and the role of individual choice in grid and group theory. In her third treatise, *In the Active Voice* (1982), she presents a symbiotic relationship between grid and group, redefines the two concepts, and offers criteria to distinguish and classify social systems.

Discovering Douglas

In the late 1980s, I became interested in the dynamics and potential of school culture. At the time, the concept of school culture was gaining increased attention in a broad range of educational literature and practice. I was intrigued with notions such as cultural leadership, values, organizational culture, and the interrelationship of these conceptions with school improvement strategies.

The more I delved into cultural issues, the more questions arose. For instance,

- What is the interrelationship of school culture and school improvement?
- How can we best comprehend, compare, and contrast variant school cultures?
- Why is school culture important to the educational process?

Three Views of Organizational Culture

In my quest for comprehending the various complexities of school culture, I realized the field of education, as well as other fields, lacked a clear and consistent definition of the term. Culture was often used interchangeably with a variety of concepts, including climate, ethos, and saga (Deal, 1993).

Educational literature regarding culture was influenced heavily by anthropology, as well as popular writings on corporate culture, such as *In Search of Excellence: Lessons from America's Best-Run Companies* (Waterman & Peters, 1988). The concept of culture was, and still is, approached from at least three differing perspectives: holistic, symbolic, and dualistic.[7]

The holistic perspective, as the name implies, is broad and encompassing in its explanation of culture. It proposes that culture should be conceptualized as part of what an organization *is* rather than what an organization *has*. That is, schools don't *have* cultures, they *are* cultures.

The symbolic view proposes that schools are social organizations composed of people with a set of shared beliefs, complex rituals and relationships, as well as collective verbal behaviors. Symbols, or manifestations of these behaviors and beliefs, are keys to understanding shared meanings, values, and activities. They are expressions of how people interact and conduct business from day to day.

In this approach, school culture is viewed simply as "the way things are done around here" (Deal & Kennedy, 1982, p. 4), and things are done through such symbols as

- stories,
- heroes and heroines,
- myths and metaphors,
- rituals and ceremonies,
- facility décor, and
- special language or jargon.

Due to the works of Terrence Deal, Kent Peterson, Allan Kennedy, and others, this approach is popular in many educational circles. It emphasizes that at the heart of any educational environment is a set of shared beliefs and values, which are personified by its heroes and heroines, maintained and reinforced by its rituals and ceremonies, shaped by the school environment, and communicated through the informal network.

A third approach, cultural duality, has roots in both of the above views. Theories that emphasize the duality of culture propose that in any given social context a person's professed knowledge, feelings, beliefs, and values are important, but his or her actions may or may not coincide with those espoused beliefs. Thus, to understand culture, one must divide it into dualistic categories:

1. the espoused beliefs and knowledge of the cultural members, and

2. the interrelationships and actions of the cultural members.

In practical terms, what cultural members espouse and what they actually do in an operational sense can be distinguished, analyzed, and explained. From this perspective, culture is a combination of ideas or theories that people use collectively and the way they act out those ideas or theories.

Culture as Seen Through Douglas's Lens

To a degree, Douglas (1982) utilizes principles and ideas from all of the above approaches. I first learned of Douglas's typology of grid and group while critiquing Lingenfelter's (1992) *Transforming Culture: A Challenge for Christian Mission* for the *Criswell Theological Journal* (Harris, 1993). In reviewing Lingenfelter's treatise, I was intrigued by the framework's value in addressing problems inherent in understanding, explaining, comparing, and contrasting cultures.

In Harris (1995), I explained how Douglas's (1982) typology enables a researcher to meet the conceptual and methodological challenges inherent in cultural inquiry:

> The idealist can use the model to better understand and explain how constructed contextual "meanings are generated, caught, and transformed" (Douglas, 1982, p. 189). The variable culturalist is provided a matrix to classify contexts and draw specific observations about individuals, their value and belief dimensions, and behavioral and symbolic variables manifested in particular environments. One of the model's most beneficial aspects is its holistic, comprehensive nature. It is designed to take into account the total social environment and individual member relationships among each other and their context. (p. 619)

Effects of the Theoretical Framework on My Research

As mentioned, I first used Douglas's theoretical framework to explore existing data and case studies generated from previous research (Harris, 1995). Consideration of using Douglas's typology or any theoretical frame in the process was a posteriori.

Initial Reluctance

In the original studies, data were organized into emergent themes or codes and constantly revisited after initial coding, until it was evident that no new themes were emerging. For Harris (1995), Douglas's (1982) theory provided alternative categories to sort various themes as well as fresh vernacular to explain cultural phenomena. In the article, although I presented direct accounts of informants and data, I selected salient excerpts from the original studies according to Douglas's prototype criteria. Also, data I deemed superfluous to illustrating grid and group were omitted from the original data sets. A major reason for those omissions was space, as I needed to explain grid and group theory and portray four environments in a space-constrained, article format.

Thus, for the construction of the article's (Harris, 1995) final case narratives, emergent topics derived from constant comparison methodology were evaluated by Douglas's (1982) criteria, and descriptive portraits representing each of the four grid and group prototypes were constructed. This a posteriori categorizing and case study construction combined authentic emergent design with the functional structure of preexisting patterns.

My next venture was to utilize and consider grid and group from other vantage points. Initially, I was reluctant to use a theoretical framework in qualitative research. I feared a priori theory and inductive inquiry might be oxymoronic. I desired neither to commit research heresy nor appear to suffer from paradigm schizophrenia.

Qualitative research asserts distinct paradigmatic assumptions regarding, among other things, the nature of reality, emergent design, transferability of findings, and holistic consideration of cause and effect relationships. For instance, qualitative researchers typically reject the notion of linear-sequential, cause-and-effect relationships and embrace the notion that entities are in a continual state of mutual, simultaneous shaping. In qualitative inquiry, distinguishing between initial cause and consequent effect is a futile effort. So, is it antithetical to use a constant, predictive framework in a research paradigm that asserts multiple constructed realities, time- and context-bound findings, and interrelational causation?

Although grid and group structure allows for a moderate degree of predictability in understanding causal relationships among culture, behavior, and thought patterns, it is not deterministic or linear in its approach to those causes. A central feature of grid and group theory is the symbiotic, mutually supportive relationship between the dimensions of grid and group as well as among the concepts of culture, behavior, and values. Moreover, Douglas (1982) has been careful to say that her theoretical framework does not call for deterministic causation. Notions of free will, choice, subjectivity, and individual worth are interwoven in the fabric of grid and group theory. An example of some of these themes can be seen in Stansberry and Harris (2005), when they explain the interrelationship between instructional technology and culture.

My reluctance to use a theoretical framework waned somewhat as my knowledge increased about grid and group and how Douglas's (1982) typology and qualitative research could be used complementarily. I also discovered a rich history of theory use in social anthropology. Not all social scientists agree, however, on the extent to which theory is valuable in anthropological research. In *The Art of Fieldwork* (see pp. 170–190), Wolcott (1995) provides a balanced discussion of theory and its significance to qualitative research and the social sciences. Although Wolcott (1995) clearly expresses caution in over-employing theory in fieldwork, he grants that theory offers strategies for coping with "the dual problem of purpose and generalization" and a means to cope with "the underlying issue tersely summarized in a two-word question always at the tip of some skeptic's tongue: So what?" (p. 189).

In my evolving use of grid and group, the framework allowed me to address the perennial "so what" question as well as provided structure and definition to research experiences. Reiterating some of Wolcott's (1995) grounds for appropriate theory use, I explain below various ways grid and group theory has influenced my research. For example, use of Douglas's (1982) typology of grid and group has

- provided convenient labels, categories, and vernacular, which has helped in expressing and comparing cultural phenomena, as well as developing thick description for broader application for single case studies and transferability issues;
- allowed for the development of a web of inquiry (I prefer to use the term, "web of inquiry," rather than "line of inquiry," as "web" connotes networks, inter-relationships, and simultaneous shaping), which I can expand upon and link to prior research, use to relate my work to the larger body of literature on school culture, and better integrate my teaching, research, and service activities;
- offered a way to gain a broader perspective of cultural research and appreciate school culture in the larger context of social anthropology;
- afforded a means to strengthen research design, better organize and present data, and recognize and convey relevant aspects of my research experience; and
- provided a lens to better perceive and identify my own biases and constructed realities I bring to each research experience.

All these factors, and especially the last, have not only enriched my research, but also deepened my understanding of qualitative inquiry. Qualitative inquiry is a value-bound enterprise. The primary instrument in qualitative inquiry is human; therefore, all data collection and analysis are filtered through the researcher's worldview, values, perspectives, and, yes, theoretical frame(s).

Either consciously or unconsciously, we all carry biases and reality constructions to research experiences. Theoretical frameworks are examples of specific constructions of reality with definite form and substance. In using grid and group theory, I have tried to be sensitive to biases in the data collection and analysis process, because any construction of reality can blind me to certain aspects of phenomena under study. I realize all observations and analyses are filtered through my worldview, values, and perspectives, which are all influenced by my extensive use of the framework.

I have had many students who, after using the theory in their dissertation say, "I now see *everything* through a grid and group lens." This realization is important. When using any theoretical framework, the researcher must understand how biases shape the inquiry and its findings and be open to those areas that may fall outside the purview of the framework's lenses. A theoretical framework, while potentially clarifying, is also imperfect and can be distorting.

As a qualitative researcher, I do not view theory as deterministically predictive. It is simply one construction of reality that might provide order, clarification, and direction to a study. In any qualitative study, the reality construction one brings to the research experience interacts with others' constructions. Therefore, a central task of the researcher is to negotiate through the layers of meaning, rather than pigeonholing individuals into particular constructions and categories of any particular framework (Merriam, 2001).

Effect on the Research Questions

Using a theoretical frame has also influenced the types of research questions I formulate. Questions addressed in much of my research have been derived from the dilemmas presented in the cultural literature. For instance, although school culture has gained amplified consideration in an expansive range of educational literature and practice, questions still exist regarding how to best understand, explain, and compare cultures.

Teacher leadership, for example, is a topic of interest for many of my students. An overarching question in a qualitative study using grid and group theory to explain teacher leadership might be: "What is the interrelationship between school culture and teacher leadership?" Correspondingly, "How is teacher leadership manifested (and/or defined) in various school contexts?"

More specifically, a typical set of research questions designed for studying teacher leadership in several schools might look like the following:

- What is the grid and group make-up of each school?
- How is teacher leadership practiced (or defined or manifested) in each school?
- What is the interrelationship of grid and group and teacher leadership?
- How useful is grid and group theory in explaining teacher leadership?

The last research question, or a derivative thereof, is vitally important to research processes. In a qualitative study, a critique of the framework's utility allows the researcher to assess theoretical constructions in light of the themes that were developed. Invariably, if rigor is employed, some phenomena may be addressed and explained directly by the theoretical framework and some data may fall outside the framework's purview. An appraisal of the framework's usefulness is crucial in explaining a particular study's significance to research, theory, and practice, thereby building upon the existing body of literature.

There is little doubt that it is useful to view schools as cultures, and an abundance of definitions attempt to explain the elusive concept. Still, problems exist in explaining how to best improve schools through, or especially, *in spite of,* their cultures. In order to successfully envision and enhance cultures of learning, certain questions must be examined, such as

- How can educators best comprehend school culture?
- Why is school culture important to the educational process?
- How can educators apply school improvement strategies to their particular and unique school cultures?

These questions have guided much of my research using grid and group analysis. The evolution of my research has recently resulted in a book, *Key Strategies to Improve Schools: How to Apply Them Contextually* (Harris, 2005), dealing with adapting improvement strategies in schools with various grid and group dynamics.

Strengths and Weaknesses of Grid and Group Analysis

In using Douglas's (1982) frame in cultural inquiry, I have found both boundaries and benefits. When I began using grid and group theory, an initial limitation was my lack of anthropological training. Consequently, I conferred with experts in the fields of sociology and anthropology, corresponded extensively with others who use the theory, and embarked on an intense reading program.

I realized quickly I could spend a large part of my career exploring intricacies and applications of the framework. This realization was not daunting, but very stimulating and motivating, because it gave direction, focus, and meaning to my work. I had a foundation from which to construct a web of inquiry and integrate various strands of my roles and responsibilities in academe.

I found many practical advantages to using Douglas's (1982) theoretical framework. For instance, grid and group theory offers four finite categories of reference, terminology to express behavioral forms, and a graphic structure to understand inter- and intra-organizational behavior. Once a category is known, with some degree of assurance, forms of behavior within each prototype can be anticipated, variance in intra-organizational actions will be reduced, and intercultural comparisons can be made. Various school cultures can be seen as corresponding to a range of ideal types, which is why grid and group theory is useful in broad analyses of school organizations.

Whereas Douglas's (1982) frame is not intended to be the summum bonum of all theoretical constructions, it does provide a helpful lens through which to view human dynamics as well as vernacular to understand, compare, and explain different school cultures. Other benefits particular to theory, research, and practice are discussed below.

Theory

Douglas's (1982) typology draws on the assertion that culture is a consistent construction of thought and action that is integrated into a unified social system. It allows researchers to view holistically the entire social system of an educational environment. Grid and group dynamics have parallels to other theories with which educators may be familiar. For instance, the Getzels-Guba (Getzels & Guba, 1957) model has been useful in conceptualizing the dynamic interaction of personal (idiographic) and organizational (nomothetic) dimensions of an open system, and has served as a framework for scores of studies. Various versions of systems theory include role theory, sociotechnical theory, and contingency theory (Owens, 2004).

Douglas (1982) offers a complementary addition to social systems' theory base. Not only are grid and group inherent in open systems, but these two coordinates also offer a mutually exclusive continuum of categories for dealing simultaneously with social behaviors in varied contexts. While grid and group theory requires a similar contextual approach to systems theory, its four classifications also provide a more variegated conception of social life within a particular social system.

Categorizing, however, can also be misleading. For instance, grid and group theory can appear to be rigid in its categorization schemes and counterintuitive to highly variable dynamics of human life. The boxes that manifest the four types may appear to suggest discrete positions, rather than dynamic social interaction. In both theory and practice, however, the dimensions of grid and group are continuous, interactive, and symbiotic.

When explaining a cultural context in terms of grid and group, it is important not to insinuate discrete, static categories, nor compartmentalize a certain school or person in a quadrant without consideration of variation. Qualitative case studies are time and context bound, and the researcher must realize that, as in any portrait of life, although the description is written to capture a particular moment in time, the actual context is continually changing. Human behavior is dynamic, complex, and extremely difficult, if not impossible, to contain and predict. Thus, the frame is not intended to portray social environments as static or motionless, but rather as vigorous and precarious dynamic processes.

Similarly, another caveat in using the theory is attempting to overclassify a system or unit of analysis. That is, while it is theoretically correct to say, "I work in a collectivist environment," this does not imply that one works in a group composed exclusively of collectivists.

Grid and group proponents are quick to mention that almost all social systems incorporate all four prototypes of social games, but not necessarily in equal proportions. Whereas an environment likely has a predominant social game, it also incorporates three other social games in complementary and/or antagonistic relationship with one another.

In my preliminary and rudimentary understanding of Douglas's (1982) method, I thought it worked best in explaining hierarchical situations. As my understanding has evolved, however, I have discovered that it also has comparable utility in theoretically reflecting situations where hierarchy is absent. I have found grid and group theory, while not a cure for all theoretical problems, works very well in reflecting and portraying a comprehensive and complex sequence of social conditions.

Research

In using a theoretical frame, one must be consciously aware of when and how the frame makes its entry into the research process. Wolcott (1995) refers to this as choosing between "theory first" or "theory later" (p. 187). He advises that the best use of theory is near the conclusion of a study, "where a self-conscious but genuine search for theoretical implications and links *begins* rather than ends" (Wolcott, p. 187).

While there is merit in this advice, I also recognize that data collection and analysis are very interactive and inclusive processes. Making sense of data occurs at the very beginning of data collection and continues throughout the study to facilitate emergent design and developing structure. Whether one chooses "theory first" or "theory later," one must allow the framework to *guide* and *inform*, rather than *determine* and *force* the emerging research design and process.

I have used grid and group analysis in a priori (i.e., "theory first") and a posteriori (i.e., "theory later") modes as well as a guide in theory construction. As mentioned, my first application of the model was a posteriori. The research for my dissertation was completed in 1990. Since I knew nothing of grid and group, I depended heavily on the cultural literature popular at the time, especially the works of Deal and Kennedy (1982), Deal and Peterson (1990), Goodlad (1984), Lightfoot (1983), and Schein (1985).

When I subsequently discovered the typology, I directly incorporated grid and group language to express prior research findings. For example, some of Douglas's (1982) criteria for grid (such as autonomy, role, and rewards) and for group (such as group allegiance and social incorporation) were useful in distinguishing particular aspects and explaining past research findings.

I was able to expand on thick descriptions with a new vocabulary. For instance, the Jewish day school was not just a school with many role distinctions and a good deal of community support, it was a "strong grid/strong-group" environment, which emphasized "achieved" rather than "ascribed" role status, where roles were "hierarchical" and "social incorporation" was strong.

Grid and group analysis has been fruitful, not only for me, but for a number of researchers. Research areas where others have incorporated the theoretical frame include interpretation of environmentalism (Douglas & Wildavsky, 1982), risk perceptions (Rayner, 1984; Wildavsky & Dake, 1990), religious communities (Carter, 2002; Lingenfelter, 1992), technology policy (Schwarz & Thompson, 1990), high-tech firms (Caulkins, 1999), work cultures (Mars & Nicod, 1983), career expectations (Hendry, 1999), and higher education (Lingenfelter, 1992).

Practice

The implications for practice follow closely on those of theory and research. Grid and group analysis is valuable to practicing educators, as it draws specific application about the value and belief dimensions of their specific context. I have found that many practicing educators identify with the way the theoretical framework explains how roles and institutional pressures constrain or confer individual autonomy and how collective participation is deemed either essential or marginal to effective work in schools.

Key Strategies to Improve Schools: How to Apply Them Contextually (Harris, 2005) is designed to help practicing educators understand the grid and group make-up of their particular school in order to employ specific school improvement strategies. Those in the day-to-day world of schooling can see that, although the dynamics of human life are highly variable, when grid and group coalesce over time, certain themes and dominant patterns of practice tend to define a particular setting. The structure and vernacular inherent in grid and group theory help educators recognize and clarify the dissonance and complexity of everyday life in educational settings.

Utilization of Another Theoretical Framework

I have considered and used one other framework in my research, Wallace's (1970, 1979) typology for revitalization movements. Anthropologist and historian Anthony Wallace (1956) developed a structure for understanding stages of acculturation under the influence of technological change. Wallace describes these stages in terms of cultural revitalization. A revitalization movement is a "deliberate, organized, conscious effort by members of a group to create a new culture" (Wallace, 1956, p. 265).

These movements are reactionary and often begin with discontented cultural members, because traditional institutions are unable to adapt and respond to social changes. The process stages of a revitalization movement are

I. Steady State
II. Period of Increased Individual Stress
III. Period of Cultural Distortion
IV. Period of Revitalization
    1. Mazeway (Worldview) Reformulation
    2. Communication
    3. Organization
    4. Adaptation
    5. Cultural Transformation
    6. Routinization
V. New Steady State

I have used Wallace's (1956) frame in two research endeavors. The first applied his concepts of revitalization movements to the evolving field of educational administration (Burlingame & Harris, 1998). The purpose was to demonstrate how Wallace's revitalization movement is a better frame than Kuhn's (1962) notion of paradigm shift, which is often used to explain the cultural changes in educational administration during the last century. In that article, we made reference to the fact that Douglas's (1982) typology could also add significant insight into how pressures influenced evolutionary transformations in leadership thought over the past 100 years.

The second undertaking explained technology adaptation in variant organizational cultures (Stansberry, Haulmark, & Harris, 2001). The twofold purpose was to demonstrate complementariness between Douglas's typology and Wallace's stages, as well as to reinforce Wallace's stages by analyzing them according to grid and group dimensions.

In Stansberry et al. (2001), we used both Douglas's (1982) framework and Wallace's (1956) stages. The dual employment of the frameworks allowed us to detail the stages of technology adaptation as well as explore the social barriers and pressures that affected those stages. Moreover, Douglas offered a means to compare and contrast significant features of the environments through the process of each cultural stage.

Free Response

Social anthropology, the study of human beings, their group relationships, and cultural forms, is where educators first borrowed conceptualizations to explain school culture. Schools are social organizations, dynamic organisms whose effectiveness is often influenced by cultural forms. Douglas's (1982) theoretical framework has deepened my understanding of and helped explain the complexities of human dynamics.

As mentioned, when I discovered Douglas's typology, I was reluctant to extensively use the framework. To my knowledge at the time, theoretical frameworks were utilized predominantly in quantitative, not qualitative, studies. The rage in qualitative research was grounded, ex post facto theory, not a priori theory.

Grounded theory is still an important feature of qualitative inquiry. Many novice researchers desiring to use qualitative methodology, however, lack the experience and preparation necessary to erect theoretical constructions from the ground up and are unfamiliar with the complexities of ex post facto theory development.

Theoretical Frameworks and Metaphor

Theoretical frameworks help shape and direct a study as well as offer means to build upon and link a study to the broader body of literature. Morgan (1997) offers a useful comparison of theory with the notion of metaphor. Metaphor is used to understand one frame of reference with another.

For instance, when we say, "he is as strong as a bull," we relate muscular characteristics of a bull to those of a person. This relational comparison offers both insight and distortion. The bull metaphor evokes images of strength, power, and robustness. Metaphor, however, can also distort the fact that the person may possibly also be slothful or overweight. To carry the idea further, to say "he is bullheaded," suggests new meaning altogether. Like theory, metaphor evokes ways of thinking and seeing, which shape our perceptions of reality.

Morgan's (1997) *theory as metaphor* premise has important implications for qualitative researchers. Theoretical frames, like metaphors, can offer valuable insight to a study and, at the same time, be restrictive, biased, and potentially misleading. In this sense, a theoretical frame is inherently paradoxical. In reference to similar paradoxical aspects of metaphor, Morgan (1997) explains: "It can create powerful insights that also become distortions, as the way of seeing created through a metaphor becomes a way of *not* seeing" (p. 5).

Also implied in the theory-metaphor assertion is that no single theoretical framework will ever offer a flawlessly clear view of any studied phenomena. A theoretical frame will highlight certain interpretations, but will also force other interpretations into the background. Nonetheless, qualitative researchers should not be dissuaded from using theory. Rather, as Morgan (1997) further elaborates on metaphor, "the challenge is to be skilled in the art of using metaphor: to find fresh ways of seeing, understanding, and shaping situations that we want to organize or manage" (p. 6).

Theoretical frameworks can be extremely helpful. In qualitative inquiry, the consideration should not be whether or not to use a theoretical frame, but rather, as Wolcott (1995) reminds, *how* and *when* theory can be best utilized in a study.

Focusing on One Theoretical Framework

In the seminary I attended, I often heard the adage: "Deepen your message before broadening your ministry." I have found this advice to be beneficial in many areas of life, including academe. To improve and deepen my research, teaching, and service activities, I have explored and employed one primary theoretical frame. Douglas's (1982) typology has become the lens, the organizing system through which I view school culture, as well as prioritize and integrate all aspects of work. It has allowed me to, in essence, deepen my message as well as offer language to communicate that message to a broad audience.

I have been, and continue to be, both student and teacher of grid and group typology. Many topics, such as teachers' voice, shared decision making, site-based management, and technology adaptation in educational systems have been explained via grid and group vernacular. For instance, cultural theory has been useful in seeking explanations to problems concerning

- why some educational practices are successful in some contexts and not successful in others; and
- how faculty and administrators from various educational environments can attend the exact same seminars and workshops, yet return to their respective settings and apply interventions in wildly variant ways.

Many courses I teach deal with some aspect of organizational theory, leadership, or qualitative research methods. I integrate grid and group in course content in a variety of ways, such as

- demonstrating the interrelationship of situational leadership and an environment's grid and group composition,
- allowing students to critique either work I have done in the area of cultural theory or an idea that could affect leadership practice,
- comparing Douglas's (1982) concepts with classical organizational theory or systems theory, and
- expanding the notion of theory use in qualitative research.

My service and consulting activities include many of Douglas's (1982) concepts, especially

- comparing an organization's grid and group composition with individual members' social game,
- emphasizing the contextualization of school improvement strategies, and
- demonstrating how variant grid and group orientations can result in conflict in educational settings.

I am, as all educators are, in the business of making sense of things. Douglas's (1982) typology of grid and group has given me direction, structure, and a holistic, integrated sense of my research teaching and service activities. It has helped me to see how concepts and actions make sense and sometimes "fit together."

I realize, however, that this notion of "fitting together" can also be a pitfall. We cannot always comprehend how all variables correlate. A qualitative researcher learns to live with a certain degree of ambiguity in his or her research endeavors. Grid and group theory functions as a useful *guide* to inform and clarify, not determine and coerce. In using Douglas's (1982) theoretical frame, I strive continually to make the crucial distinction between understanding how some things *might* fit and insisting that everything *does* fit in the theoretical frame.

Although my focus has been primarily on one typology, I realize that no single theoretical framework offers a flawless, universal view of the world. If a perfect framework did exist, my own biases, imperfections, and reality constructions would distort the research process, anyway.

Notes

1. In those studies, specific research topics included: decentralization, shared leadership, teachers' voice, instructional technology adaptation, inclusion, application of school improvement strategies, and other areas dealing with school leadership. A central, two-fold assumption in all these studies is that organizational culture

exerts a powerful force on its members and activities; and understanding an environment's interconnected roles, rules, and relationships requires a framework that considers and explains the pressures and dynamics of culture.

2. In *Doing Naturalistic Inquiry* (Erlandson, Harris, Skipper, & Allen, 1993), we detail methodological steps of selected case studies.

3. In Douglas's (1982) treatise, a fifth alternative, "the hermit," is presented. Hermits live out the social game of total self-reliance and separation from all group interaction (i.e., zero grid, zero group). Thus far, I have not used this category in research, as my unit of analysis is typically school organizations rather than individuals, per se. For an understanding of the hermit lifestyle in grid and group theory, I direct the reader to Ellis's (1993) *American Political Cultures* and Thompson, Ellis, and Wildavsky's (1990) *Cultural Theory*.

4. In *Key Strategies*, I also use sports illustrations to explain the variant social classification inherent in grid/group analysis.

5. I use the terms "prevailing mindset" and "social game" interchangeably. Both refer to Douglas's important notion of "cultural bias," which concerns interpreting and judging phenomena in terms particular to one's own culture. People of a culture tend to make assumptions about conventions, including conventions of language, dress, customs, and other cultural symbols. Often they can mistake these notions for universal norms or laws of nature. Social games are much more than games or parts in a play. They reflect a particular bias that we have about the right way to live our collective life. S. G. Lingenfelter (1992) offers an expanded explanation of the term social games, which is, in part, below:

> Each of the social games has far reaching implications for our life and worldview. . . . The structure of a social game leads participants to adopt a related set of assumptions and values that are elaborated in their worldview. . . . Each social game has a peculiar cultural bias, and only one bias can be right. (p. 35)

6. I offer a detailed discussion of the evolution of Douglas's theory in *Toward a Grid and Group Interpretation of School Culture* (Harris, 1995). For further reading on the subject, I direct the reader to Thompson, Ellis, and Wildavsky (1990), Gross and Rayner (1985), Lingenfelter (1992), and Spikard (1989).

7. I detail and evaluate these three approaches in both publications cited (Harris, 1995, 2005). Culture can be explained from a variety of vantage points. The reader may obtain further insight from the following works: Marshall Sashkin and Herbert Walberg's, (1993) *Educational Leadership and School Culture;* Tomoko Hamada and Willis Sibley's (1993) *Anthropological Perspectives on Organizational Culture;* Lee Bolman and Terrence Deal's (2003) *Reframing Organizations: Artistry, Choice, and Leadership;* and Sonja Sackmann's (1991) *Cultural Knowledge in Organizations: Exploring the Collective Mind.* Sackmann explains cultural perspectives in terms of (1) holistic, (2) variable, and (3) cognitive. She also reminds the reader that "the boundaries between these three perspectives are not completely clear-cut. Overlaps exist . . ." (p. 18), and application depends heavily on purpose and context.

References

Bernstein, B. (1964). Social class, speech systems and psychotherapy. *British Journal of Sociology, 15*(1), 54–64.

Bernstein, B. (1970). *Class, codes, and control: Toward a sociological theory of speech.* London: Routledge and Kegan Paul.

Bolman, L. G., & Deal, T. E. (2003). *Reframing organizations: Artistry, choice, and leadership* (3rd ed.). San Francisco: Jossey-Bass.

Burlingame, M., & Harris, E. L. (1998). Changes in the field of educational administration in the United States from 1967 to 1996 as a revitalized movement. *Journal of the British Educational Management & Administration Society, 26*(1), 21–34.

Carter, T. L. (2002). *Paul and the power of sin: Redefining 'beyond the pale.'* Cambridge, UK: Cambridge University Press.

Caulkins, D. D. (1999). Is Mary Douglas's grid/group analysis useful for cross-cultural research? *Cross-Cultural Research, 33*(1), 108–128.

Deal, T. E. (1993). The culture of schools. In M. Sashkin & H. J. Walberg (Eds.), *Educational leadership and school culture* (pp. 3–18). Berkeley, CA: McCutchan.

Deal, T. E., & Kennedy, A. (1982). *Corporate cultures: The rites and rituals of corporate life.* Reading, MA: Addison-Wesley.

Deal, T. E., & Peterson, K. D. (1990). *The principal's role in shaping school culture.* Washington, DC: U.S. Department of Education, Office of Educational Research and Improvement.

Douglas, M. (1970). *Natural symbols: Explorations in cosmology* (1st ed.). New York: Random House.

Douglas, M. (1973). *Natural symbols: Explorations in cosmology* (2nd ed.). New York: Basic Books.

Douglas, M. (1982). *In the active voice.* London: Routledge and Kegan Paul.

Douglas, M., & Wildavsky, A. (1982). *Risk and culture.* Berkeley, CA: University of California Press.

Ellis, R. J. (1993). *American political cultures.* New York: Oxford University Press.

Erlandson, D. A., Harris, E. L., Skipper, B. L., & Allen, S. D. (1993). *Doing naturalistic inquiry: A guide to methods.* Newbury Park, CA: Sage.

Getzels, J. B., & Guba, E. G. (1957, Winter). Social behavior and the administrative process. *The School Review, 65,* 423–441.

Goodlad, J. I. (1984). *A place called school: Prospects for the future.* New York: McGraw-Hill.

Gross, J., & Rayner, S. (1985). *Measuring culture: A paradigm for the analysis of social organization.* New York: Columbia University Press.

Hamada, T., & Sibley, W. E. (Eds.). (1993). *Anthropological perspectives on organizational culture.* Lanham, MD: University Press of America.

Harris, E. L. (1993). [Review of the book *Transforming culture: A challenge for Christian mission*]. *Criswell Theological Journal, 5*(6), 159–160.

Harris, E. L. (1995). Toward a grid and group interpretation of school culture. *Journal of School Leadership, 5,* 617–646.

Harris, E. L. (2005). *Key strategies to improve schools: How to apply them contextually.* Lanham, MD: Rowman & Littlefield.

Hendry, J. (1999). Cultural theory and contemporary management organization. *Human Relations, 52*(5), 557–577.

Kuhn, T. S. (1962). *The structure of scientific revolutions.* Chicago: University of Chicago Press.

Lightfoot, S. L. (1983). *The good high school: Portraits of character and culture.* New York: Basic Books.

Lincoln, Y. S., & Guba, E. G. (1985). *Naturalistic inquiry.* Beverly Hills, CA: Sage.

Lingenfelter, S. G. (1992). *Transforming culture: A challenge for Christian mission.* Grand Rapids, MI: Baker Book House.

Mars, G., & Nicod, M. (1983). *The world of waiters.* London: Allen and Unwin.

Merriam, S. B. (2001). *The new update on adult learning theory: New directions for adult and continuing education* (No. 89). San Francisco: Jossey-Bass.

Morgan, G. (1997). *Images of organization* (2nd ed.). Thousand Oaks, CA: Sage.

Owens, R. G. (2004). *Organizational behavior in education: Adaptive leadership and school reform* (8th ed.). Boston: Allyn & Bacon.

Peters, I. J., & Waterman, R. H. (1988). *In search of excellence: Lessons from America's best-run companies.* New York: Warner Books.

Rayner, S. (1984). Disagreeing about risk: The institutional cultures of risk management and planning for future generations. In S. G. Hadden (Ed.), *Risk analysis, institutions, and public policy* (pp. 150–169), Port Washington, NY: Associated Faculty Press.

Sackmann, S. A. (1991). *Cultural knowledge in organizations: Exploring the collective mind.* Newbury Park, CA: Sage.

Sashkin, M. J., & Walberg, H. J. (Eds.). (1993). *Educational leadership and school culture.* Berkeley, CA: McCutchan.

Schein, E. N. (1985). *Organizational culture and leadership.* San Francisco: Jossey-Bass.

Schwarz, M., & Thompson, M. (1990). *Divided we stand: Redefining politics, technology, and social choice.* Philadelphia: University of Pennsylvania Press.

Spikard, J. V. (1989). A guide to Mary Douglas's three versions of grid/group theory. *Sociological Analysis, 50*(2), 151–170.

Stansberry, S. L., & Harris, E. L. (2005, Spring). Understanding the interrelationship of instructional technology use and organizational culture: A case study of a veterinary medicine college. *Journal of Veterinary Medical Education, 32*(1), 25–37.

Stansberry, S. L., Haulmark, M., & Harris, E. L. (2001, November). *A grid and group explanation of higher education faculty use of instructional technology.* Paper presented at the Rocky Mountain Educational Research Association Conference, Las Cruces, NM.

Thompson, M., Ellis, R., & Wildavsky, A. (1990). *Cultural theory.* Boulder, CO: Westview.

Wallace, A. F. G. (1956). Revitalization movements. *American Anthropologist, 58,* 264–281.

Wallace, A. F. G. (1970). *Culture and personality* (2nd ed.). New York: Random House.

Wallace, A. F. G. (1979). Revitalizing movements. In W. A. Lessa & E. Z. Vogt (Eds.), *Reader in comparative religion: An anthropological approach* (pp. 421–429). New York: Harper & Row.

Wildavsky, A., & Dake, K. (1990). Theories of risk perception: Who fears what and why? *Daedalus, 119*(4), 41–60.

Wolcott, H. F. (1995). *The art of fieldwork*. London: AltaMira.

9

Adapting Bourdieu's Field Theory to Explain Decision-Making Processes in Educational Policy

Carol A. Mutch

Introduction

This chapter outlines the way a particular theoretical framework—that of field theory—has come to permeate my research and thinking to the point where I constantly visualize settings, from everyday encounters to complex power plays, in terms of field, capital, and *habitus*. This chapter will outline how I have adapted and used Pierre Bourdieu's framework and I will discuss several pieces of research in which I have used the social field model, to illustrate the usefulness of this theory to my areas of interest and research. I will conclude with an analysis of the model's strengths and limitations and indicate aspects of the theory still to be explored.

An Overview of the Study: *Social Studies in the New Zealand Curriculum*

The main study I will describe (Mutch, 2004a) focuses on the writing of the highly controversial 1997 social studies document, *Social Studies in the*

New Zealand Curriculum. In this study, I was able to supplement historical research and document analysis with a series of semi-structured interviews with curriculum writers, ministerially appointed advisers, reference groups, and social studies educators all involved in the development process. My aim was to document the path that this document took before it reached completion. This particular curriculum development was highly convoluted and contested. The document was fully rewritten three times before all parties were satisfied. I saw this development of interest not only to the New Zealand educational community but also to scholars interested in wider issues of curriculum development. The social field model allowed me to express the themes of my study—context, complexity, and contestation—in a vivid manner. I reconfigured the idea of a social field as a model of "curriculum construction as a social field" and developed a diagrammatic representation in which the players were portrayed along a "line of tension," vying for control over the object of the process—in this case, determining the contents of the social studies curriculum.

Briefly (as it is explained in more detail in the next section), a "social field" needs to have clearly delineated boundaries. Each setting of the field in this study has a temporal boundary, a particular purpose to be achieved in that time frame, and a recognizable set of players. Players use "capital" to gain access to and to position themselves on the field.[1] *"Habitus"* determines the rules by which the game is played and the way players communicate and interact. The time frame for the first setting—the writing of the first version of *Social Studies in the New Zealand Curriculum* (Ministry of Education, 1994)—was from late 1993 until late 1995. The purpose was to prepare a new social studies curriculum for the compulsory schooling sector in New Zealand and the players included those who set, monitored, completed, and evaluated the task. The second setting of this field occurred in 1996 (Ministry of Education, 1996). The task this time was to revise the newly published curriculum and the players had similar roles but the field included new individuals holding those roles. The final setting was 1997 (Ministry of Education, 1997)—the task to prepare a version of the social studies curriculum that would meet favor from both sides of the hotly contested debate. Again, there were similar roles but changed membership. The external forces at work were historical, political, economic, and social. The notion of curriculum presage (Print, 1993) highlights the personal, professional, and wider social and political influences that shape the thoughts and actions of curriculum developers. For example, the writers of the first version were influenced by a range of historical forces—New Zealand's liberal progressive educational history, prior processes of curriculum development, and the legacy of influential educationalists. In more recent history (since 1984, in particular), there has been a strong economically driven political influence over curriculum decision making. In the New Zealand context, the treasury produced lengthy briefing papers for governments in the 1980s, giving their suggestions for improving educational outcomes and efficiencies. Socially and culturally, the writers—especially of the first (Ministry of Education, 1994) and final (Ministry of Education, 1997) versions—were influenced by their responsibilities under the Treaty of Waitangi (the recognition of Maori, the indigenous people, as equal partners), their awareness of the growing multicultural population, the importance of gender issues in education, and their commitment to the need for equal educational opportunities and outcomes for all sectors of society.

On the field, the major groups vied for control over curriculum content. The Ministry of Education, reporting to the politically appointed minister of education, was one powerful group. Educational institutions and organizations of varying kinds were also influential groups—but often with widely divergent factions. Smaller players included the various social and political lobby groups, the strongest at this time being the Business Roundtable. The major line of tension was political—between the supporters of new right economic policies and those opposing this ideology, described in this study as the liberal left.

Version 1: *Social Studies in the New Zealand Curriculum* (Draft)

In 1993, the Ministry of Education called together a Policy Advisory Group to set the parameters for the development of *Social Studies in the New Zealand Curriculum* (Ministry of Education, 1994). Two conveners were then appointed to set up a writing team.

At this point, the notions of field, capital, and *habitus* allow important aspects to be elaborated upon. Who was granted entry to the field and why? Which ideological positions were favored and why? Who was excluded and why? What particular capital did members bring and how was this valued? Once the field was set, how was consensus achieved and what factors kept dissension at bay? What forces from outside this micro-field influenced what happened within?

Figure 9.1 shows, by placement of the main players, that the main line of tension was between the Ministry of Education and the writers. The ministry wished to prepare a curriculum that would meet the needs of all sectors of society but, in particular, would be in line with the pervasive ideology that focused on improving New Zealand's economic competitiveness. The writing team, on the other hand, represented the other end of the ideological

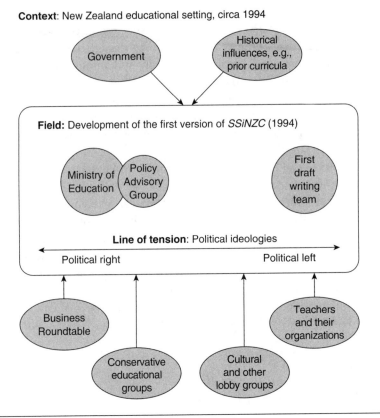

Context: New Zealand educational setting, circa 1994

Figure 9.1   Setting of the field for the writing of the first version of *Social Studies in the New Zealand Curriculum* (*SSiNZC*, 1994).

continuum, coming from liberal-progressive, feminist, critical, postcolonial, and postmodern theoretical perspectives.

Personnel within the ministry began as the most powerful group. They selected the Policy Advisory Group and the successful proposal team. Control over the framing of communication resided with the ministry. Every working draft was reviewed by the ministry's Contract Review Committee and the Policy Advisory Group. Members of the first version writing team proved to be equally powerful, however, in promoting the version of social studies closest to their views of current New Zealand society and best practice in social studies pedagogy. The writing team conveners took great care to select a writing team that was culturally inclusive, gender inclusive, and representative of location, discipline, and sector. Entry to the field was granted, therefore, to people who met these inclusive criteria. Capital included attributes such as actual classroom experience, expertise in a relevant area, research in related fields, the ability to work on a team, and particular value was placed on knowledge of Maori culture and protocol.

Version 2: *Social Studies in the New Zealand Curriculum* (Revised Draft)

After extensive trials in schools, public submissions, and media debate, this second version of *Social Studies in the New Zealand Curriculum* (Ministry of Education, 1996) was withdrawn. There were strong critiques from conservative and business groups. In terms of framing the communication, the ministry regained control, directing all feedback on the document to be forwarded to them to be analyzed by their appointee. In response to the feedback, the ministry appointed a single writer to amend the first draft. Again field theory helps describe how the field came to be set differently, how the power balance had altered, why the consultative, collaborative model was discarded, and the capital that was most highly valued in the new setting. In this setting of the field (see Figure 9.2), we can see that the ministry is still powerful but the new writer has entered the field. The original writers have, however, been marginalized, and the Policy Advisory Group (PAG) has minimal influence.

The newly commissioned writer was, at that time, an educational consultant who brought capital such as her considerable experience in curriculum development, and was seen by the ministry as being able to provide an objective stance in relation to the revision process. As a newcomer to the setting of the field, she was not bound by the *habitus* of the previous writing team and could, therefore, set up her own procedures and consultation process. The Business Roundtable also entered the field of play. Their education watchdog group, the Education Forum, ran a highly visible campaign to discredit the first version of the curriculum. As stated earlier, the first version (Ministry of Education, 1994) writing team and the Policy Advisory Group were sidelined.

The publication of the second version released a backlash of criticism, most notable of which was a well-known social studies educator taking a case to the Race Relations Conciliator on the grounds that the second version was racist in its portrayal of Maori history and culture.

Version 3: *Social Studies in the New Zealand Curriculum* (Final)

As outlined earlier, the second version of *Social Studies in the New Zealand Curriculum* (Ministry of Education, 1996) was not to be the last. This time

Context: New Zealand educational setting, circa 1996

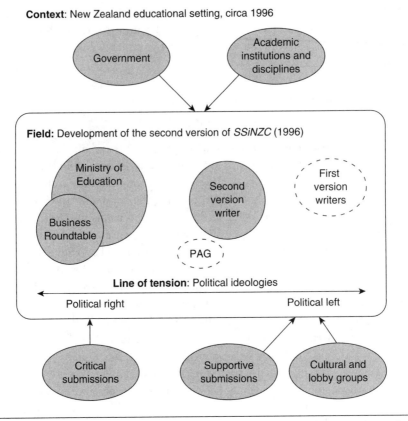

Figure 9.2   Setting of the field for the writing of the second version of *Social Studies in the New Zealand Curriculum* (*SSiNZC*, 1996).

Note: PAG = Policy Advisory Group.

there was more dissatisfaction from the liberal left (especially teachers; teacher unions; subject associations, such as the Federation of Social Studies Associations; and more liberal-minded academics). Members of the Business Roundtable, however, were still not content—they wanted social studies removed from the curriculum altogether. The Ministry of Education convened a third writing team. The version this team compiled was to become the final one (Ministry of Education, 1997). How does field theory help us interpret this new setting of the field? What capital was valued this time? What was the *habitus* of the new group? Who was included and who was excluded and why? Figure 9.3 shows the changes in field placement.

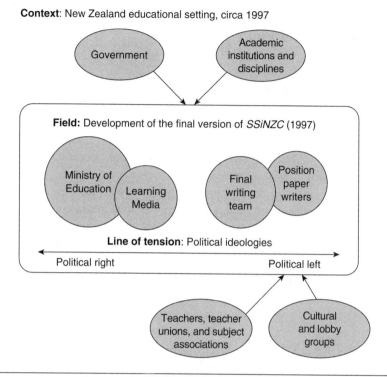

Figure 9.3   Setting of the field for the writing of the final version of *Social Studies in the New Zealand Curriculum* (*SSiNZC*; 1997).

The capital that the next writing team brought was that most had been involved in the first version (Ministry of Education, 1994) or later consultation, that is, they were knowledgeable about social studies and they understood the nature of the task. They also provided broader representation in the way that had been so highly valued in the composition of the first writing team. The *habitus* of the new team came, therefore, to mirror that of the first version writing team.

The internal and external influences have changed in this setting of the field. Teachers' voices are stronger and the Business Roundtable has been removed, but the ministry's publications branch, Learning Media, which attempted to exercise editorial control over both the content and format, has appeared. In the end, however, the writers claimed victory over the framing of communication and control over the object of the task—determining the content and format of the social studies curriculum.

The Theoretical Framework:
Bourdieu's Social Field Theory

The model of a social field, as I have used and adapted it over the years, is synthesized from a selection of theoretical literature. The notions of a social field, capital, and *habitus* are taken from Bourdieu (1990, 1993, 1999; Bourdieu & Passeron, 1977). The notion of framing is taken from Bernstein (1971, 2000). I have also, at times, used the notions of "insiders" and "outsiders" from Lave and Wenger (1991) and discourse (for example, from Foucault, 1981). The idea of using Bourdieu's notions of field, capital, and *habitus* in relation to educational policy is taken from Ladwig (1994), but I have extended this notion of the social field and adapted and refined Bourdieu's notions, in particular, to explicitly delineate positions and actions within this field.

A "social field" is similar to a field of play. Bourdieu (cited in Earle, 1999, p. 185), in fact, describes *habitus* as "what in sport one calls a feel for the game" and in Bouveresse (1999) as "*le sens du jeu*," so this analogy is not inappropriate. Bourdieu (1993), describing it as game and the participants as players, writes,

> The new players have to pay an entry fee which consists in recognition of the value of the game (selection and co-option always pay great attention to the indices of commitment to the game, investment in it) and in (practical) knowledge of the principles of the functioning of the game. (p. 74)

The field is a common ground on which the action occurs and this ground has boundaries where entry is blocked by existing holders of power. Within the field, players have positions that have both roles to be enacted and status carried with them. These positions, however, can be challenged at any time. There is a network of negotiated actions and relations between positions, and the players (be they individuals or institutions) vie for possession of, or influence over, the object at stake (for example, control of educational policy making or curriculum content). How the players are invited to participate, or allowed access, uses the notion of "capital." This capital is specific to the field and could be social, political, economic, cultural, or symbolic. Who has what capital, and in what amounts, sets up the hierarchically distributed power structure. As Bourdieu (1993) explains,

> The structure of the field is a state of the power relations among the agents or institutions engaged in the struggle, or, to put it another way, a state of the distribution of the specific capital which has been accumulated in the course of previous struggles and which orients subsequent strategies. (p. 73)

Habitus is a set of dispositions that are commonly held by members of a social group and these subjectively created attitudes, beliefs, and practices bind the members together so that they can identify and communicate with each other. It also allows them to recognize, and be recognized by, outsiders. As Bourdieu (1990) explains, "*habitus* is an infinite capacity for generating products—thoughts, perceptions, expressions, and actions—whose limits are set by the historically and socially situated conditions of its production" (p. 443). Similarities can be seen between Bourdieu's concepts of field, capital, and *habitus* and those of Bernstein (1971, 2000), who refers to the pedagogical relationship in similar terms. He talks of the places in which action takes place as sites that are identifiable by their distinct boundaries and practices. He also talks of the frame of the relationship. This determines the selection, organization, timing, pacing, and direction of the transmission of information. "Framing is about *who* controls *what*. . . . Framing is concerned with *how* meanings are to be put together, the forms by which they are to be made public, and the nature of the social relationships that go with it" (Bernstein, 2000, p. 12; emphases in the original). The elements of my adaptation of the model of a social field (see Figure 9.4) are as follows:

- The social field model is used to portray the complex, contextual, and contested interactions at a particular time or during a particular process—for example, in the realms of educational policy or curriculum construction.
- A social field can operate at a macro-level (for example, in national and international contexts) or at a micro-level (within a particular group or setting) and there will be overt and covert links to wider social contexts and related fields.
- The field sits within a context. The context needs to be adequately described. What are the historical, social, cultural, political, or economic factors that have led to this setting of the field?
- The field also needs to be clearly described. What are its boundaries? Who is allowed access? Who determines who has access? What is the capital that the players bring? How does this allow them entry to or position them on the field?
- The reason for the field's creation needs to be explained. What is the purpose that brings this setting of the field into being? What is expressed as being "at stake" both explicitly and implicitly?
- How the field operates also needs explanation. What is its "*habitus*"? How are rules made? How are decisions made? How are conflicts handled?
- The positioning of the players on the field needs to be described. How do they position themselves in relation to one another? Where are the alliances? Who are the players (or factions) in the stronger or weaker positions? How might these positions change? How might these positions be displayed along a continuum or line of tension?

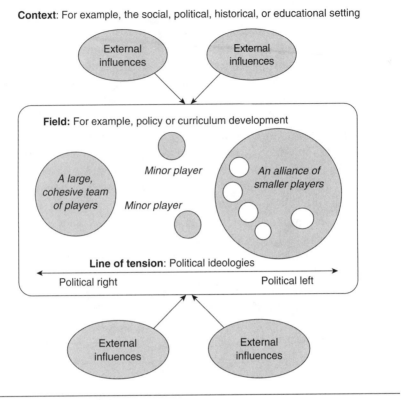

Figure 9.4   A generic diagram of a social field.

My Introduction to the Theoretical Framework

Bourdieu's field theory comes from the discipline of sociology and Bourdieu, himself, was chair of sociology at the Collège de France, although he is often considered to have been a philosopher (see, for example, Shusterman, 1999). I took sociology in my undergraduate degree in the early 1970s and became familiar with the work of Durkheim and Weber and terms such as culture, society, and role. Later as a teacher in schools, I eagerly embraced the 1977 New Zealand social studies curriculum, which was strongly influenced by the "new social studies" movement in the United States (especially *Man: A Course of Study*, Bruner, 1966, and the work of Taba, Durkin, Fraenkel, and McNaughton, 1971). In the United Kingdom the work of Lawton, Campbell, and Burkett (1971) was influential. I taught the themes of cultural difference, interaction, social control, and social change. In the 1980s, my career path turned from being a teacher to being a teacher educator.

As I upgraded my qualifications, I was introduced to critical theory, with its emphasis on who gains and holds the power in social and political interactions and how this is used to advantage some groups and disadvantage others. As I was teaching social studies education, it seemed logical that I should review these theoretical concepts and their relevance to the development of the social studies curriculum. I first met Bourdieu's theory in 1996 when conducting historical research into the early development of the New Zealand curriculum, and social studies, in particular (see Mutch, 1998). I was looking for a theoretical explanation for the tensions within society that seemed to pull education in conflicting directions. A colleague gave me a copy of an article by James Ladwig (1994), an Australian educational researcher, in which he proposed a model of "educational policy as a social field" based on Bourdieu's notion of a social or cultural field. Ladwig claimed that the educational reforms of the 1980s revealed the maturation of educational policy as a social field with its own autonomy and rewards. I read and pondered how this might relate to my study. I went on to read some of Bourdieu's work in more detail (for example, Bourdieu, 1993; Bourdieu & Passeron, 1977) and then experimented with these ideas by representing the "field" two dimensionally and the groups on it diagrammatically. In my initial study, field theory allowed me to show how groups placed themselves on the field in relation to each other and how this changed over time. I could then theorize around the changing fortunes of the various groups and the factors that influenced these changes.

The first study I undertook using this model as an analytic framework (Mutch, 1998) examined educational decision making in the early days of New Zealand's formal education system (1814–1877). As this was my first attempt at using a visual portrayal of the model, I had not yet developed it as thoroughly as in the explanation earlier in this chapter, but the two settings of the social field in this study showed clearly how the power and influence of particular groups changed over time, and, in this particular case, how the number of players and complexity of their interactions also increased over time.

My next piece of historical research (Mutch, 2000) looked at particular developments in social studies and used the development of the 1977 social studies syllabus as a case study of how individuals within a curriculum writing team similarly positioned themselves and sought to keep their own agendas to the fore. This study (Mutch, 2000) drew mainly upon a report by Jim Lewis (1980) and focused on a social field at a micro-level. Lewis was a key participant in the writing of the 1977 social studies syllabus (Department of Education, 1977). His knowledge of the participants, their roles, their influence (and factors that had influenced them), and of the lines of communication and interaction provided an illuminating insight into the inner workings of the group. Exploring the social field at a micro-level highlighted the hierarchical distribution of people within a narrower context. It also showed more clearly the outside influences, an idea I was to explore more fully in later research.

Effects of the Framework
on the Research I Undertake

My most recent research (Mutch, 2004b) has moved away from social studies education back to educational policy making in a more general sense but in contemporary settings. As part of a wider international comparative study of educational policymakers and their conceptions of education for the future, I interviewed elite policymakers in New Zealand. In this case, I did not attempt to find alternative models, as I knew the social field model would be adaptable for my purposes, and, indeed, the project was conceived and the interview questions framed with such an analysis in mind. The interview questions referred to such concepts as power, influence, and control. In this case, when conducting the analysis, I returned to the earlier "educational policy as a social field" form and portrayed the findings without a line of tension. Outlining the study here shows how the concepts of social field, capital, and *habitus* were to the fore all the way through the project. The context for this study is temporally located in New Zealand in 2003, the year the interviews were conducted. Influences from outside include the effects of the prior decades of educational reforms and the influence that these reforms are still having nationally and worldwide.

In this research, the government of the day was politically center-left. In the field diagram (see Figure 9.5), the government is shown alongside the Ministry of Education (its bureaucratic machine) as the key policymakers, with the secretary for education as the intersection between the two organizations. The other stakeholders in the process—the community and the education sector—are shown as broken lines to represent the fact that they are loose amalgamations of various groups whose members are sometimes at odds with each other. Research providers are shown as an emerging group that policymakers saw as becoming a more integral part of the process.

In terms of the capital that granted access to the field at the time, the government had access, and pole position, due to the public mandate that it had through democratic elections. The personnel at the ministry were granted access to the field as they were employed as public servants to carry out the government's wishes, but at the same time they were able to exert some influence of their own. The community was entitled to a say because it elected the government. The education sector's relationship to policy making was by

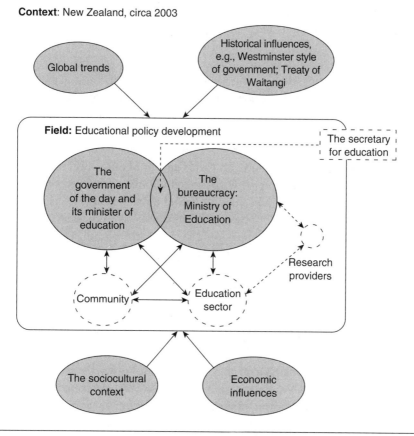

Figure 9.5   Educational policy in New Zealand as a social field.

virtue of the expectation that it would be the day-to-day implementers of the policy. The research organizations gained access because of their emerging relationship to educational policy. Within the community sector, particular individuals or groups had a place because of their relationship to other stakeholders, because of their lobbying ability, or because of the government's wish for representative consultation and involvement.

Habitus, which ensures that players are able to remain on the field and adequately communicate with other participants, is related in this setting to knowing what, knowing who, and knowing how. First, *knowing what* includes knowing the legislation, knowing the channels for participating in policy making, and understanding the process and its variations and vagaries. Second, *knowing who* means getting beneath the surface and knowing who the "movers and shakers" are and who to talk to to make your voice count. Third, is *knowing how*: how to approach the right people; how to use the submissions process to your advantage; and how to keep abreast of current initiatives and emerging issues.

The final aspect is the framing of communications. The arrows on the diagram represent the flow of communication. Although shown here as a reciprocal flow, depending on the times, the circumstances, and the issues, this can vary. Sometimes, the communication can cease altogether and sometimes alliances can form that effectively undermine or silence other voices. At other times, less prominent voices can make themselves heard.

This study (Mutch, 2004b) shows how the social field framework can underpin research from beginning to end. The aim of this aspect in the larger project was to ask quite explicitly for the elite policymakers to outline the process as they saw it, to indicate who played a part in these decisions, and where they felt the balance of power lay. The questions were framed with the outcome of displaying the findings on a social field diagram. How it might look and what adaptations might be necessary were not yet determined, but the selection of the topic, the questions to be asked, and the analytic framework to be employed all arose out of my interest in the social field model.

Incorporating Other Theoretical Frameworks

Being a qualitative researcher in the main, I do not always start out with a theoretical framework—a theoretical position, yes, best described as tending toward social constructionism, that is, the belief that our versions of the world are socially, culturally, and historically constructed and situated (Burr, 1995). Once I have gathered my data, extracted my themes, and begun the analysis, I usually ask that typically qualitative question, "What does this remind me of?" I have not always used social field theory in answer to this question.

In the study of the 1997 social studies curriculum described earlier (Mutch, 2004a), I explored a range of other theoretical models—Walker's (1972, cited in Print, 1993) naturalistic curriculum development model, Marsh's (1997) stakeholder classification, and McGee's (1997) dynamic curriculum development model. These all illuminated *parts* of the process, but none allowed me to explore and express the positioning and repositioning of the key players and the influences on them and their decisions in the way the Bourdieu model did, especially given the nature of the research topic. When I wanted to explain the curriculum development process, and why the Bourdieu model faltered in this particular case, I looked at a model that more clearly outlined the steps in the process and hence chose the McGee (1997) model with its situational analysis stage to make my point clearer. When I wanted to show "curriculum presage" (what curriculum developers bring to the process in terms of their beliefs, understandings, and aims), this was where the Walker

(1972, cited in Print, 1993) model proved useful as it outlined the stages of platform, deliberation, and design. When I wanted to specify who the players were that made up the groups, factions, and alliances, I used the Marsh (1997) stakeholder classification as a way of detailing players and their roles. In the end, however, the social field model was the only one that allowed me to adequately describe, analyze, and visually portray the development of *Social Studies in the New Zealand Curriculum* as a highly contested process with constant changes in personnel.

Displaying settings of the field diagrammatically helped to identify changes in the locus of power over time, and to trace the changing fortunes of groups inside and outside the field. A model such as this supports the view of Ozga (2000), who takes "a different more diffuse view of policy as a *process* rather than a product, involving negotiation, contestation, or struggle between different groups who may lie outside the formal machinery of official policy-making" (p. 2). The social field model highlighted the official forces (for example, the Ministry of Education) and the unofficial forces (i.e., the Business Roundtable) that were to impact the process. This model best portrayed the fluidity of individuals and/or groups competing for positions of strength or influence in the decision-making process. In this study, the players were described as using strategies of compromise, contingency, and expediency. The model also allowed me to discuss other themes arising out of the study—those of polarization, factionalization, collaboration, and marginalization.

This model does not always resonate with my research findings and other theories or models may need to be used in its place; but where the research findings show interactions, power plays, tensions, or contested decision making, I find it difficult to go past the concept of a social field. In fact, I now sit in meetings or follow events in the news, viewing them in my head as individuals or groups placing themselves on a particular field. I then watch their strategies to advance their causes, defend their current positions, set up alliances, or discredit other players. I have even tried to explain the notion of a social field to my son who was watching one of those reality television shows where people are left to survive by their wits in some exotic location!

Strengths and Limitations of Bourdieu's Social Field Model

The studies outlined in this chapter (Mutch, 1998, 2000, 2004a, 2004b) show the usefulness and flexibility of the field model for the kinds of research I undertake. One strength of this model, therefore, is that it is not *pre*scriptive; it is *de*scriptive. Rather than telling how things should be done (as in my area where many traditional curriculum development models do), it allows multiple processes and complex interplays to be described. This means that it can be adapted to a range of contexts to explain what is happening internally and externally. The three key elements are very important. The concept of field allows the researcher to detail the context in which the action is taking place and to put boundaries around the place of action. The concept of capital explains who gets to play, why, and how. The concept of *habitus* can be used to describe and analyze the strategies of the players in each particular context.

The model can show a snapshot in time or it can show changes over time. The diagrammatic expression of the model makes the theoretical framework visually clearer and argumentatively stronger. The model can be expanded to include complementary notions such as framing (Bernstein, 1971, 2000) or insiders/outsiders (Lave & Wenger, 1991). The placement on the field can indicate positions and relationships (i.e., ideological stances). The size of the representations can indicate the size (quantitatively) or the strength (qualitatively) of the group on the field. The use of the line of tension allows settings where powerful ideological forces are pitted against each other to be portrayed.

Limitations of the model are that it can appear a little dense and complex at the outset and needs careful explanation—but this is where the diagrammatic version comes into its own. The diagrammatic representation, which I generally find to be a strength, can also be seen as a limitation. It could be seen as too reductionist in that it takes away the "authentic voices" and "rich description" so highly prized by qualitative researchers. It could reduce a whole interview transcript, for example, to a small dot on a diagram. A participant's passionate and emotionally charged story could end up being portrayed as a geometric shape, the complex interactions displayed as an arrow. In order to overcome this concern, it is necessary to support the theorizing with authentic data (excerpts from transcripts, field notes, or documents). It is also important that a reader is convinced that the theorizing is credible, that the researcher has not just selected data that fits the model. The contradictions and anomalies must also be discussed and portrayed. The diagrammatic representation could be considered too static. Shusterman's words (1999, discussing Dyke's assessment of Bourdieu, 1999) could be used to critique my interpretation:

> Bourdieu's theory of the dynamics of *habitus* (not a rigidly fixed or mechanical habit) and of field (not a stationary space but a dynamic field constituted by struggles over changing positions) demonstrates that social structures must be understood not as static, typological and hard-edged but rather as dynamic formations of organized diachronic complexity, poised between stability and change. (p. 8)

Another limitation of the social field model is that it could be seen as too functionalist. Participants are reduced to their roles—their unique individualities and personalities become anonymous. Their words are portrayed as coming from a position rather than from a living, breathing human being. The social field model, especially my variation with the line of tension, can be seen as too polarizing, pitting ideologies against each other. Reducing individuals or groups to positions and then portraying them statically on a diagram sets their stances in concrete, so to speak. The vacillations, waverings, and overlaps as people reconsider and adapt their views and positions cannot be easily shown.

It is also difficult to show the complexities *within* a group or individual (without going into micro-micro-levels). As participants can only be shown once for each setting, their position is determined, placed, and labeled. In real life, people are much more complex and multifaceted than they appear on these field diagrams. Critics of Bourdieu, in fact, raise several of these concerns about Bourdieu's theory as he applies it in his own writing. Margolis (1999) critiques Bourdieu's use of the dualisms and binarisms he sought to challenge. Bohman (1999) finds his explanations "functionalist" and his theory unable to explain "theoretical reflection, cultural conflict, and social change" (pp. 220–228), whereas Butler (1999) claims that Bourdieu privileges the social field in a way that fails to recognize opportunities for social transformation.

Despite these limitations—which must be acknowledged but can be lessened with awareness, careful consideration, and explanation—social field theory has much to offer in terms of portraying complex positioning and interaction. There are also boundless ways this model could be developed. I find the static nature of the presentation limiting and would love to explore computer-generated, three-dimensional moving images. Although technology can do this, the academic world is not yet set up to receive and embrace such nontextual representations as the norm. Within the limitations of two-dimensional portrayal, there are still possible nuances to explore, for example, displaying influential forces on an axis or matrix rather than by a single line. As I re-read Bourdieu, I am struck that there are other concepts that could be included in my model, for example, "cultural production" or "field of reception." For the time being, there is plenty to keep me interested in, and challenged by, the social field model.

Conclusion

In this chapter, I have demonstrated the usefulness of a theoretical model for moving research findings out of the case-bound specifics into broader understandings of human interactions. It is also helpful if the selected model is flexible enough to suit a range of contexts and adaptable enough to include complementary notions from other theorists. In my case, the theory I have chosen to discuss, social field theory (drawing mainly on Bourdieu), has come to influence how I visualize everyday interactions, as well as determining relevant research topics and influencing their design. The three important concepts of field, capital, and *habitus* have helped me to detail the place of action, the players, and their strategies in contested decision-making processes. In this chapter, I have also promoted the usefulness of visual portrayals of complex theories. Although this, and any theory for that matter, has limitations, and in this case the visual portrayal could be seen to exacerbate these, they can be overcome or minimized by the supporting discussion and with sound evidence from the data. For this model, I have suggested the limitations as over-reduction of data; a static representation; a seemingly functionalist approach; the polarization of the forces being displayed; and the inability to show the complexities within players or groups as well as between them.

Finally, I think too often we are frightened of theories (and theorists, especially ones as esteemed as Bourdieu); but I would like to argue that if we use their theories or models with sensitivity, adapting them to suit our purposes while keeping their integrity intact, they are wonderfully illuminating tools. Bourdieu, himself (1992, cited in Webb, Schirato, & Danaher, 2002), has argued about his theories that

> These tools are only visible through the results they yield. . . . The ground for these tools . . . lies in research, in the practical problems and puzzles encountered and generated in the effort to construct a phenomenally diverse set of objects in such a way that they can be treated, thought of, comparatively. (p. 47)

My use of Bourdieu's field theory has certainly been employed within such a spirit of inquiry. Theories are always evolving, and should be tested, adapted, updated, and challenged. This is our contribution as qualitative researchers to understanding and explaining our world in multiple and diverse ways.

Note

1. Although Bourdieu and others speak of being "in" a field, I found that once I had visualized it diagrammatically and compared it to a field of play, in the sense of a game or sport, "on" seemed more appropriate.

References

Bernstein, B. (1971). On the classification and framing of educational knowledge. In M. Young (Ed.), *Knowledge and control* (pp. 79–115). London: Collier-Macmillan.

Bernstein, B. (2000). *Pedagogy, symbolic control and identity: Theory, research and critique.* Lanham, MD: Rowman & Littlefield.

Bohman, J. (1999). Practical reason and cultural constraint: Agency in Bourdieu's theory of practice. In R. Shusterman (Ed.), *Bourdieu: A critical reader* (pp. 129–152). Oxford, UK: Blackwell.

Bourdieu, P. (1990). *The logic of practice.* Stanford, CA: Stanford University Press. (Reprinted in *Social theory. The multicultural and classic readings,* pp. 52–58, by C. Lemert, Ed., 1999, Boulder, CO: Westview)

Bourdieu, P. (1993). *Sociology in question.* London: Sage.

Bourdieu, P. (1999). The social conditions of the international circulation of ideas. In R. Shusterman (Ed.), *Bourdieu: A critical reader* (pp. 220–228). Oxford, UK: Blackwell.

Bourdieu, P., & Passeron, J. (1977). *Reproduction in education, society and culture.* London: Sage.

Bouveresse, J. (1999). Rules, dispositions and the *habitus.* In R. Shusterman (Ed.), *Bourdieu: A critical reader* (pp. 45–63). Oxford, UK: Blackwell.

Burr, V. (1995). *An introduction to social constructionism.* London: Routledge.

Butler, J. (1999). Performativity's social magic. In R. Shusterman (Ed.), *Bourdieu: A critical reader* (pp. 113–128). Oxford, UK: Blackwell.

Department of Education. (1977). *Social studies syllabus guidelines, Forms 1–4.* Wellington, NZ: Government Printer.

Earle, W. (1999). Bourdieu nouveau. In R. Shusterman (Ed.), *Bourdieu: A critical reader* (pp. 175–191). Oxford, UK: Blackwell.

Foucault, M. (1981). The order of discourse. In R. Young (Ed.), *Untying the text* (pp. 51–76). London: Routledge and Keegan Paul.

Ladwig, J. (1994). For whom this reform? Outlining educational policy as a social field. *British Journal of Sociology, 15*(3), 341–363.

Lawton, D., Campbell, J., & Burkett, V. (1971). *Schools Council's working paper 39: Social studies 8–13.* London: Schools Council.

Lewis, J. (1980). The Form 1–4 social studies syllabus: Planned or? In D. Ramsay (Ed.), *Curriculum issues in New Zealand* (pp. 111–156). Wellington, NZ: New Zealand Educational Institute.

Lave, J., & Wenger, E. (1991). *Situated learning.* Cambridge, UK: Cambridge University Press.

Margolis, P. (1999). *Habitus* and the logic of practice. In R. Shusterman (Ed.), *Bourdieu: A critical reader* (pp. 64–83). Oxford, UK: Blackwell.

Marsh, C. (1997). *Perspectives: Key concepts for understanding curriculum: Vol. 1.* London: Falmer.

McGee, C. (1997). *Teachers and curriculum decision-making*. Palmerston North, NZ: Dunmore.

Ministry of Education. (1994). *Social studies in the New Zealand curriculum* (Draft). Wellington, NZ: Learning Media.

Ministry of Education. (1996). *Social studies in the New Zealand curriculum* (Revised draft). Wellington, NZ: Learning Media.

Ministry of Education. (1997). *Social studies in the New Zealand curriculum* (Final). Wellington, NZ: Learning Media.

Mutch, C. (1998, January 11–14). The long and winding road: The development of the new social studies curriculum. In *Ten years on: Reforming New Zealand education*. Proceedings of the New Zealand Educational Administration Society Biennial Conference (pp. 340–361). Christchurch, NZ: New Zealand Educational Administration Society.

Mutch, C. (2000, April 24–28). *The struggle for ideological control over curriculum: Two New Zealand examples*. Paper presented at the American Educational Research Association's Annual Conference, New Orleans, LA.

Mutch, C. (2004a). Curriculum construction as a social field. Mapping the process of the development of the New Zealand social studies curriculum. *Curriculum Perspectives, 24*(3), 22–33.

Mutch, C. (2004b, November 24–26). *Educational policy in New Zealand: Who pays the piper?* Paper presented at the New Zealand Association for Research in Education Conference, Wellington, NZ.

Ozga, J. (2000). *Policy research in educational settings: Contested terrain*. Buckingham, UK: Open University Press.

Print, M. (1993). *Curriculum development and design*. St. Leonards, NSW, Australia: Allen and Unwin.

Shusterman, R. (1999). Introduction: Bourdieu as philosopher. In R. Shusterman (Ed.), *Bourdieu: A critical reader* (pp. 1–13). Oxford, UK: Blackwell.

Taba, H., Durkin, M. C., Fraenkel, J. R., McNaughton, A. H. (1971). *A teacher's handbook to elementary social studies. An inductuve approach* (2nd ed.). Reading, MA: Addison-Wesley.

Webb, J., Schirato, T., & Danaher, G. (2002). *Understanding Bourdieu*. Crow's Nest, NSW, Australia: Allen and Unwin.

10

On Politics and Theory: Using an Explicitly Activist Theory to Frame Educational Research

Catherine A. Lugg

Remember, when you wake up in bed with a person of the same sex, you are now in politics. (Rivera, 1999b, p. 1198)

S ometimes, publishing opportunities for your research can literally fall into your lap. And, if you are very lucky, you can be given the professional opportunity of a lifetime. In November of 2001, I was asked to develop a manuscript that examined the issues of gender, sex, sexuality, and the politics of U.S. education to be included in a special issue of *Educational Administration Quarterly*. At the time, I had been reading for well over 10 years in the areas of law, social history, the politics of education, and how these relate to the lives of queer Americans. History, sociology, psychology,

EDITORS' NOTE: Quotations from Valdes, F. (1995) are reprinted from *California Law Review*, 83(1) by permission of the University of California, Berkeley. Copyright © 1995 by the *California Law Review*.

law, and social work all have wonderfully rich research literatures. Little could be found, however, in the educational administration and educational policy literatures on lesbian, gay, bisexual, transgendered, transsexual, and/or intersexual people (i.e., queer people); their issues; and how these can influence the politics of education. More specifically, these two professional areas were remarkable—if not notorious—for their near absolute silence on queer issues. For example, the first queer-positive law review article appeared as early as 1979. By contrast, in educational administration, the first queer-themed and broadly available article appeared in 1999. It was written by Colleen Capper and published in *Educational Researcher,* which is not dedicated to educational administration per se.

My article (Lugg, 2003b), "Sissies, Faggots, Lezzies and Dykes," was part of a special issue of *Educational Administration Quarterly* devoted to looking at new paradigms in the politics of education research. Traditionally, the politics of education literature has been dominated by theories imported from political science. Furthermore, although gender had been addressed, the politics of education literature had long ignored educational politics and policy as they related to sexuality. My charge was to incorporate issues of sex, sexuality, and gender, and draw possible implications for educational politics and policy in the United States.

I also had my own agenda, which included demonstrating how anti-queer prejudice was part of the woof and weave of public schooling, and, in particular, how devastating this prejudice can be for queer and non-queer children and adults. After presenting the overwhelming evidence on this specific point, I then offered some realistic-to-idealistic options for better school policies and practices. Such an activist policy agenda is, again, atypical for most social science research. As Rhonda Rivera's pungent quote presented at the beginning of this chapter underscores, however, I had a duty to take an activist stance. Whether I liked it or not, my status as an OUT Queer American academic working in a professional field that has been defined by homophobia (Blount, 1998, 2005; Lugg, 2003a) means that whatever research I do, it will be seen as *inherently* political. Consequently, I long ago decided I had best define the work I did before someone else did it for me.

Unlike other chapters in the present book, which are based on more typical qualitative research, my chapter represents a historical approach to educational research. To put a bit of a crass gloss on this, unlike most qualitative researchers, many historians, including the present author, prefer their research subjects to be quite dead.[1] Consequently, a historian is forced to look for artifacts or *primary sources* such as diaries; personal and professional correspondence; newspaper accounts; government documents, including memos, minutes of meetings, arrest reports and criminal complaints, health and safety data, public health records, and court decisions; church, synagogue, and mosque records; as well as unedited sound and video recordings. Historians also rely on *secondary sources,* which include scholarly accounts such as biographies; political, social, and/or legal histories; film and audio documentaries; but also autobiographies and memoirs. "Doing" historical research involves sifting and sorting through these literatures using both primary and secondary sources, shifting back and forth between the two large sets of materials. Historians ultimately weave these disparate sources together to build a coherent story. Thus, my study, on which this chapter is based, is somewhat analogous to a review of the literature—if an inordinately large literature review. Nevertheless, the present chapter demonstrates clearly how theory might affect and be used in the conduct of historical research.

Overview of the Framework

> Queer. Sissy. Dyke. Tomboy. What do these vulgar terms have in common? Why do they sting? And, perhaps more curiously, why do they carry a common sting?
>
> Our childhood memories confirm that these epithets, and the stereotypes that they invoke, travel through American society as synonyms. For many, these words resonate in memories harkening back to days in the school yard. They conjure remembered peers, or perhaps youthful selves, who were chosen to sustain and survive the common ridicule of their perceived transgressions against a sex-ordered world. Clearly, the synonymity of these terms, and others like them, informed the social order into which we were inducted as children (Valdes, 1995, pp. 5–6).

For this article (Lugg, 2003b), I had to "frame" the wide-ranging material in a manner that would be understandable to people who might be totally ignorant of queer issues, history, and politics—much less the incredible complexities of "queer theory," writ large. Because the article seemed most directly related to educational policy and political issues, I chose queer legal theory as the theoretical framework for making the issues understandable. By design, it is user-friendly—as much as any postmodern theory can be considered "user friendly."

Queer legal theory, as a theoretical lens or set of lenses, emerged in the mid-1990s in response to larger political and legal events (Valdes, 1995). It is part of a larger movement within the U.S. academy of legal scholars who are concerned with issues of social justice. Unlike many theoretical frames found in the social sciences, queer legal theory does not expect the researcher to remain "neutral" on issues of social justice and queer Americans. As such, queer legal theory embraces an *explicitly activist stance,* which is consistent with some contemporary legal theories (Kairys, 1998).

Queer legal theory (QLT) springs from the intersection of several strains of progressive thought in legal theory, including feminist legal theory, critical race theory, critical legal studies, and gay and lesbian legal theory (Valdes, 1995, 1997, 1998). It draws on feminist legal theory's commitment to disestablishing patriarchy, critical race theory's dedication to unmasking the deep racist structures within U.S. society and life, critical legal theory's examination of how class structures are perpetuated and reinforced, and gay and lesbian legal theory's understanding of how heteronormativity (the notion that the entire world is non-queer—or that it should be) is reproduced, while queer identity and individuals are eliminated (Hutchinson, 1997, 1999, 2000, 2001; Valdes, 1995, 1997, 1998).

QLT moves beyond these theories in distinct and important ways. The theory rejects the tendency toward gender essentialism that underpins much of feminist legal theory (Harris, 1990; Valdes, 1995), the heteronormativity reflected in early critical race theory's analyses (Hutchinson, 1999, 2001), the over-reliance on class as the sole analytic variable in critical legal theory (Valdes, 1995), and the inherently racist and classist assumptions reflected in gay and lesbian legal theory, and gay legal theory in particular (Hutchinson, 1997, 1999, 2000; Valdes, 1995, 1998).

QLT is dedicated to eliminating those U.S. legal and social structures that privilege and enforce heterosexuality, patriarchy, white supremacy, and class advantage, with the legal and social liberation of sexual minorities—queers—as its principal focus (Valdes, 1995). Furthermore, queer legal theory acknowledges many different ways "to be," and it is fiercely anti-essentialist in its theoretical outlook. Drawing on the burgeoning medical research on sex, sexual identity, and sexuality, and the explosion of research that considers gender as performance, QLT understands that orientation, identity, sex, and gender are highly variable. U.S. law, however, considers sex as the only proper jurisdictional category—both fixed and dichotomous (Valdes, 1995, 1998). According to QLT, there is no one way to be female or male, or queer, or for that matter, African American or white (Hutchinson, 1997, 1999, 2000, 2001; Valdes, 1995, 1997, 1998).

Two concepts of QLT that are critical to understanding its anti-essentialist stance are *intersectionality* and *multidimensionality.* Intersectionality comes from the work of those critical race theorists who examine the unique lives of women of color who have experienced discrimination and violence. Many times, women of color experience discrimination because of their race *and* because of their sex (Crenshaw, 1991). Yet, courts tend to recognize only the racism or the sexism in the discriminatory and/or violent acts, negating the fact that these women live at the intersection of both race and sex (Hutchinson, 1999, 2000, 2001). Intersectionality theorists argue that disentangling sex from race (or race from sex) becomes an act of essentialism. Intersectionality theorists also disavow the common assumption of more mainstream legal theorists, which include notions that there is one way to be "raced" (African American male),[2] and one way to be "sexed" (white female; see Hutchinson, 1999, 2000).

Multidimensionality moves beyond intersectionality by pushing the analysis to be more inclusive, considering class and orientation as well as sex/gender. Multidimensionality acknowledges that to be "queer" can hold multiple meanings and can be experienced quite differently from person to person. It also posits that individuals have multiple identities: One is not just "queer"—one also may be male, working class, and Asian. Similarly, people who are "non-queer" also hold multiple identities, and some of these may be held in common with queer people. Other aspects are distinct to a given individual's own multilayered position and life experiences (Hutchinson, 1999, 2000, 2001). Queer legal theory adherents have used both intersectionality (Valdes, 1995) and multidimensionality (Hutchinson, 1997, 1999, 2000, 20001; Valdes, 1998) as analytic tools.

Finally, queer legal theory questions the cultural and legal demands that individual members of a given minority group, or members of multiple minority groups, assimilate, convert, cover, or "pass"—hide or distort one's identity—particularly queers (Rush, 1997; Yoshino, 1998, 2002). "Passing" has been a survival strategy for many oppressed people, at least for those who could pass as white, male, Protestant, and/or non-queer. Hence, when the United States was governed by strict racial apartheid, some light-skinned blacks passed as "white" to gain access to jobs and decent housing (Rush, 1997; Yoshino, 1998, 2002). Likewise, some Jews and Catholics have been forced to pass as Protestants.

Queer legal theorists view such demands "to pass" as inherently discriminatory, undermining personal integrity and autonomy while eroding and denying an individual's legal and political rights (Hutchinson, 1999; Valdes, 1995; Yoshino, 1998, 2002). Queer people, in particular, are told repeatedly they must pass as non-queer to be hired, to visit their partners in the hospital, to *not* be bullied and harassed in school (*Nabozny v. Podlesny*, 1996), and so forth. In somewhat more enlightened situations, queers are cautioned that they must "cover" their identities (Yoshino, 2002). They do not have to hide or deny their identity—they just cannot talk about it. Mere mention is considered "flaunting." The U.S. military's ban on queer personnel under the rubric of "Don't Ask, Don't Tell," would be one example of covering. The final and most regressive form of assimilationist bias would be "converting," where a queer person undergoes some sort of "reparative" therapy, to change their identity from queer to non-queer. While converting is not as common for queers as it once was (Katz, 1992), queer children remain at risk for compulsory conversion (see Cruz, 1999; Goishi, 1997; Hicks, 1999).

Like other social justice–oriented legal theories, QLT aims its theoretical analyses at legal and regulatory systems (like public schools), in hopes of disestablishing those structures and practices that oppress queer people. It is expressly future-oriented in its approach (Valdes, 1995). One strategy for working toward a progressive future is to re-examine history and legal precedents for important clues as to how homophobic and heteronormative structures have been woven into governmental institutions. It is this final point that made QLT particularly helpful in my examination of educational politics and policy.

A final appeal of QLT specifically, and queer-positive legal research in general, is the tradition of provocatively titled law review articles, which range from "Our Straight-Laced Judges" (Rivera, 1979/1999a), to "Reasoning About Sodomy" (Halley, 1993), to "Queers, Sissies, Dykes, and Tomboys" (Valdes, 1995). Not only are these titles arresting-to-incendiary, but also the content of each pushes readers to expand their analytic horizons. Consequently, each time I have employed QLT, I have made a rhetorical and analytic nod to these theoretical and activist roots.

Sifting and Sorting Considerations

> Queer legal theory can be positioned as a race-inclusive enterprise, a class-inclusive enterprise, a sex-inclusive enterprise, and a gender-inclusive enterprise, as well as a sexual orientation-inclusive enterprise. . . . Queer legal theory must connote an activist and egalitarian sense of *resistance to all forms of subordination,* and it also must denote a sense of unfinished purpose and mission. (Valdes, 1995, p. 354; emphasis added)

I was convinced QLT was appropriate for educational policy and politics because both are influenced by the law—particularly judicial decisions. Because the judiciary, at both the federal and state levels, has been driving most of the civil rights gains and losses for queer Americans, it was vital that I examine landmark court decisions, the reasoning behind them—particularly *Bowers v. Hardwick* (1986)—and explore how the educational politics and policy environments reacted to these events.

Another compelling point regarding the use of QLT is its commitment to liberatory practice—not just for queers, but also for all historically marginalized peoples (Valdes, 1995). Sexual minorities do remain a central focus, but given QLT's understandings of how unstable, fluid, and multidimensional identity can be, it also pays attention to issues of race, class, sex, gender, religion, dis/ability, and so on. Again, QLT rejects the traditional notions of research neutrality or objectivity, noting that U.S. law has distributed very real benefits and punishments that historically have favored some identity groups over others (Crenshaw, 1991; Eskridge, 1999; Kairys, 1998; Novick, 1988; Valdes, 1995). Justice has not been blind; rather it has been selectively myopic.

Queer legal theory draws on two aspects of scholarly research: history and detailed case analysis. QLT also builds a strong narrative, which can include storytelling that is rooted in both fiction and nonfiction (see Valdes, 1995),[3] court cases, and legal opinions. As Francisco Valdes wrote,

> Queer legal theory must supplement the use of social science scholarship with narrative scholarship. Queer legal theory must compile and employ narratives, or counter-narratives, to air in legal venues the stories of sexual minority lives caught in the legal system for one reason or another. Using narratives, like using social sciences data, can help combat conflationary prejudice and stereotypes by focusing decisionmakers on facts and weaning them away from fictions, but its special power is in the capacity of stories to elicit a sense of empathy with sexual minority equality claims and in its corollary ability to root both action and theory in reality.
>
> By capturing the humanity, complexity, and diversity of Queer lives and Queer legal issues, the use of narratives can dramatize in concrete, compelling, and undeniable ways the injustice of heterosexism to help inform and guide the actions of legal decisionmakers. But narratives also can help ensure that Queer legal theory is grounded in and textured by the everyday realities of sex/gender inequality and discrimination. The use of narratives on the whole thus serves to make Queer legal scholarship both persuasive to decisionmakers and responsive to lived realities. (1995, p. 366)

Because of its use of history, a strong narrative, and legal precedent (*stare decisis*), QLT greatly appealed to my own sensibilities as a historian and policy scholar. Consequently, for "Sissies, Faggots" I needed to write a historical component as well as sketch the legal complexities involved (Lugg, 2003b).

On the actual materials used, I drew heavily on the law review literature and case law, as well as scholarship in education, gender studies, history, media studies, psychology, political science, science, sociology, and selected materials by queer activists. Due to time constraints, most of my data came from secondary sources, with court decisions largely serving as my primary sources. This material was organized both thematically (at the beginning and conclusion of the paper) as well as chronologically (see Lugg, 2003b, the section entitled "A Short Queer History of U.S. Public Education").

Using QLT, I sifted the wide-ranging materials focusing on the topics of U.S. public education, gender, sex, and sexuality. Remember, for over 10 years I had been reading in the area of sexuality. When I would read anything that covered queers and public education (students, teachers, policies, etc.), I tended to underline the passage in pencil and then note the page number in the front of the book or beginning of the article. I also had been using the search engine LexisNexis to search the law review literature on common QLT terms, including "gays and lesbians," "public schools," "homophobia," "queer theory," "queer legal theory," and "sodomy laws." Those articles that received "matches" were downloaded to my computer archive. Then, court cases discussed in the law review literature were downloaded. I conducted similar searches using the academic search engines ProQuest, EBSCOhost, and JSTOR,[4] as well as the search engine in the weekly periodical *Edweek* (from 1980 to 2002), downloading the pertinent materials to my hard drive. Using such a wide-ranging and longitudinal approach gave me more materials than I could hope to use.

I further filtered the results using a differing aspect of queer legal theory. These materials (largely secondary, but with some primary sources) had to take a *liberationist* or *social justice* approach to issues of sexuality, sex, gender, and U.S. public schools. This quickly limited the materials I could use. For example, the gay conservative columnist Andrew Sullivan (1996) authored the book *Virtually Normal,* which is a politically conservative argument for gay rights (his language). As such, one could argue that he employs a "social justice" approach. Yet, his stances on gender and sex (biology) verge on being regressive, and I found his views on race and class profoundly disturbing. Sullivan is also dismissive of the radical roots of queer activism in the United States, which are found in the late 1940s Communist Party (see D'Emilio, 1983). Consequently, I excluded Sullivan's writings.[5]

Some Cautions

Unlike social theory that is rooted in sociology, political science, and/or psychology, QLT is not predictive in a quantitative sense. In the quantitative social sciences, the goal for research is to have a strong enough sample (or samples) so that one can generalize to larger populations. In legal research, one can and must draw implications from a single court decision (case), or multiple court decisions, or in some instances, seemingly disparate and unrelated decisions, and then apply these findings to the entire jurisdiction (a state, region, and/or nation—depending on the court involved). Law and legal reasoning are all about establishing legal precedence from court decisions (*stare decisis*)[6] and then applying these analyses to larger jurisdictional units. Ultimately, one looks for legal precedence—even in a solitary court case—on which to base policy recommendations and decisions.

Furthermore, whereas the use of legal precedence might seem at first blush comparable to qualitative notions of "transferability" of findings (given similar contexts and research questions; see Marshall & Rossman, 1999), applied legal theories have a function all of their own. Because they have immediate real-world applications, legal theories go in areas no social scientist (either quantitative or qualitative) would dare to tread. Consequently, for conventional social scientists another weakness of queer legal theory is its embrace of storytelling, particularly the use of fictitious moral parables. Also, QLT's embrace of postmodern theory, which posits that all human identity is unstable and contested (e.g., Judith Butler, 1990) can be migraine inducing.

"Predictability," or the power to forecast how a given court will decide a future legal case, has been highly problematic for any legal theory, and this includes QLT. This is an ironic situation given the legal doctrine of *stare decisis*—relying on and adhering to prior court decisions. But another tradition of the U.S. judicial system is independence, and judicial independence has been zealously guarded by the judiciary for well over 200 years. For example, U.S. Supreme Court justices, on their own and working collectively, have been surprisingly unpredictable at times—much to the angst of legal theorists (see Kairys, 1998). Even *originalists*—who claim to hold the most predictable and constitutionally consistent approach and who view legal challenges from the standpoint of "How would the founding fathers decide this case?"—can arrive at wildly divergent decisions regarding the very same case.[7] Nevertheless, the majority of the justices deciding any case establishes the precedent that must be followed. Unlike social science, legal decisions ultimately come down to a matter of votes.[8]

An example of using a single decision as a basis for practice can be drawn from the U.S. Supreme Court's recent decision in *Lawrence v. Texas* (2003). This landmark decision invalidated all laws banning consensual sodomy, overturning the prior Supreme Court decision in *Bowers v. Hardwick* (1986). *Lawrence* has significant implications for educational politics and policies because states that maintained bars on consensual sodomy usually did so to harass queer Americans (see Eskridge, 1999). Prior to *Lawrence*, states with laws barring consensual sodomy had the legal right to revoke the licensure for queer educators because they were, by definition, self-confessed criminals, and in some instances, self-confessed felons (Lugg, 2003a, 2003b, 2005). Of course, felons are barred from holding any state-approved license, from working as a surveyor to beautician, lawyer, teacher, principal, or school superintendent. Yet, drawing on *Lawrence*, all of these policies and regulations limiting queers in public employment are now invalid. My reasoning is drawn from a solitary case—an *N* of one—which is normally dangerous ground for a social scientist. Nevertheless, I can be fairly confident in my analysis because there is no legal method to enforce what has been ruled unconstitutional.[9]

Other limitations with employing QLT include some surprising logistical problems. At one point, as I was e-mailing versions of the manuscript back and forth to *Educational Administration Quarterly's* then-editor, Jane Clark Lindle, her e-mail account was frozen for 3 hours. We discovered that we had run afoul of the University of Kentucky's "net nanny,"[10] which prohibited certain words or terms to be used when using e-mail and accessing the World Wide Web. Because I had used the title "Sissies, Faggots, Lezzies and Dykes" (Lugg, 2003b) in the subject line at one point, the software automatically closed her account. Professor Clark Lindle could neither send nor receive any e-mail. How many other scholarly theories can claim such real-world disruptive power?

Some Final Observations on History, Law, and Theory

> All historians, including those who pretend to be objective, write with an agenda for their own times: to promote or prevent social change, to glorify or vilify particular people or societies. (Pencak, 2002, p. 3)[11]

Given my training as a historian, I am inclined to use social theory as a hypertensive patient uses salt: judiciously and very sparingly. Contrary to Marx's, Engels's, and Santayana's pronouncements, history does not repeat itself (Burke, 1992). That said, social, political, economic, and cultural structures; themes; categories; and understandings are remarkably long-lived and span generations of human existence (Foucault, 1982). Whereas individual events do not reoccur, important themes, ideas, regimes, and beliefs continually play out in expected, as well as in novel and unexpected, ways (see Foucault, 1982; Sharpe, 2001). Furthermore, laws, like history, develop and evolve within specific contexts—contexts that can be surprisingly idiosyncratic, yet inextricably bound to a given political culture. And these cultures do develop their broader themes, icons, symbols, and metaphors (Edelman, 1995; Lugg, 1999; Pencak, 2002).

As I see it, the historian's task, to the best of her/his ability (Novick, 1988), is to reconstruct a broken mirror that once reflected a given reality or sets of realities. Theory can aid this task in helping sort out which fragments are likely to fit together, sometimes in novel and unanticipated ways. It can also distort the shattered lens, however, by filtering out critical pieces. Consequently, the final product, which is a reconstruction, can be aided or further muddled by the use of theory (Burke, 1992; Pencak, 2002). As the historian Peter Burke observed in his book *History and Social Theory,* "Sociologists, for example, are trained to notice or formulate general rules and often screen out the exceptions. Historians learn to attend to concrete detail at the expense of general patterns" (1992, p. 3). The goal for historians is to use theory to uncover these patterns that occur over time—without losing too much of the unique detail of specific people and events.

As a historian, I also need to be aware of my own assumptions and presumptions as I undertake any historical exploration. Although objectivity is an impossible ideal, I am obligated to be fair to the material and individuals I present (Novick, 1988; Pencak, 2002). It is also imperative that I present my own understandings and approach to the research project near the start of any manuscript, if for nothing else, to give an unsuspecting reader "fair warning."

These were the theoretical lenses, under Queer legal theory, that I brought to "Sissies, Faggots, Lezzies and Dykes" (Lugg, 2003b). Given my training as a historian, queer legal theory appealed to me because of its sheer utility in linking law, educational policy, and U.S. public schools to the larger political and historical environments.

Notes

1. Historians who employ oral history are obviously exempt from this observation.

2. The majority of white Americans do not see themselves as "raced"—although this notion flies in the face of history and U.S. jurisprudence. There is burgeoning research in this area called, "critical white studies" (see Delgado & Stefanic, 1999).

3. Some strands of history have also embraced storytelling. I do not mean "oral history," which relies on eyewitness accounts of past events. Beginning in the 1970s, historian Hayden White advocated that history become more like literature, with historians striving to tell "plausible stories" and worrying less about the rules of evidence (see Novick, 1988).

4. During the time of my data collection and writing, Sage publications (*Educational Administration Quarterly, Education and Urban Society, Education Policy,* etc.) could be found via EBSCOhost or ProQuest. With the advent of its own proprietary database, however, Sage has withdrawn its publications from these academic databases.

5. I did use a few primary sources that were profoundly queer-hostile, but they were used as examples to demonstrate a larger political point of queers viewed as "social contagion" (see Lugg, 2003b).

6. *Stare decisis* is a Latin term meaning "to stand by things decided." In U.S. jurisprudence, this means lower courts are bound by Supreme Court decisions. Furthermore, the U.S. Supreme Court will generally, but not always, uphold prior decisions unless the justices can be provided compelling evidence as to why the prior precedent was incorrect. This was the case in the *Lawrence v. Texas* (2003) decision, which overturned *Bowers v. Hardwick* (1986; see Lugg, 2005).

7. Which was the case in *Lawrence v. Texas*. In the 6–3 decision, the Supreme Court justices generated four separate opinions: five wrote with the majority (Kennedy, with Ginsberg, Breyer, Stevens, and Souter); one wrote a separate concurrence (O'Connor), and there were two separate dissents (Scalia, with Rehnquist; and Thomas, writing separately).

8. One of the best judicial vote-counters was Supreme Court Chief Justice Earl Warren, who carefully shepherded the U.S. Supreme Court's decision making of *Brown v. Board of Education* (1954). Because the Court was going to overturn the legal precedent of segregation established in *Plessy v. Ferguson* (1896), Warren carefully lobbied all of his fellow justices until he was sure the Court's decision would be unanimous. In contrast, Chief Justice William Rehnquist presided over a highly factionalized court marked by numerous 5–4 decisions. This situation has implications vis-à-vis *stare decisis*. It is fairly daunting for successive courts to invalidate 9–0 decisions—and this is why Earl Warren lobbied mightily for the *Brown* decision to be unanimous. Overturning a 5–4 decision is a far more manageable prospect.

9. This does not mean that some misguided individuals will not try to enforce these bans. And the U.S. law review literature is rife with examples of extrajudicial enforcement of unconstitutional practices. If the ensuing case went to a federal court, however, the court would have to bow to the strictures of *Lawrence v. Texas* (Lugg, 2005).

10. University "net nannies" are the bane of any queer researcher's existence because they can effectively block any Web-based searching, including surfing through university databases. Not surprisingly, I use my own computer hardware, software, and Internet account, doing the vast majority of electronic research at home.

11. Bill Pencak, Professor of History at Pennsylvania State University, was one of my mentors as a doctoral student, and he introduced me to the world of semiotics. Over the last 15 years, I have taken many of my methodological and theoretical cues from his work. I have been fortunate to have him as both a colleague and dear friend.

References

Blount, J. M. (1998). *Destined to rule the schools. Women and the superintendency, 1873–1995*. Albany: State University of New York Press.

Blount, J. M. (2005). *Fit to teach: Same-sex desire, gender and school work in the twentieth century*. Albany: State University of New York Press.

Bowers v. Hardwick, 478 U.S. 186 (1986).

Brown v. Board of Education (Brown I), 347 U.S. 483 (1954).

Burke, P. (1992). *History and social theory.* Ithaca, NY: Cornell University Press.

Butler, J. (1990). *Gender trouble: Feminism and the subversion of identity.* New York: Routledge.

Capper, C. A. (1999). (Homo)sexualities, organizations, and administration: Possibilities for in(queer)y. *Educational Researcher, 28*(5), 4–11.

Crenshaw, K. W. (1991). Mapping the margins: Intersectionality, identity politics, and violence against women of color. *Stanford Law Review, 43,* 1241–1299.

Cruz, D. B. (1999). Controlling desires: Sexual orientation conversion and the limits of knowledge and law. *Southern California Law Review, 72,* 1297–1400.

Delgado, R., & Stefanic, J. (Eds.). (1999). *Critical race theory: The cutting edge.* Philadelphia: Temple University Press.

D'Emilio, J. (1983). *Sexual politics, sexual communities: The making of a homosexual minority in the United States, 1940–1970.* Chicago: University of Chicago Press.

Edelman, M. (1995). *From art to politics.* Chicago: University of Chicago Press.

Eskridge, W. N., Jr. (1999). *Gaylaw: Challenging the apartheid of the closet.* Cambridge, MA: Harvard University Press.

Foucault, M. (1982). *Archeology of knowledge.* New York: Pantheon.

Goishi, M. (1997). Legal & social responses to the problems of queer youth: Unlocking the closet door: Protecting children from involuntary civil commitment because of their sexual orientation. *Hastings Law Journal, 48,* 1137–1182.

Halley, J. E. (1993). Reasoning about sodomy: Act and identity in and after *Bowers v. Hardwick. Virginia Law Review, 79,* 1721–1779.

Harris, A. P. (1990). Race and essentialism in feminist legal theory: *Stanford Law Review, 42,* 581–615

Hicks, K. A. (1999). "Reparative" therapy: Whether parental attempts to change a child's sexual orientation can legally constitute child abuse. *American University Law Review, 49,* 505–547.

Hutchinson, D. L. (1997). Out yet unseen: A racial critique of gay and lesbian legal theory and political discourse. *Connecticut Law Review, 29,* 561–645.

Hutchinson, D. L. (1999). Ignoring the sexualization of race: Heteronormativity, critical race theory and anti-racist politics. *Buffalo Law Review, 47,* 1–116.

Hutchinson, D. L. (2000). "Gay rights" for "gay whites"? Race, sexual identity, and equal protection discourse. *Cornell Law Review, 85,* 1358–1391.

Hutchinson, D. L. (2001). "Intersectionality," "multidimensionality," and the development of an adequate theory of subordination. *Michigan Journal of Race & Law, 6,* 285–317.

Kairys, D. (Ed.). (1998). *The politics of law: A progressive critique.* New York: Basic Books.

Katz, J. N. (1992). *Gay American history: Lesbians and gay men in the U.S.A.—A documentary history* (Rev. ed.). New York: Meridian.

Lawrence v. Texas, 539 U.S. 558 (2003).

Lugg, C. A. (1999). *Kitsch: From education to public policy.* New York: Falmer.

Lugg, C. A. (2003a). Our straight-laced administrators: LGBT school administrators, the law, and the assimilationist imperative. *Journal of School Leadership, 13*(1), 51–85.

Lugg, C. A. (2003b). Sissies, faggots, lezzies and dykes: Gender, sexual orientation and the new politics of education. *Educational Administration Quarterly, 39*(1), 95–134.

Lugg, C. A. (2005). *Thinking about sodomy: Public schools, panopticons and queers.* Unpublished manuscript. New Brunswick, NJ: Rutgers University.

Marshall, C., & Rossman, G. B. (1999). *Designing qualitative research* (3rd ed.). Thousand Oaks, CA: Sage.

Nabozny v. Podlesny, 92 F.3d 446 (7th Cir. 1996).

Novick, P. (1988). *That noble dream: The "objectivity" question in the American Historical Association.* New York: Cambridge University Press.

Pencak, W. (2002). *The films of Derek Jarman.* New York: McFarland & Company.

Plessy v. Ferguson, 163 U.S. 537 (1896).

Rivera, R. (1999a). Our straight-laced judges: The legal position of homosexual persons in the United States. *Hastings Law Review, 50,* 1015–1178. (Original work published 1979)

Rivera, R. (1999b). Our straight-laced judges twenty years later. *Hastings Law Review, 50,* 1179–1198.

Rush, S. E. (1997). Equal protection analogies—Identity and "passing": Race and sexual orientation. *Harvard Blackletter Journal, 13,* 65–106.

Sharpe, J. (2001). History from below. In P. Burke (Ed.), *New perspectives on historical writing* (2nd ed., pp. 25–42). University Park: Pennsylvania State University Press.

Sullivan, A. (1996). *Virtually normal: An argument about homosexuality.* New York: Vintage.

Valdes, F. (1995). Queers, sissies, dykes, and tomboys: Deconstructing the conflation of "sex," "gender," and "sexual orientation" in Euro-American law and society. *California Law Review, 83,* 3–37.

Valdes, F. (1997). Queer margins, queer ethics: A call to account for race and ethnicity in the law, theory, and politics of "sexual orientation." *Hastings Law Journal, 48,* 1293–1341.

Valdes, F. (1998). Beyond sexual orientation in queer legal theory: Majoritarianism, multidimensionality, and responsibility in social justice scholarship or legal scholars as cultural warriors. *Denver University Law Review, 75,* 1409–1464.

Yoshino, K. (1998). Assimilationist bias in equal protection: The visibility presumption and the case of "Don't Ask, Don't Tell." *Yale Law Journal, 108,* 485–571.

Yoshino, K. (2002). Covering. *Yale Law Journal, 111,* 769–939.

Conclusion: Coming Full Circle

Norma T. Mertz
Vincent A. Anfara, Jr.

A ny serious consideration of research methods in social science runs squarely into basic issues of the relationship between theory and the research process. Whether one approaches the research process from a quantitative or qualitative perspective, theory has an important role to play. This book was designed to highlight that role, to step into the conceptual confusion and misunderstanding surrounding the nature and role of theory in qualitative research and to address, directly and by example, what a theoretical framework is, how it is used in qualitative research, and how it affects such research. The contributing authors provide accessible, understandable, self-conscious descriptions of the use of theoretical frameworks in a wide range of qualitative studies. In this way, they allow the reader to "see" contextually how such frameworks are used, and to be able to then go to the published research on which the descriptions are based, to assess what has been said against what has been reported. It is clear from their descriptions, that theory makes an enormous difference in how we practice qualitative research.

We see the role of theory in qualitative research as basic, central, and foundational, whether consciously recognized or even identified. It influences the way the researcher approaches the study and pervades almost all aspects of the study. It is a "lens," as two contributors (Harris, Chapter 8; Henstrand, Chapter 1) note, framing and shaping what the researcher looks at and includes, how the researcher thinks about the study and its conduct, and, in the end, how the researcher conducts the study. Other contributing authors used equally powerful metaphors to describe the role theory plays in qualitative research: a sieve (Fowler, Chapter 3), a roadmap (Kearney & Hyle, Chapter 7), and reconstructing a broken mirror (Lugg, Chapter 10). These metaphors are powerful devices for understanding the relationship of theory and research and providing insightful "ways of thinking" and "ways of seeing" (Morgan, 1986, p. 12). To greater and lesser extents, the contributing authors demonstrate the pervasive nature of theory in their qualitative research studies. Clearly, not every contributor speaks to the effect of the theory they used on every aspect of their study, but some do, and collectively, they make this pervasiveness evident.

Although an increasing number of educational researchers practice and/or are being trained in the use of qualitative methods, we are mindful that the role of theory in such research has long been denied or obscured. Indeed, if acknowledged, theory was perceived to be the *product* of qualitative research. We live now in a period characterized by the "loss of theoretical innocence" (Flinders & Mills, 1993, p. xi). Our faith in "immaculate perception," as Flinders and Mills so eloquently put it, is on the wane. Qualitative researchers cannot opt out of attending to theory or of examining the role it plays in their research. Research cannot be conducted without the conscious or unconscious use of underlying theory (Broido & Manning, 2002; Papineau, 1979). Indeed, Garrison (1988) contends that those who claim to do atheoretical research do one of the following: hold the theories tacitly; hold them explicitly but do not make them public; or "pack structural concepts that properly belong to theory into their methodology where they are hidden from their view" (p. 24) and ours.

As suggested by the contributing authors, the role of theory in qualitative research extends beyond the confines of a particular study. It situates qualitative research clearly within the scholarly conversation, adds subtlety and complexity to what appear at first glance to be simple phenomena, and allows for building a repertoire of understandings, diverse perspectives, of the same phenomenon. Interestingly enough, this positions social science research more in line with research in the natural sciences. "Philosophers of science have repeatedly demonstrated that more than one theoretical construction can always be placed upon a given collection of data," although noting that "the invention of alternates is just what scientists seldom undertake except during the pre-paradigm stage of their science's development and at very special occasions during its subsequent evolution" (Kuhn, 1970, p. 76).

Let us turn now to a discussion of what the contributors to this book offer readers in their quest to more fully understand the role of theory in qualitative research. This concluding discussion is structured around two questions posed in the introduction:

- How do I find a theoretical framework?
- What effects does it have on my research?

In addition to answering these questions, we offer some suggestions for accomplishing what has been discussed.

How Do I Find a Theoretical Framework?

The problem of finding a theoretical framework is not confined to students or neophyte researchers. Even seasoned qualitative researchers have been known to have manuscripts returned to them with questions about the theoretical framework that guided their study. Students of qualitative research as well as experienced researchers sometimes find themselves at a loss in the process of selecting a theoretical framework. They often expect it to appear or to magically drop into their laps. Admittedly, finding a theoretical framework, especially one that works well for the phenomenon being studied, is not always an easy process. Although you may be lucky and find one quickly and painlessly, or even have one handed to you by a professor for your thesis or dissertation, the fact remains that in all likelihood you will have to actively search for a theoretical framework. No doubt, this pursuit will be characterized by much reading, possible discussion with colleagues, and finding, reflecting upon, and discarding several potential theoretical frameworks before one is finally chosen. And whereas some researchers use a particular theoretical framework for an extended period of time (Harris, Chapter 8; Merriam, Chapter 2), others change frameworks with each study undertaken.

In response to the dilemma of finding a theoretical framework, the contributing authors in this book offered a wide spectrum of "hows"—from total chance (Karpiak, Chapter 6), to a suggestion from a colleague (Mutch, Chapter 9), to putting two heads from two different fields together (Bettis & Mills, Chapter 4; Mills & Bettis, Chapter 5), to being well-read in education and other fields of study, for example, economics, political science, sociology, anthropology, psychology, and so on (Harris, Chapter 8). In short, there is no one tried and true way of finding a theoretical framework.

Many of the authors report that an "ah-ha" experience accompanied the finding of the theoretical framework they used—that it fit, made sense, and resonated with their thinking. They revealed that the theoretical framework they had found provided "ways of thinking" and "ways of seeing" (Morgan, 1986, p. 12) that unveiled understandings of the phenomena being studied in novel and interesting ways.

A good approach to beginning to find a theoretical framework might be to study a scholarly journal that requires its authors to identify the theoretical framework used. One journal that fits this criterion is *Educational Administration Quarterly*. If readers were to look at volume 37, issue 1, published in February 2001, for example, it is interesting to note that the Pounder and Merrill article uses job choice theory to study job desirability of the high school principalship; Ortiz applies the theory of social capital to interpret the careers of three Latina superintendents; Nestor-Baker and Hoy employ practical intelligence and tacit knowledge to study school superintendents; and Geijsel, Sleegers, Van den Berg, and Kelchtermans use professional development, decision making, and transformational leadership to analyze conditions that foster the implementation of large-scale innovation programs in schools. Each of these articles has a section entitled theoretical framework or conceptual framework, two phrases that are often used interchangeably, in which the researchers describe the theory they used. We encourage readers to spend some time looking at published research and identifying the theoretical frameworks used as a way to stimulate thinking about theories and their relationship to research projects.

Qualitative researchers are encouraged to be persistent in the search for theoretical frameworks and to think beyond the confines of their disciplinary focus. Consider how theories from economics, sociology, political science, anthropology, and other fields of study might thoughtfully be used to study phenomena in interesting and distinctive ways.

What Effect Does the Theoretical Framework Have on My Research?

In discussing the effects of a theoretical framework on the research process, the contributors to this book offered interesting insights. A theoretical framework has the ability to (1) focus a study, (2) reveal and conceal meaning and understanding, (3) situate the research in a scholarly conversation and provide a vernacular, and (4) reveal its strengths and weaknesses.

Focus a Study. The ability of a theoretical framework to focus a study involves a number of issues. First, qualitative researchers often feel overwhelmed by the mountains of data (e.g., interview transcripts, documents, observation/ field notes) that can be collected. By acting as a "sieve" (Fowler, Chapter 3) or a "lens" (Harris, Chapter 8; Hendstrand, Chapter 1), the theoretical framework assists the researcher in the process of sorting through these data. Second, the theoretical framework "frames" every aspect of a study from the questions asked (Mutch, Chapter 9), to the sample selected (Merriam, Chapter 2), to the analysis derived (Hendstrand, Chapter 1; Merriam, Chapter 2). The concepts, constructs, and propositions that are part and parcel of a theory help the researcher in formulating these component parts of the research process. Third, qualitative researchers are keenly aware of the existence of subjectivity and bias in their research. The theoretical framework helps the researcher to control this subjectivity by the self-conscious revisiting of the theory and a concomitant awareness that one is using a particular perspective (Harris, Chapter 8; Hendstrand, Chapter 1). Fourth, the theoretical framework provides powerful concepts that may be used in the coding (Mills & Bettis, Chapter 5) and the analysis of the data (Merriam, Chapter 2).

The degree to which the contributing authors recognized and were able to write about the effects of the theoretical framework on their research varied. As stated earlier, we hold that every aspect of the qualitative research process—from the questions asked to the analysis of the data—is affected by the theoretical framework. It influences every choice we make during the research process and guides the researcher's thinking about the phenomenon under investigation. In short, the theoretical framework forces the researcher to be accountable to ensure that the methodology, the data, and the analysis are consistent with the theory.

In considering what advice might be useful, we encourage qualitative researchers to thoroughly understand the theoretical framework chosen to "frame" their study. Consider potential problems you might encounter in attempting to import and apply a theory from another field (e.g., economics, political science), in particular its applicability and fit. Investigate how other researchers have used the theory to see if and how it has been applied to research in your field. Be self-conscious about the ways the theoretical framework affects every aspect of the research process. Indeed, it might prove useful to document these effects in a journal kept during the research project.

Reveal and Conceal Meaning and Understanding. The contributing authors noted the ability of the theoretical framework to reveal and conceal meaning and understanding. As Eisner (1985) reminded us, "When you provide a window for looking at something, you also . . . provide something in the way of a wall (pp. 64–65). Although we acknowledge that theories can allow us to see familiar phenomena in novel ways, they can also blind us to aspects of the phenomena that are not part of the theory. As part of theory's ability to reveal and conceal, we are cognizant that a theoretical framework can distort the phenomena being studied by filtering out critical pieces of data (Lugg, Chapter 10).

Researchers need to recognize this characteristic of a theoretical framework and give serious thought to what is being concealed. This ability to reveal and conceal makes it all the more important for researchers to tell their readers, if possible, what is concealed. This is, after all, the essence of a study's delimitations. Although the choice of a theoretical framework clearly delimits a study, we have seen little recognition of this fact in theses and dissertations or in journal articles.

In the real world, few have time to engage in the following activities, but we feel it important to mention them nonetheless. Consider designing a study with one theoretical framework and then redesigning it using an alternative framework. What effect does this have on the questions asked? What effect might the differing frameworks have on the analysis derived? How will your data collection strategies change? A little more realistic exercise would involve getting a colleague to study the same phenomenon using a different framework (see Bettis & Mills, Chapter 4; Mills & Bettis, Chapter 5). Again, how did the different frameworks affect the research processes? One would imagine that the more "ways of thinking" and "ways of seeing" (Morgan, 1986, p. 12), that is, theoretical frameworks, that are employed in our attempts to understand some reality would ultimately bring us closer to an understanding of that reality, an ontological issue we do not want to debate at this time.

Situate the Research in a Scholarly Conversation and Provide a Vernacular. In the process of advancing knowledge, the theoretical framework allows researchers to situate their research and knowledge contributions in a scholarly conversation (Bettis & Mills, Chapter 4; Fowler, Chapter 3). It allows us to talk across disciplines (Hendstrand, Chapter 1) using the known and accepted language of the theory. It is this established language that assists in making meanings of the phenomena being studied explicit. The theoretical framework also provides convenient labels and categories that help in explaining and developing thick descriptions and a coherent analysis (Harris, Chapter 8).

In reflecting upon this effect of the theoretical framework, it is important for qualitative researchers to learn the language of the theory being used and to use it precisely and clearly. It is also necessary to make every attempt to state your contributions to the scholarly conversation without overreaching appropriate parameters—parameters that will be dictated by the data you have collected and the analysis you have formulated. Part of participating in this scholarly conversation and documenting your contribution involves looking carefully at the relationship between your study and the theory you have used. Does your research support the existing theory, does it advance the theory in some meaningful and important way (Fowler, Chapter 3), or does it refute the theory? These are important questions that should not be avoided in this discussion.

Reveal Its Strengths and Weaknesses. As the contributing authors reflected on the effects of the theoretical framework on their research, it became evident that no theoretical framework adequately describes or explains any phenomena (Fowler, Chapter 3; Merriam, Chapter 2). Some of the contributors expressed concern about the power of a theoretical framework to be too reductionistic, stripping the phenomenon of its complexity and interest (Mutch, Chapter 9), or too deterministic, forcing the researcher to "fit" the data into predetermined categories (Harris, Chapter 8). Indeed, others have been concerned about the power of the existing literature on a topic to be "ideologically hegemonic" (Becker, 1986), making it difficult to see phenomena in ways that are different from those that are prevalent in the literature. Other contributors to this book discussed the fact that strengths and weaknesses provide sufficient reason to employ multiple frameworks in one study (Kearney & Hyle, Chapter 7).

Researchers need to be prepared for the strengths and weaknesses being revealed during the process of conducting a research project. Questions will be raised that need to be addressed. Whereas the "fit" of the theoretical framework for a study may become evident, it may in fact become necessary to discard the theoretical framework and start the process of searching for a new one. Researchers need to be wary of dropping data in light of assessing the strengths and weaknesses of any theory. It could be these data that help in the advancement of the theory or in its being refuted.

The relationship between theory and qualitative research remains complicated. We hold it is impossible to observe and describe what happens in natural settings without some theory that guides the researcher in what is relevant to observe and what name to attach to what is happening. As noted by Schwandt (1993), the theory allows us to "enter the field with a theoretical language and attitude" (pp. 11–12). Qualitative forms of inquiry demand that theory (i.e., theoretical frameworks) be used with imagination and flexibility. As John Dewey (1934) noted, it is part of our need to reeducate our perceptions.

References

Becker, H. S. (1986). *Writing for social scientists: How to start and finish your thesis, book, or article.* Chicago: University of Chicago Press.

Broido, E. M., & Manning, K. (2002). Philosophical foundations and current theoretical perspectives in qualitative research. *Journal of College Student Development, 43*(4), 434–445.

Dewey, J. (1934). *Art as experience.* New York: Perigee.

Eisner, E. W. (1985). *The educational imagination* (2nd ed.). New York: Macmillan.

Flinders, D. J., & Mills, G. E. (Eds.). (1993). *Theory and concepts in qualitative research: Perceptions from the field.* New York: Teachers College Press.

Garrison, J. (1988). The impossibility of atheoretical science. *Journal of Educational Thought, 22,* 21–26.

Geijsel, F., Sleegers, P., Van den Berg, R., & Kelchtermans, G. (2001). Conditions fostering the implementation of large-scale innovation programs in schools: Teachers' perspectives. *Educational Administration Quarterly, 37*(1), 130–166.

Kuhn, T. (1970). *The structure of scientific revolutions* (2nd ed.). Chicago: University of Chicago Press.

Morgan, G. (1986). *Images of organizations.* Newbury Park, CA: Sage.

Nestor-Baker, N. S., & Hoy, W. K. (2001).Tacit knowledge of school superintendents: Its nature, meaning, and content. *Educational Administration Quarterly, 37*(1), 86–129.

Ortiz, F. I. (2001). Using social capital in interpreting the careers of three Latina superintendents. *Educational Administration Quarterly, 37*(1), 58–85.

Papineau, D. (1979). *Theory and meaning.* Oxford, UK: Clarendon.

Pounder, D. G., & Merrill, R. J. (2001). Job desirability of the high school principalship: A job choice theory perspective. *Educational Administration Quarterly, 37*(1), 27–57.

Schwandt, T. E. (1993). Theory for the moral sciences. In D. J. Flinders & G. E. Mills (Eds.), *Theory and concepts in qualitative research: Perceptions from the field* (pp. 5–23). New York: Teachers College Press.

Index

About the Editors

Vincent A. Anfara, Jr., is Associate Professor of Educational Administration and Supervision at The University of Tennessee, Knoxville. He received his PhD in educational administration from the University of New Orleans in 1995. Before entering the professoriate, he taught for 23 years in both middle and high schools in Louisiana and New Mexico. His research interests include middle school reform, leadership in middle schools, issues related to student achievement, and qualitative research methods. He is past President of the American Educational Research Association's Middle Level Education Research Special Interest Group and the Chair of the National Middle School Association's (NMSA) Research Advisory Board. His research has been published in *Educational Researcher, Education and Urban Society, School Leadership, Leadership and Policy in Schools,* and the *NASSP Bulletin.* His most recent books include *From the Desk of the Middle School Principal: Leadership Responsive to the Needs of Young Adolescents* (2002, Scarecrow Press) and *The Encyclopedia of Middle Grades Education* (2005, Information Age Publishing). He is the Series Editor of *The Handbook of Research in Middle Level Education,* copublished by Information Age Publishing and the NMSA.

Norma T. Mertz is Professor of Higher Education at The University of Tennessee, Knoxville. She received her EdD in curriculum and teaching from Teachers College, Columbia University, with a collateral in anthropology and education. Before becoming a faculty member in educational administration at The University of Tennessee, she prepared teachers to work in urban, inner-city schools in Michigan and New York City as an Assistant Professor at Eastern Michigan University and Hunter and Brooklyn Colleges; and was an Assistant Director of the Race Desegregation Assistance Center and Director of the Sex Equity Assistance Center. Her research centers on gender and leadership, mentoring, and organizational socialization, and has been published in *Educational Administration Quarterly, Urban Education, Journal of School Leadership, Planning and Changing,* and *Communications of the ACM.*

About the Contributors

Pamela J. Bettis is Assistant Professor in the Cultural Studies and Social Thought in Education program at Washington State University. Her areas of research include the social context of education and how gender operates in schools. She is the coauthor of *Cheerleader! An American Icon* (2003) and *Geographies of Girlhood: Identities In-Between* and has had work published in *Sociology of Education, Gender & Society, Educational Foundations,* and *Sex Education.*

Frances C. Fowler was a classroom teacher and union leader in Tennessee before she received her PhD in educational administration from The University of Tennessee, Knoxville, in 1990. In that same year, she accepted a position in the Department of Educational Leadership at Miami University of Ohio, where she is currently Professor and the Director of Graduate Studies for her department. She teaches courses about the politics of education and education policy and has published extensively in this area. Her textbook, Policy Studies for Educational Leaders: An Introduction, is in its second edition

Edward L. Harris has served as teacher, coach, and administrator in public and private schools as well as Associate Dean for the College of Education at Oklahoma State University. He earned a PhD in educational administration from Texas A&M University and currently holds the Williams Chair of Educational Leadership at Oklahoma State University. His research, teaching, and service activities focus on school culture and leadership. He is the author of *Key Strategies to Improve Schools: How to Apply Them Contextually* (2005).

Joyce L. Henstrand has been a language arts teacher, department chair, and high school principal. In her current role as Director of Instruction in the Reynolds School District in Fairview, Oregon, she focuses on improvement of instruction especially in reading and writing. She earned a BA in

English literature at SUNY at Buffalo and a PhD in educational policy and management from the University of Oregon. Her case study described in this book was given the annual dissertation award by the American Education Research Association Division A in 1992.

Adrienne E. Hyle received her doctorate from Kansas State University in 1987 and began her faculty career at Oklahoma State University that same year. Her research interests include change and gender issues in K-through-20 educational settings. Theory has played a large part in the design and analysis of explorations in these settings, as well as in her students' doctoral research. Current research interests include exploring our understandings of learning in cohort and off-site contexts.

Irene E. Karpiak is Associate Professor of Adult and Higher Education in the Department of Educational Leadership and Policy Studies, University of Oklahoma. She teaches graduate-level courses on the adult learner, adult learning and development, transformative learning, and chaos and complexity in adult education. Her scholarly interests draw on qualitative, interpretive, and narrative methods. Her research into autobiography and the life stories of adult learners have enriched her understanding of learning, transition, and change, and have furthered her appreciation of the ways in which crises, crossroads, and chaos can further personal growth and transformation.

Kerri S. Kearney has a professional background in both education and corporate America and began her faculty career at Oklahoma State University in 2004. She holds an MBA in management and an EdD in educational administration. Her research interests focus on leadership and change across a variety of organizational and individual contexts. Current research interests include exploring the role of individually held values in leadership and the use of arts-based methodologies in qualitative research.

Catherine A. Lugg is Associate Professor of Education at the Graduate School of Education, Rutgers University, and serves as an Associate Director for Publishing, University Council for Educational Administration. She is also a Senior Associate Editor for the *Journal of Gay and Lesbian Issues in Education*. Recent publications include "One Nation Under God? Religion and the Politics of Education in a Post 9/11 America" in *Educational Policy*.

Sharan B. Merriam is Professor of Adult Education at the University of Georgia in Athens, where her responsibilities include teaching graduate courses in adult education and qualitative research methods, and supervising graduate student research. Merriam's research and writing activities have focused on the foundations of adult education, adult development, adult learning, and qualitative research methods. For 5 years, she was coeditor of *Adult Education Quarterly,* the major research and theory journal in adult education. She is a three-time winner of the prestigious Cyril O. Houle World Award for Literature in Adult Education. In 1999, she was a Senior Fulbright Scholar to Malaysia.

Michael R. Mills is Assistant Professor of Higher Education at the University of South Florida, where he teaches courses on the organization, administration, and finance of universities and colleges. His research and writing focus on the role of organizational culture, sensemaking, and identity in institutional responses to external stimulations such as policy changes. He earned his doctorate from the University of Michigan, his master's degree from the New School for Social Research, and his baccalaureate from Centre College. He had 10 years of experience in institutional research and academic administration before entering the professoriate.

Carol A. Mutch is currently an administrator at the Christchurch College of Education in Christchurch, New Zealand. She has oversight of research and postgraduate programs in teacher education. Her research interests relate to educational policy, curriculum development, and social education. Carol has recently published a research text, *Doing Educational Research: A Practitioner's Guide to Getting Started* (New Zealand Council for Educational Research Press, 2005), which aims to provide a step-by-step guide for teacher-researchers to make sense of and engage in research in their classrooms.